T0329400

# CAMBRIDGE LIBRARY COLLECTION

*Books of enduring scholarly value*

## Travel and Exploration

The history of travel writing dates back to the Bible, Caesar, the Vikings and the Crusaders, and its many themes include war, trade, science and recreation. Explorers from Columbus to Cook charted lands not previously visited by Western travellers, and were followed by merchants, missionaries, and colonists, who wrote accounts of their experiences. The development of steam power in the nineteenth century provided opportunities for increasing numbers of 'ordinary' people to travel further, more economically, and more safely, and resulted in great enthusiasm for travel writing among the reading public. Works included in this series range from first-hand descriptions of previously unrecorded places, to literary accounts of the strange habits of foreigners, to examples of the burgeoning numbers of guidebooks produced to satisfy the needs of a new kind of traveller - the tourist.

## Selections from the Works of the Baron de Humboldt, Relating to the Climate, Inhabitants, Productions, and Mines of Mexico

Alexander von Humboldt (1769–1859) was one of the most respected scientists of his time; Darwin called him 'the greatest scientific traveller who ever lived'. From 1799 Humboldt spent five years exploring the Americas, reporting his findings in thirty volumes, published over a period of more than twenty years from 1805. His *Essai Politique*, describing northern New Spain, particularly Mexico, was one of the first studies of a single country written to take account of both its history, its society and its political development. In 1824, the English mining engineer John Taylor published this abridged translation, combining it with passages from Humboldt's *Geognostical Essay on the Superposition of Rocks* in order to provide a focussed account of Mexico's mining concerns and opportunities. Including detailed maps, this work contains exhaustive statistics, particularly with regard to trade, agriculture and mining, alongside geographical studies and observations on the population and government.

Cambridge University Press has long been a pioneer in the reissuing of out-of-print titles from its own backlist, producing digital reprints of books that are still sought after by scholars and students but could not be reprinted economically using traditional technology. The Cambridge Library Collection extends this activity to a wider range of books which are still of importance to researchers and professionals, either for the source material they contain, or as landmarks in the history of their academic discipline.

Drawing from the world-renowned collections in the Cambridge University Library, and guided by the advice of experts in each subject area, Cambridge University Press is using state-of-the-art scanning machines in its own Printing House to capture the content of each book selected for inclusion. The files are processed to give a consistently clear, crisp image, and the books finished to the high quality standard for which the Press is recognised around the world. The latest print-on-demand technology ensures that the books will remain available indefinitely, and that orders for single or multiple copies can quickly be supplied.

The Cambridge Library Collection will bring back to life books of enduring scholarly value (including out-of-copyright works originally issued by other publishers) across a wide range of disciplines in the humanities and social sciences and in science and technology.

# Selections from the Works of the Baron de Humboldt, Relating to the Climate, Inhabitants, Productions, and Mines of Mexico

Alexander von Humboldt
Edited by John Taylor

CAMBRIDGE
UNIVERSITY PRESS

CAMBRIDGE UNIVERSITY PRESS

Cambridge, New York, Melbourne, Madrid, Cape Town,
Singapore, São Paolo, Delhi, Tokyo, Mexico City

Published in the United States of America by Cambridge University Press, New York

www.cambridge.org
Information on this title: www.cambridge.org/9781108033749

© in this compilation Cambridge University Press 2011

This edition first published 1824
This digitally printed version 2011

ISBN 978-1-108-03374-9 Paperback

# SELECTIONS

FROM

## THE WORKS OF THE BARON DE HUMBOLDT,

RELATING TO THE

## CLIMATE, INHABITANTS, PRODUCTIONS,

### AND MINES

OF

# MEXICO.

———

WITH NOTES

By JOHN TAYLOR, Esq.

TREASURER TO THE GEOLOGICAL SOCIETY, ETC.

———

LONDON:

PRINTED FOR

LONGMAN, HURST, REES, ORME, BROWN, and GREEN,

PATERNOSTER-ROW.

———

1824.

PRINTED BY RICHARD TAYLOR,
SHOE-LANE, LONDON.

# INTRODUCTION.

THE object of this work is to present in a condensed form some of the information which is displayed at large in two celebrated works * of M. le Baron de Humboldt. This peculiarly gifted traveller, after traversing countries whose future importance to Europe his discriminating foresight enabled him to predict, gave to the world descriptions of these vast territories, which, while they astonish us by the extent of research, and the varied science they display, are rendered even more valuable by the accurate truth and the candid and manly spirit which pervade them. To those who may now for the first time be

---

* Political Essay on the Kingdom of Mexico or New Spain ; and Geognostical Essay on the Superposition of Rocks.

a

inquiring into Mexican affairs,—whether for
the purpose of engaging their money in any
of the enterprises for working the mines of
that country, or with the more interesting view
of seeking in it a place of residence where
their skill and experience may become useful
in the great plans which are meditated, and
may, at the same time, be made subservient
to their own emolument and advancement,—
it will be most satisfactory to know that the
details which are here laid before them, come
from a person whose authority has never been
questioned, and whose relations are daily
confirmed by many who have since visited
the country.

I received permission to submit to the
Baron de Humboldt some questions relative to the mines, to which he has had the
kindness to return answers the most explicit,
and evincing the most profound knowledge
of the subject. In the earlier part of his life
he had the direction of some important mines
in Germany : it will therefore be the more
satisfactory to those who, like myself, are especially interested in this part of the inquiry,

to know that the information contained in
this volume comes from one on whose judgement the most entire reliance may be placed.
I must also add, that these Selections from
his works have been made with his knowledge
and approbation. I am conscious that it is
a liberty I ought not to have taken but from
the consideration that the abridgement may
now be useful to numbers who could not have
availed themselves of the works at large. Valuable as M. de Humboldt's writings are, he
has never made them a source of profit to
himself, and it may truly be said that public
utility is with him the leading object. Ac-
tuated by this disinterested feeling, he has constantly refused the most advantageous offers
to engage himself in any concerns connected
with Mexico, that his mind might remain un-
biassed by any consideration of personal interest. I have said thus much, that those
who are inclined to attach weight to any
statements which I may lay before them,
may know the respectability of my authority
for many things which wear so flattering
an aspect, as to excite a suspicion that they

have been brought forward to serve a particular purpose.

I have also to acknowledge the liberality of Messrs. Longman and Co., for permitting the free use of Mr. Black's translation of M. de Humboldt's *Essai politique*, from which most of the following sheets are compiled. This has enabled me to lay the work before the public much sooner than I could otherwise have done. I have adapted the technical language more to the comprehension of my English mining readers, than that of the translation would be found to be. In doing this, constant reference has been made to the original; and the figures and measurements have been reduced to those denominations which are most in use among us. My own engagements not leaving me time sufficient for the task of selection and arrangement, it has in a great measure fallen upon a friend who undertook it for me; and I am conscious that the public will be gainers by this circumstance.

My attention is not now drawn to the mines of Mexico for the first time: several years ago I studied some of these very works; which

I was led to do by the desire of comparing the lodes or veins in that country with those which had come under my own observation.

I was then struck with their size or width, with the great productiveness of particular parts, with the similarity of many circumstances with those which miners every where think favourable symptoms, and above all with the greatness of the profits under a system of management of the worst kind. I observed that little or no machinery was employed, and that what there was, seemed to be of the rudest description, that no attempt was made to abridge labour, or to save expense, and that under the old government, obstacles to improvement of the most formidable kind existed. Attempts were indeed sometimes made : but when it is considered that all these were likely to interfere with the profit of Viceroys, or provincial Governors, who, under the court of Spain, enjoyed the privilege of making the people pay at the highest rate for articles of the greatest necessity, it is not surprising that these attempts were stifled and rendered abortive. With the

richest mines in the world, with a splendid
college for instructing miners, and with a
code of laws which pretended to encourage
them, Mexico made no advances in the science of working its mineral treasures; while
England, with only metals of inferior value,
without any public institution for instruction
of this sort, and even without books upon the
subject, has within a few years raised the art
of mining to a perfection heretofore unknown,
and has carried it on in spite of difficulties not
to be met with elsewhere.

I long ago formed the opinion which I now
entertain, that if the skill and experience in
mining which we possess, and the use of our
engines, could ever be applied to the mines of
Mexico, the result would be that of extraordinary profit.

At that time the Old Government still held
its sway over this interesting country : no
hope, therefore, existed in my mind of ever
seeing the attempt made; in later years the
country has been struggling with its former
masters, and it now seems likely that, having
emancipated itself from their yoke, it will con-

solidate a government more adapted to the wants and interests of the people ; how far it may succeed, and with what measure of wisdom and moderation, I do not pretend to foresee. A failure in produce, similar to that experienced in the mines of Cornwall 60 or 80 years ago, before the application of the steam-engine, had already given a considerable check to the prosperity of the mines ; and in the year 1810, at the commencement of the civil commotions in Mexico, they experienced a fatal blow by the interruption to industry produced by internal war. The proprietors no longer received their usual revenues, and the mines becoming full of water, the whole country was impoverished, and at the return of better times the necessary capital for renewing the works did not exist. This is the cause of the application to other countries on the part of the Mexican proprietor, and the reason of his willingness to alienate a part of his interest in a mine for the sake of that assistance which he bargains for in return.

The state of affairs is then changed since M. de Humboldt wrote; and it might be expected that in now laying before the public a revised Selection from his works, some alteration in those parts relating particularly to the effects of the Government should have been made: but upon consideration this was not deemed advisable; the reader will therefore bear in mind that the descriptions relate to a former period, and not to the present one.

A writer in one of our newspapers has commented on the extraordinary spectacle of a vast country, teeming with the precious metals, applying to the inhabitants of a northern island, comparatively barren in native wealth; for assistance in the extraction of its treasures. It is, indeed, a striking proof that the richest gifts of nature are useless without the industry and intelligence requisite to bring them into action, and that such industry and intelligence are only to be looked for where property is secure and rational liberty is enjoyed.

I had occasion, again, about the year 1819, to consider some circumstances connected with the Mexican mines, owing to the intention of a respectable house in London to send out a steam-engine to be employed in one of them. A number of interesting papers were then submitted to me, some of them warranted by the name of Don Fausto d'Elhuar, formerly President of the College of Mines at Mexico, and now resident at Madrid. My opinion of the benefits to be expected from such undertakings was much confirmed, and I saw a disposition to favour them on the part of the resident proprietors. I then advised the necessary measures to be taken : an engine was constructed and sent out, accompanied by a miner from Cornwall, Robert Phillips ; and this was, I believe, the first equipment of the kind that reached this part of Spanish America. Owing to several circumstances, the engine was not sent to the mine it was intended for, and considerable delay occurred before it reached the place of its ulterior destination ; but it is now erected in the mine of Conception in the Real Catorce. I had lately a letter from Phillips, who was in good health and spirits ; and the undertaking, as far as I can learn, is likely to be a very successful one.

At the present moment the difficulties I

have alluded to arising from the policy of the former Spanish Government are removed, and it seems probable that the New Government, whatever form it may assume, will follow the direction of its own interests and of the wishes of the people, and will give encouragement to foreign aid in working the mines. The property in them, like that of mines in England, is private; the contracts are therefore made with individuals, many of whom have considerable influence; the State only interferes in taking a duty on the metals when exported, which has lately been lowered with respect to silver from $29\frac{1}{2}$ per cent. to 6 per cent.

Various commercial establishments from this country have been made of late in Mexico, and English gentlemen are resident there; a channel of communication has thus been opened, through which negotiations with England have been carried on for grants or shares in some of the principal mines, and abundant capital has been raised to work them with effect.

The first Company seems to have originated with a proposal from Don Lucas Alaman, a leading minister in the Mexican Government. It was first promulgated in Paris, under the title of the " Franco-Mexican Company;" but not succeeding there, it was transferred hither, and after some time, and some alteration in the original plan, is now established under the name of the *United Mexican Association*, with a capital of 240,000*l*. in 600 shares of 40*l*. each. The object of this Company is said to be principally to purchase ores and smelt and refine them; it also, according to the prospectus, meditates the working mines, but it does not appear to have yet actually engaged any.

I should think the establishment of a Company to purchase ores of the smaller mines, and to refine them upon a well-conducted system, a promising undertaking; but as I am unacquainted with the details of the plan, I of course refrain from giving any further opinion.

The Company next established is called the " Anglo-Mexican Association," which having actually contracted for some of the

most extensive and productive concerns, has
raised a proportionate capital by a subscrip-
tion of one million in 10,000 shares of 100*l.*
each. This Company has done me the honour
to consult me on its arrangements; it is governed by twelve Directors of great respectability, and the preparations are in considerable forwardness. The mines undertaken by
this association are principally in the Real of
Guanaxuato, concerning which a great deal
of information will be found in the following
pages. Its situation, north-west of the city of
Mexico, will be seen by a reference to the map.

The great mine of Valenciana is in this
district; of this M. de Humboldt speaks frequently, and ample details as to its produce
and other circumstances will be laid before
the reader. It is situated upon a lode, or vein,
which has been extensively worked, and upon
which the Company has other mines, called
Tepeyac, Rayas, Cuta and Serena; it has also
one which seems to be in another lode, called
La Luz, at no great distance: they are nego-
tiating for other mines, which will complete

an undertaking of great magnitude, and adequate to warrant a large and .effective establishment.

Valenciana was a dry mine when M. de Humboldt was there, and it has thus been carried to an extraordinary depth; it was holed to Tepeyac, which let down water into it, and since the troubles in 1810 has been gradually filling. There is no adit, and the engines must therefore lift to the surface, where in all probability the stream will be very useful in dressing. Tepeyac will be drained at the same time, and other engines are provided for the smaller mines.

The modes of dressing and particularly of crushing the ores are very imperfect; it is therefore probable, and has indeed been stated from good authority, that large quantities of the former waste lying there, will pay well for working over. Steam stamping engines are constructing for this purpose, and will probably soon enable the proprietors to make some returns.

Instead of smelting, the Mexicans have generally used the process of extracting the sil-

ver by the use of mercury, which is called
amalgamation: a full description of this mode
will be found, and of the enormous expense
and difficulties attending it.   There is good
reason to believe, that by dressing the ores as
clean as possible in the first instance, so as to
effect a considerable reduction of their bulk,
by a better application of fuel either in good
reverberatory furnaces, or in the blast hearths
used in the north of England, the silver ores
may be smelted with a certain quantity of
lead, and afterwards tested off: dispatch and
economy will thus be promoted without any
serious loss of the precious metals.

The Anglo-Mexican Association has also
contracted for a mine, called Purissima, in
the Real de Catorce before mentioned, which
will be found in the northern part of the map.
This is very near the mine where Robert
Phillips now is, upon which the steam-engine
has been erected.

This district has been very rich, and considerable expectations are, probably with justice,
entertained with respect to the future profit.

The third Company is of a more private nature, and is formed of individuals who possess the largest interest in the mines of this country. As I direct the administration of their affairs at home, they have wished me to manage this undertaking abroad, and to organize the establishment which will proceed to Mexico to carry on the works. From among their numerous valuable agents and connexions here, I shall not find this a difficult task. I trust that those who undertake to represent the respective Companies will do credit to their choice, and will show that improvements may be carried into effect without that indiscretion or precipitancy which might cause disgust and opposition.

This last Company is known by the title of " The Adventurers in the Mines of Real del Monte," which is a district about sixty miles north of the city of Mexico. They have agreed with the agent of the Count Regla for his mines on the Biscaina vein and others connected with it. They also have taken the mine of Moran from the proprietor, Thomas Murphy, Esq., who was long resident in Mexico.

The Company's agents will proceed directly to the mines, and engines and proper machinery will be immediately prepared to follow them. The reader will find in the subsequent pages some notice of the mines of Real del Monte on the Veta Biscaina, which is the great lode on which they are worked. Moran is on the same lode, and this mine is curious as having been the only one in which pumps were tried in Mexico. These were worked by a pressure engine (*machine à colonne d'eau*) erected by a German engineer : it succeeded in drawing out the water with 9 inch pumps, 6 feet stroke ; and it appears that when it worked 12 hours out of 24, it kept the water clear: the stream, however, which supplied the power was quite insufficient, except in the rainy season, which lasts in Mexico but about three months in the year; the machine was therefore useless, and the mine was abandoned.

The number of mines in Mexico is very great; there are many very important ones besides those engaged by the Companies now formed, and others not even noticed in the following pages, which have been exceedingly rich, and may become so again. There is no natural rivalry in the business of mining in a district where there is room for the exertions of all ; the produce is easily disposed of without injurious competition, and the effect of increased production upon prices is so gradual, that all will participate in its advantages before the consequent depression will be sensibly felt.

No foolish jealousies, therefore, ought to prevail ; English miners will carry out the same friendly feelings as exist in their own country, where mutual assistance is cordially afforded, and where the improvement designed by one is freely exhibited to all. Common danger is said to be a bond of union; and the usual risks and uncertainties of mining are sufficient in themselves to induce co-operation in order to overcome them.

Many unforeseen difficulties may be found in a new country, and time, patience, and discretion may be required to avoid and surmount them. New processes or modes of working should be introduced with caution,

and prejudices should be respected, rather
than the success of the undertaking should
be endangered by injudicious attempts at
premature alterations. After the value of
an improvement is known and acknowledged,
no objection will be made to its adoption :
there are few cases where proof of this kind
may not be given by small beginnings, and a
gradual progress towards perfection may thus
be made. The advance may be somewhat
slower, but it will be proportionably more
sure. The whole business of mining is expe-
rimental ; hardly a shaft is sunk or a level
driven, but it is, as we properly say, for the
purpose of trial. The modes in which such
trials or experiments may be made, may
be various, and there are few but have
something to recommend them, or which do
not deserve some consideration. A skilful
miner knows how to select and combine such
operations, and the most unskilful may be
guided into the right path by temperate advice and judicious example. I would insist
much on this point for the consideration of
such persons as may go from England, be-

cause I have seen well-devised projects, even in this country, endangered by hasty and indiscreet measures which encouraged opposition or jealousy.

The Mexican people will eventually be much benefited by the application and use of our steam-engines, and probably by some other improvements we may carry with them. They invite our assistance in a friendly manner, and there is no doubt that the enlightened part of the nation will regard us favourably: we ought to do our part to deserve their confidence and support; a connexion may thus be established which may be beneficial to the present and future generations of both countries. It is impossible to calculate to what extent the exchange of the varied and precious productions of the Mexican soil and climate, for those furnished by English industry and capital, may be hereafter carried.

A perusal of this little book will show what advantages Mexico has received from Nature, and that, as it is free from the embarrassments of a slave population, there is a

fair probability that under a liberal and equi-
table Government it may rise to a dignity in
the scale of enlightened nations, which its extent, position, and internal wealth entitle it to
hold.

One of the principal difficulties in the application of machinery will arise from the
weight of the parts, and the labour of convey-
ing them through the country to the mines
which are at considerable distances from the
coast. The principal roads are mentioned by
M. de Humboldt, and the improvements contemplated, or in part executed; they are
still, however, in places, very bad for wheel
carriages, and most of the internal commerce
is carried on by the use of mules loaded with
the goods they transport; a mode which will
be inapplicable to many articles and to their
conveyance into deep mines. Nothing is more
important to a country than good roads, especially in a country like Mexico, where the
elevation of the table-land will probably pre-
clude the use of canals: it may be hoped that,
under more tranquil and prosperous political
circumstances, the Government will attend to

and devise means for improvements in this important matter.

The subject for the greatest consideration with English miners will be that of fuel, both as it relates to the power to be employed to drain the mines—for which nothing but steam-engines can in our present state of knowledge be contemplated, and as it regards the reduction of the ores. If it should be found that the supply of this most essential article is not too limited, we may indeed promise ourselves considerable success; and we may hope to benefit Mexico not only by our machinery, but by substituting a more economical mode of extracting the precious metals.

Amalgamation is at present the favourite process, and as long as fuel is scarce it may probably remain so; it may even be difficult to overcome prejudice in this respect, and hazardous to venture on hasty measures to alter the practice: but I am of opinion, that if coal in particular, perhaps even turf, which I am told exists in some parts, can be procured, —silver, and perhaps gold also, may be obtained without waste, by the use of means infinitely less expensive than quicksilver.

Various passages in the work will show not only the great charge of this material, which, being hitherto only produced in Spain and Germany, is of very limited supply; but that in fact the silver mines of Mexico have been frequently and most seriously embarrassed for want of it; and this is confirmed to me by recent and authentic information. It will appear from the tables hereafter given, that the produce of gold and silver has been reduced when mercury was scarce, and that on the contrary the Mexican mines flourished when it was abundant. To guard against such variations, I know that it will be necessary for each establishment to keep at all times a large stock of this article at the mines; and that thus, besides the risks of plunder and waste, a greater capital than would otherwise be required must be provided and locked up in a distant country.

As notice will be taken of this subject in the work itself under the proper heads, I shall content myself with insisting strongly on the necessity of great attention to the operations of dressing or washing the ores. If fuel be scarce, or if quicksilver be expensive, it must be expedient to carry the process of dressing to the furthest point we can, without losing too much of the precious metal :—I say without losing too much, because I know that any kind of dressing must produce some waste; and none but persons who are in possession of all the facts, and can balance one with another, can understand this part of the business. The Assay Office must be frequently consulted, and every thing taken into the account. In England we have different modes of dressing, and they have regulated themselves by gradual experience according to circumstances : fuel with us is cheap; and therefore with copper ores, where fire will refine the metal with less waste than any other mode, we wash but little. In the case of tin ores, which will bear water without much chance of loss, and where the purity of the metal must be obtained by separating it from all other metallic substances before it goes into the furnace, we clean the ores very accurately. We are induced to dress our lead ores also well, because the metal being easily volatilized and dissipated by strong heats, we endeavour to free the ores from other more infusible substances.

In silver ores we have not much practice, although in some raised from mines of which I have the superintendance in Cornwall, I observe that they bear the water pretty well: my opinion formed upon my past experience, therefore, is, that the waste which will unavoidably result from making them very clean, must be risked under the present circumstances of the Mexican mines; and that the object kept principally in view must be the reduction of the bulk of the ore to its minimum; and this, whether amalgamation be employed or smelting. Silver is indestructible in the fire, and in a strong heat lead will attract it from all other mixtures, and be a faithful carrier to other processes by which it is easily and expeditiously refined.

The operations of dressing, to be conducted

properly, must have the aid of peculiar machinery, and the advantage of skilful persons to direct. The mechanical part of the business seems to be very rude in Mexico, and wholly inadequate to perform what is required in a proper manner : our stamping mills, crushing rollers, and other apparatus will be of the greatest use, and of general application ; but these will do but little, unless directed by competent judgement and experience. The persons proper to manage dressing in Mexico, will in my opinion be found amongst those who are brought up in our tin mines. Copper and lead ore dressers will not be attentive enough to minute particulars.

The prospect of advantage to the capitalists who embark their money in mining in Mexico is subject to be clouded by many doubts respecting the political circumstances of a new Government, the difficulty of exercising controul over establishments to which great discretionary powers must be confided at a formidable distance from home, and the impediments likely to arise from the prejudices

or avarice of the Mexicans. These, however, though serious risks, may perhaps be
overrated by many; and I am inclined to
think may be moderated by a prudent selection of the agents who are to represent
British interests in Mexico. The proprietors
of the mines there in making their grants,
and the Government in their laws relating to
property of this kind, will consult their own
interest in a faithful and liberal encouragement of foreign aid; and I know of no good
reason to doubt that this will be afforded.
On the part of those to whom the direction
and working of the mines in Mexico are in-
trusted, there ought to be unremitting attention to carry on their operations with vigour
and effect, rendering to the proprietors, with
the portion of the profits to which they are
entitled, an example of skilful management
and an exact observance of the rights of all
parties concerned.

With a good understanding founded on
such a basis, and with discretion on the part
of those who may direct the affairs of the
Companies at home and abroad, I can see no

obstacle to the prosperity of these mines, which does not equally present itself in the case of those in remote counties of England.

If no unforeseen circumstances arise to disturb the arrangements which are made for the conduct of the undertakings, and if I am to look to the mining risk simply, I cannot come to any other opinion, than that this is very small, or rather I should say that the expectation of profit is a large one.

The veins are of an unusual width, and have in many cases been worked on in several points for a great length, and are proved extensively ; the quantity of ore which has been raised is enormous ; the quality, though not (as M. de Humboldt says) in itself rich, because the mass is so great, may yet be deemed comparatively so, when reduced in bulk, as it may be, and when considered with relation to what English mines produce ; the metals are of the highest value, while the expenses need no be greater than they would be in the same place for mines worked in veins inferior in the quantity or quality of their produce.

These advantages are so great that they

may compensate for many errors and many
difficulties; and if such occur at first, as in
all probability they may, I cannot but in-
dulge sanguine expectations that zeal, patience and skill will overcome them, and that
finally the enterprise will be as profitable as
the risks encountered may fairly require it
should be.

I freely admit that I am deeply interested
in the success of these adventures, that I feel
an unusual degree of anxiety for their success,
and that to this end I shall gladly contribute
the utmost exertion of my humble efforts.  I
may therefore be considered a partial adviser.
I have endeavoured, however, to leave the
facts as I found them, standing on authority
which has not been questioned.  From these,
judicious readers will draw their own conclu-
sions.

JOHN TAYLOR.

Bedford Row,
12th March, 1824.

# RECENT MEMORIAL

## TO

# THE SOVEREIGN CONGRESS

### OF

# MEXICO.

————◆————

SINCE the completion of this work, I have been favoured with the following extract of a memorial presented to the Government of Mexico at a very late period, by an enlightened and liberal minister of that country, Don Lucas Alaman, and which I have the greatest pleasure in making public. It is remarkable for the justness of the views it gives of the means of encouraging their great sources of national wealth ; and if such principles are acknowledged and acted upon, which there is no good reason to doubt, I will venture to predict that foreign capital will be employed with confidence, and with benefit to the country where it is employed as well as to that which may supply it, the advantage to each particular Company who may

undertake mines, being of course more or less
as they may prudently and skilfully manage their
affairs.                                              J. T.

*Extract from the Report of the Minister for Foreign Affairs
and of the Interior to the Sovereign Constituent Congress assembled in Mexico, 1st November 1823, (received by a late arrival from Mexico.)*

## ARTICLE INDUSTRY.

### MINES.

It is a principle admitted by all writers on political economy, that the most direct encouragement
that can be given to agriculture and to industry, is
to facilitate the consumption of the produce of the
one, and the sale of the manufactures of the other.
If the mines be considered amongst us under this
point of view, it will be found that nothing contributes so much as they do to the prosperity of those
essential branches of the public riches. The great
number of people that are occupied in them, the
animals that are employed in the working of the
machinery, and in transporting the ores, the consumption that arises therefrom of grain, as well as
of soap, paper, iron, &c., give a powerful impulse
to agriculture, the arts, and to commerce. If
practical illustration be necessary to prove those
facts, which are doubted only by men whose minds
are preoccupied by the paradoxical assertions of
systematic economists, they may be found on a
comparison of the state of our mining provinces,

such as Guanaxuato and Zacatecas, previous to the
year 1810 and at the present period. Abundance
and prosperity then reigned throughout both of
them. The agriculturist found in those famous
reales (districts) a ready and certain market for his
produce ; the smith, the carpenter, the mason, a
constant employment for his industry ; the merchant an extensive consumption for the goods which
he introduced ; and the treasures drawn from the
bowels of the earth were distributed throughout and
revivified the most distant provinces in payment for
the soap, wood, salt, magistral, horses and mules,
that were brought from all parts. The nature of
our ores is also a powerful cause of these happy results ; they are generally poor in metal, and most
abundant in quantity, and require for their manufacture a great quantity of machinery and ingre-
dients ; and it may therefore be said that the miner
merely draws forth funds to distribute them freely
among the labourers, merchants and artisans ; and
we must naturally conclude that the prosperity of
these classes depends principally upon the impulse
given to them by the mines, which in our notion
are thus the acting principle of all the other branches
of industry.

From this it is to be inferred that the encouragement which is given to the former revolves
indirectly in favour of the latter ; and if it be
intended to animate the one, we must begin by
giving a stimulus to the other. These principles

occasioned the reduction of duties granted by the
Spanish Cortes, and confirmed by the Provincial
Junta, a reduction that has unexpectedly preserved
the mines at this time, and which may greatly
contribute to re-establish them.

We may flatter ourselves that we shall speedily
see them once more in a flourishing condition.
Several foreign capitalists are ready to invest large
funds in draining and working the principal mines,
which, from the disastrous consequences of the war,
have been overflowed and not regularly worked.
The steam engines, which it is intended to introduce, and of which two are now erecting, the one in
Temascaltepec and the other in Real de Catorce,
will powerfully contribute to so important a result.
The former Sovereign Congress, with the intention
of facilitating contracts of supply with opulent foreigners, with whom some have already been con-
cluded, abolished the laws and articles of the ordi-
nance which prohibited them from acquiring property in mines, although it wisely limited the power
which it granted to them for that purpose to those
mines only which they may supply, without being
able to denounce others, or to attempt to discover
new ones. This measure will be a new stimulus to
the introduction of funds for the supply of this
branch, which it so much needs, and which it cannot procure by other means.

The " Tribunal of Mines," which, according to
the terms of its constitution ought to have been a

bank of supply, by creating for this important object under its direction, a fund out of the duty of one rial per mark of silver, cannot at the present time afford any assistance to the miners, and which they so imperatively stand in need of, as from causes which the limits I am obliged to prescribe to this memorial do not allow me to dilate upon. Such a fund not only does not exist, but, on the contrary, this body is loaded with a debt, the interest of which cannot be paid out of the produce of the aforesaid duty.

Another of the means of encouragement which it would be proper to grant to this important branch, so soon as circumstances shall permit, is the establishment of exchange houses, which formerly existed, and the creation of new ones on these points where it may be most expedient.—They facilitate the activity of the circulation, and thereby the frequent employment of the same capital, which may be said to multiply itself by being repeatedly invested, thus avoiding the necessity of increasing the number of mint houses, the quantity of which must greatly augment the expenses of coinage.

# CONTENTS.

———◆———

# CONTENTS.

## CHAPTER V.

## CHAPTER VI.

## CHAPTER VII.

## CHAPTER VIII.

## CHAPTER IX.

## CHAPTER X.

## CHAPTER XI.

## CHAPTER XII.

# CONTENTS.

## CHAPTER XIII.

## CHAPTER XIV

## CHAPTER XV.

## CHAPTER XVI.

## CHAPTER XVII.

The marginal references of the original to the various works and documents by which the author confirms his statements, are omitted in this little work. It is presumed that any one who wishes to verify a fact which appears to him suspicious, will not think it too much trouble to consult the original, or Mr. Black's translation.

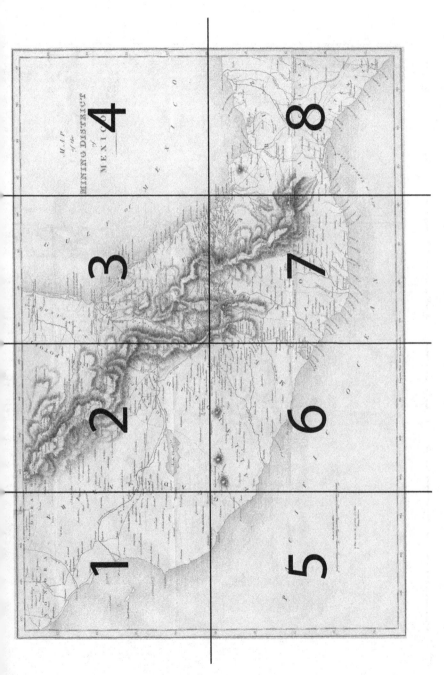

Key to following pages

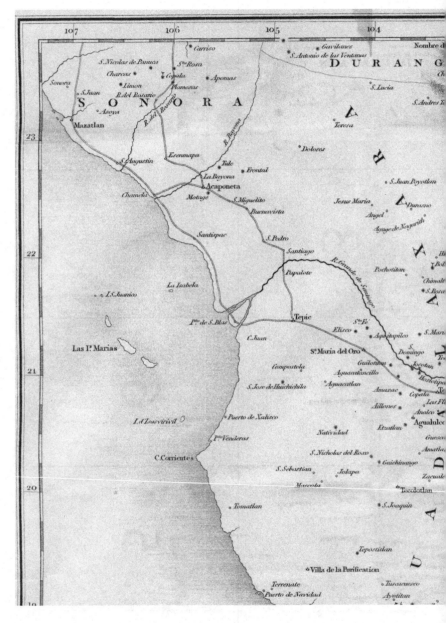

1

3

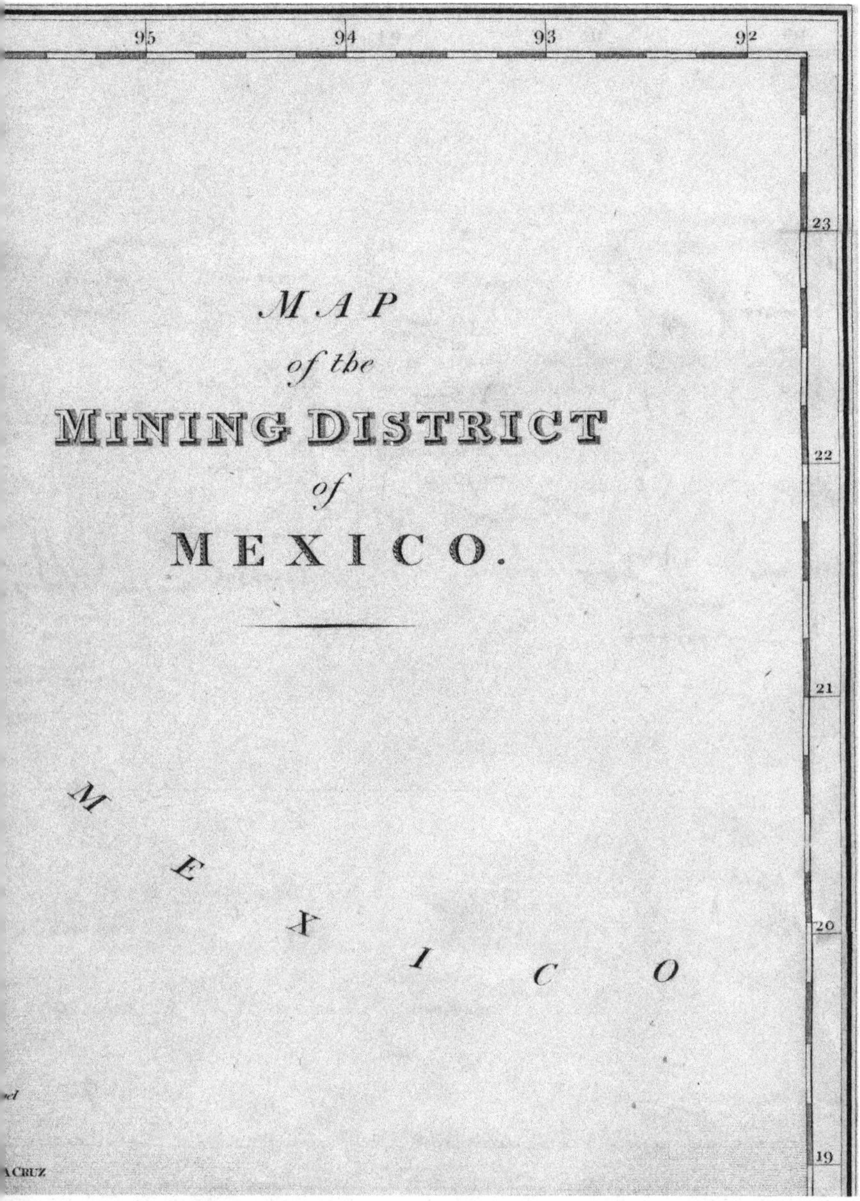

23

# MAP
*of the*
# MINING DISTRICT
*of*
# MEXICO.

22

21

M

E

X

I

C

O

20

*el*

A CRUZ

19

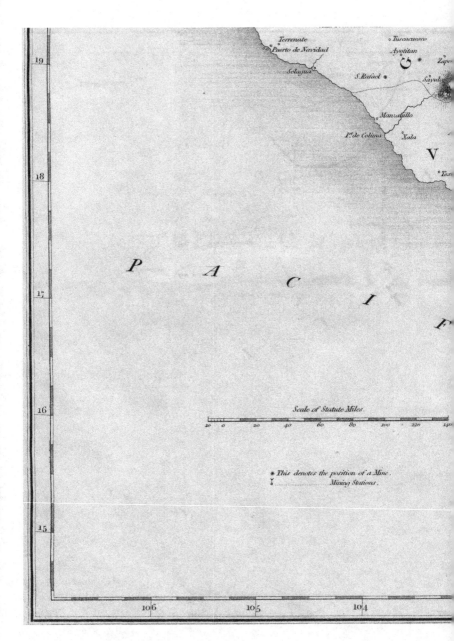

19

Terrenate
Puerto de Navidad
Selagua
S. Rafael
Manzanillo
Pᵗ de Colima
Xala

Tuscacuesco
Ayotitan
Zapo
Sayula

V

18

Texr

P        A        C        I        F

17

16

Scale of Statute Miles.

20    0    20    40    60    80    100    120    140

* This denotes the position of a Mine.
⚲ ............. Mining Stations.

15

106                    105                    104

5

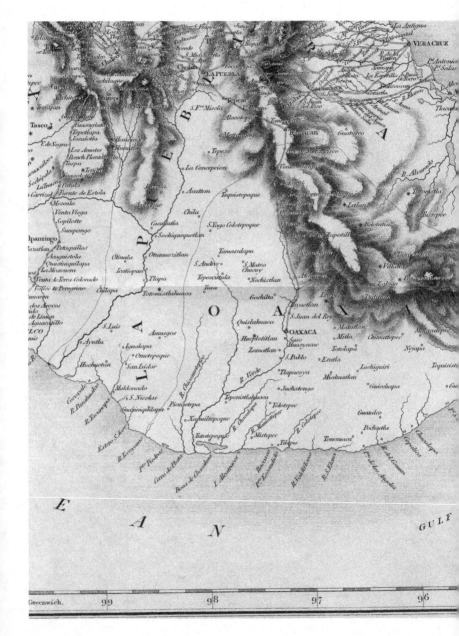

# SELECTIONS

# MEXICO.

## CHAPTER I.

*Kingdom of Mexico—situation—territorial division—favourable position of mining districts—rivers—lakes—roads.*

AMONG the colonies subject to the king of Spain, Mexico occupies the first rank, both on account of its territorial wealth, and on account of its favourable position with Europe and Asia. We speak here merely of the political value of the country, considering it in its actual state of civilization, which is very superior to that of the other Spanish possessions. Many branches of agriculture have undoubtedly attained a higher degree of perfection in the province of Caraccas than in New Spain. The fewer mines a colony has, the more is the industry of the inhabitants turned towards the productions of the vegetable kingdom. The fertility of the soil is greater in the provinces of Cumana, of New Barcelona, and Venezuela, on the banks of the lower Orinoco, and in the northern parts of New Grenada, than in the king-

B

dom of Mexico, of which several regions are barren, destitute of water, and incapable of vegetation. But when we consider the greatness of the population of Mexico, the number and proximity of its considerable cities, the enormous value of its metallic produce, and its influence on the commerce of Europe and Asia;—when we examine the imperfect state of cultivation observable in the rest of Spanish America, we are tempted to justify the preference which the court of Madrid has long manifested for Mexico above its other colonies.

The denomination of New Spain designates, in general, the vast extent of country over which the viceroy of Mexico exercises his power. Using the word in this sense, we are to consider as northern and southern limits the parallels of the 38th and 10th degrees of latitude.

The advantages afforded by this vast empire, from the wealth of its natural productions, the fertility of its soil, the facility which a man possesses there of choosing, with thermometer in hand, in a space of a few square leagues, the temperature or climate which he believes the most favourable to his age, his physical constitution, or to the species of cultivation to which he is most attached, appear to be unrivalled. Nothing can exceed the beauty of those delicious countries, situated half way up the ascent, in the region of oaks and pines, between 3,000 and 5,000 feet above the level of the sea; where a perpetual spring reigns, where the most delicious fruits of the Indies are cultivated beside those of Europe, and where these enjoyments are troubled neither by a multitude of insects, nor by the fear of the yellow fever (*vomito*), nor by the frequency of earthquakes. There does not exist a region in which man, with less labour, can supply more abundantly the wants of a numerous family.

In the short statistical account we shall give of New Spain, we shall confine ourselves to those subjects which are interesting considered with relation to the important science of political economy. The face of a country, the grouping of its mountains, the extent of its plains, the elevation which determines their temperature; every thing, in a word, which regards the construction of the earth, has the most intimate connexion with the progress of the population and the welfare of its inhabitants. It is this construction which influences the state of agriculture, varied according to the variations of climate, the facility of internal commerce, more or less favoured by the nature of the ground : lastly, the military defence, on which depends the external safety of the colony. These are the only considerations which can render geological descriptions interesting to the statesman, when he calculates the territorial force and riches of nations.

The Kingdom of New Spain, to which the capital city and seat of government has given the name of the Kingdom of Mexico, the most northern part of all Spanish America, extends from the 16th to the

38th degree of north latitude. The length of this vast region, in the direction of S.S.E. to N.N.W., is about 1,800 miles; its greatest breadth lies under the 30th degree. From the Red River in the province of Texas, to the island of Tiburon on the coasts of the intendancy of Sonora, it measures from east to west 1,100 miles. This space of seventy-nine degrees equals not only the length of all Africa, but even much surpasses the breadth of the Russian empire, which includes about a hundred and sixty-seven degrees of longitude, under a parallel of which the degrees are not more than half the degrees of the equator.

In its present state New Spain is divided into twelve intendancies, to which we must add three other districts, very remote from the capital, which have preserved the simple denomination of provinces. These fifteen divisions are,

I. UNDER THE TEMPERATE ZONE, 738,000
    square miles, with 677,000 souls, or rather
    less than one inhabitant to the square mile.
  A. REGION OF THE NORTH, an interior region.
    1. *Provincia de Nuevo Mexico*, along the
       Rio del Norte to the north of the parallel
       of 31°.
    2. *Intendencia de Nueva Biscaya* to the
       south-west of the Rio del Norte, on the
       central table-land which declines rapidly
       from Durango towards Chihuahua.

B. Region of the north-west, in the vicinity of the Great Ocean.

3. *Provincia de la Nueva California,* or north-west coast of North America, possessed by the Spaniards.

4. *Provincia de la Antigua California.* Its southern extremity enters the torrid zone.

5. *Intendencia de la Sonora.* The most southern part of Cinaloa, in which the celebrated mines of Copala and Rosario are situated, also passes the tropic of Cancer.

C. Region of the north-east, adjoining the Gulf of Mexico.

6. *Intendencia de San Luis Potosi.* It comprehends the provinces of Texas, la colonia de Nuevo Santander and Cohahuila, El Nuevo Reyno de Leon, and the districts of Charcas, Altamira, Catorce, and Ramos. These last districts compose the intendancy of San Luis properly so called. The southern part, which extends to the south of the Barra de Santander and the Real de Catorce, belongs to the torrid zone.

II. UNDER THE TORRID ZONE, 328,500 square miles, with 5,160,000 souls, or rather more than 15 inhabitants to the square mile.

D. Central region.

7. *Intendencia de Zacatecas,* excepting the

part which extends to the north of the mines of Fresnillo.

8. *Intendencia de Guadalaxara.*
9. *Intendencia de Guanaxuato.*
10. *Intendencia de Valladolid.*
11. *Intendencia de Mexico.*
12. *Intendencia de la Puebla.*
13. *Intendencia de Vera Cruz.*

E. REGION OF THE SOUTH-WEST.

14. *Intendencia de Oaxaca.*
15. *Intendencia de Merida.*

The divisions in this table are founded on the physical state of the country. We see that nearly seven eighths of the inhabitants live under the torrid zone. The population becomes thinner as we advance towards Durango and Chihuahua. In this respect New Spain bears a striking analogy to Hindostan, which in its north parts is bounded by regions almost uncultivated and uninhabited. Of five millions who inhabit the equinoctial part of Mexico, four-fifths live on the ridge of the Cordillera, or table-lands, whose elevation above the level of the sea equals that of the passage of Mount Cenis.

New Spain, considering its provinces according to their commercial relations, or the situation of the coasts, is divided into three regions.

I. PROVINCES OF THE INTERIOR, which do not extend to the ocean.

1. *Nuevo Mexico.*
2. *Nueva Biscaya.*
3. *Zacatecas.*
4. *Guanaxuato.*

II. MARITIME PROVINCES *of the eastern coast* opposite to Europe.
  5. *San Luis Potosi.*
  6. *Vera Cruz.*
  7. *Merida,* or *Yucatan.*

III. MARITIME PROVINCES *of the western coast* opposite to Asia.
  8. *New California.*
  9. *Old California.*
 10. *Sonora.*
 11. *Guadalaxara.*
 12. *Valladolid.*
 13. *Mexico.*
 14. *Puebla.*
 15 *Oaxaca.*

These divisions will one day possess great political interest, when the cultivation of Mexico shall be less concentrated on the central table-land or ridge of the Cordillera, and when the coasts shall become more populous. The maritime provinces of the west will send their vessels to Nootka, to China, and the East Indies. The Sandwich islands, inhabited by a ferocious but industrious and enterprising people, appear destined to receive Mexican rather than European colonists. They afford an important *entrepôt* to the nations who carry on commerce in the Great Ocean. The inhabitants of New Spain and Peru have never yet been able to profit by their advantageous position on a coast opposite to Asia and New Holland. They do not even know the productions of the South Sea islands. The bread-fruit tree, sugar-cane of Otaheite,—that precious reed, the cultivation of which has had such a happy influence on West India commerce,—will one day be received by them from Jamaica, the Havannah, and Caraccas, and no longer from the adjoining islands. What efforts have not been made by the United States of North America, within the last ten years, to open a communication with the western coast, with that same coast on which the Mexicans possess the finest ports, but without activity and without commerce!

According to the ancient division of the country, the *Reyno de Nueva Galicia* contained more than 126,000 square miles, and nearly a million of inhabitants: it included the intendancies of Zacatecas and Guadalaxara *, as well as a small part of that of San Luis Potosi. The regions now known by the denomination of the seven intendancies of Guanaxuato, Valladolid or Mechoacan, Mexico, Puebla, Vera Cruz, Oaxaca, and Merida, formed,

* With the exception of the most southern part, which contains the volcanos of Colima and the village of Ayotitan.

along with a small portion of the intendancy of San Luis Potosi*, the *Reyno de Mexico*, properly so called. This kingdom consequently contained more than 243,000 square miles, and nearly four millions and a half of inhabitants.

Another division of New Spain, equally ancient and less vague, is that which distinguishes *New Spain, properly so called*, from the *provincias internas*. To the latter belongs all to the north and north-west of the kingdom of Nueva Galicia, with the exception of the two Californias; consequently, 1. the small kingdom of Leon; 2. the colony of New Santander; 3. Texas; 4. New Biscay; 5. Sonora; 6. Cohahuila; and 7. New Mexico. The *provincias internas del Vireynato*, which contain 70,326 square miles, are distinguished from the *provincias internas de la Comandancia* (of Chihuahua), erected into a *capitania general* in 1779, which contain 534,375 square miles. Of the twelve new intendancies, three are situated in the *provincias internas*, Durango, Sonora, and San Luis Potosi. We must not, however, forget that the intendant of San Luis is only under the direct authority of the viceroy for Leon, Santander, and the districts near his residence, those of Charcas, Catorce, and Altamira. The governments of Cohahuila and Texas make also part of the intendancy of San Luis

---

* The most southern part, through which the river of Panuco runs.

Potosi ; but they belong directly to the *coman-dancia general de Chihuahua*. The following tables will throw some light on these very complicated territorial divisions. Let us divide all New Spain into

A. *Provincias sujetas al Virey de Nueva España ;* 531,927 square miles, with 5,477,900 souls: the ten intendancies of Mexico, Puebla, Vera Cruz, Oaxaca, Merida, Valladolid, Guadalaxara, Zacatecas, Guanaxuato, and San Luis Potosi (without including Cohahuila and Texas).

The two Californias.

B. *Provincias sujetas al Comandante general de provincias internas,* 534,375 square miles, with 359,200 inhabitants :

The two intendancies of Durango and Sonora ;
The province of Nuevo Mexico ;
Cohahuila and Texas.

The whole of New Spain, 1,066,302 square miles, with 5,837,100 inhabitants.

We have given this brief outline of the territorial divisions of the whole of this vast empire: but as it forms no part of our purpose to extend the views of our readers beyond those intendancies which are the seat of the great mining operations, we shall, in the more detailed description which follows, confine ourselves principally within the intendancies of Guanaxuato, Mexico, Zacatecas, San Luis

Potosi, Valladolid, and Guadalaxara. The only instance in which we shall exceed this boundary, is in that of Vera Cruz, which is interesting as the province through which all the riches of the interior pass to Europe.

The chain of mountains which form the vast table-land of Mexico, is the same with that which, under the name of the Andes, runs through all South America; but the construction, I may say the skeleton (*charpente*), of this chain varies to the south and north of the equator. In the southern hemisphere, the Cordillera is every where torn and interrupted by fissures, like open furrows not filled with heterogeneous substances. If there are plains elevated from 10,000 to 12,000 feet, as in the kingdom of Quito, and further north in the province of los Pastos, they are not to be compared in extent with those of New Spain, and are rather to be considered as longitudinal valleys bounded by two branches of the great Cordillera of the Andes: while in Mexico it is the very ridge of the mountains which forms the table-land; and it is the direction of this plain which designates, as it were, that of the whole chain. Peru and the kingdom of New Grenada contain transversal valleys, of which the perpendicular depth is sometimes near 5,000 feet. The existence of these valleys prevents the inhabitants from travelling except on horseback, a-foot, or carried on the shoulders of Indians (called *cargadores*); but in the kingdom of New Spain carriages roll on to Santa

c 2

Fe in the province of New Mexico, for a length of more than 1,500 miles. On the whole of this road there were few difficulties for art to surmount.

The table-land of Mexico is in general so little interrupted by valleys, and its declivity is so gentle, that as far as the city of Durango, in New Biscay, 420 miles from Mexico, the surface is continually elevated from 5,600 to 8,900 feet above the level of the neighbouring ocean. This is equal to the height of Mount Cenis, St. Gothard, or the Great St. Bernard.

A remarkable advantage for the progress of national industry arises from the height at which nature, in New Spain, has deposited the precious metals. In Peru the most considerable silver mines, those of Potosi, Pasco, and Chota, are immensely elevated, and border upon the region of perpetual snow. In working them, men, provisions, and cattle, must all be brought from a distance. Cities situated in plains, where water freezes the whole year round, and where trees never vegetate, can hardly be an attractive abode. Nothing can determine a freeman to abandon the delicious climate of the valleys to insulate himself on the top of the Andes, except the hope of amassing wealth. But in Mexico, the richest veins of silver, those of Guanaxuato, Zacatecas, Tasco, and Real del Monte, are at moderate elevations of from 5,000 to 6,000 feet. The mines are surrounded with cultivated fields, towns, and villages; the neighbouring sum-

mits are crowned with forests; and every thing facilitates the acquisition of this subterraneous wealth.

None of the plains of New Grenada, Quito, or
Peru exceed 360 square miles. Of difficult access,
and separated from one another by deep valleys,
they are very unfavourable for the transport of goods
and internal commerce. Crowning insulated summits, they appear like islands in the middle of the
aërial ocean. Those who inhabit these frozen plains
remain fixed there, and dread to descend into the
neighbouring regions, where a suffocating heat prevails, prejudicial to the primitive inhabitants of the
higher Andes.

In Mexico, however, the soil assumes a different
aspect. Table-lands of a great extent, but of a surface no less uniform, are so approximated to one
another, that they form but a single plain on the
lengthened ridge of the Cordillera: such is the
table-land which runs from 18° to 40° of north
latitude. Its length is equal to the distance from
Lyons to the tropic of Cancer, which traverses the
great African desert. This extraordinary plain appears to decline insensibly towards the north.

Further to the north of the parallel of 19°, near
the celebrated mines of Zimapan and the Doctor,
situated in the intendancy of Mexico, the Cordillera takes the name of Sierra Madre; and then
leaving the eastern part of the kingdom it runs to
the north-west, towards the cities of San Miguel el
Grande and Guanaxuato. To the north of this

last city, considered the Potosi of Mexico, the Sierra Madre becomes of an extraordinary breadth. It divides immediately into three branches, of which the most eastern runs in the direction of Charcas and the Real de Catorce, and loses itself in the new kingdom of Leon.

In travelling from the capital of Mexico to the great mines of Guanaxuato, we remain at first for 30 miles in the valley of Tenochtitlan, elevated 7,500 feet above the level of the sea. The level of this beautiful valley is so uniform, that the village of Gueguetoque, situated at the foot of the mountain of Sincoque, is only 32 feet higher than Mexico. The hill of Barientos is merely a promontory which stretches into the valley. From Gueguetoque we ascend near Botas to Puerto de los Reyes, and from thence descend into the valley of Tula, which is 380 feet lower than the valley of Tenochtitlan, and across which the great canal of evacuation of the lakes San Christoval and Zumpango passes to the Rio de Moctezuma and the Gulf of Mexico. To arrive at the bottom of the valley of Tula, in the great plain of Queretaro, we must pass the mountain of Calpulalpan, which is scarcely 9000 feet above the level of the sea, and is consequently less elevated than the city of Quito, though it appears the highest point of the whole road from Mexico to Chihuahua. To the north of this mountainous country begin the vast plains of S. Juan del Rio, Queretaro, and Zelya, plains covered with villages and con-

siderable cities. Their mean height equals that of
Puy de Dôme in Auvergne, and they are near 90
miles in length, extending to the foot of the metalliferous mountains of Guanaxuato.

In the midst of so many advantages bestowed by
nature upon New Spain, it suffers in general, like
Old Spain, from the want of water and navigable
rivers.

In the whole equinoctial part of Mexico there
are only small rivers, the mouths of which are of
considerable size. The narrow form of the continent prevents the collection of a great mass of
water. The rapid declivity of the Cordillera
abounds more properly with torrents than rivers.
Mexico is in the same state with Peru, where the
Andes approach so near to the coast as to occasion
the aridity of the neighbouring plains. Among
the small number of rivers in the southern part
of New Spain, the only ones which may in time
become interesting for internal commerce are, 1.
The Rio Guasacualco, and the Rio Alvarado, both
to the south east of Vera Cruz, and adapted for
facilitating the communication with the kingdom
of Guatimala; 2. The Rio de Moctezuma, which
carries the waters of the lakes and valley of
Tenochtitlan to the Rio de Panuco, and by which,
forgetting that Mexico is elevated above 7,000 feet
above the level of the sea, a navigation has been
projected between the capital and the western
coast; 3. The Rio de Zacatula; 4. The great

river of Santiago, formed by the junction of the
rivers Lerma and las Laxas, which might carry the
flour of Salamanca, Zelaya, and perhaps the whole
intendancy of Guadalaxara, to the port of San
Blas, or the coast of the Pacific Ocean.

The lakes with which Mexico abounds, the
greater part of which appear annually on the decline, are merely the remains of immense basins
of water, which appear to have formerly existed
on the high and extensive plains of the Cordillera.
We shall merely mention the great lake of Chapala
in New Gallicia, of nearly 1,400 square miles,
double the size of the lake of Constance; the
lakes of the valley of Mexico, which include a
fourth part of its surface; the lake of Patzcuaro,
in the intendancy of Valladolid, one of the most
picturesque situations which I know in either
continent; and the lakes of Mextitlan and Parras
in New Biscay.

The roads of Mexico are either carried along
the central table-land itself, from Oaxaca to Santa
Fe, or they lead from the table-land towards the
coast. The former serve to carry on a communication between the towns on the ridge of the
mountains, in the coldest and most populous region of the kingdom; the latter are destined for
foreign commerce, and for the intercourse which
subsists between the interior and the ports of Vera
Cruz and Acapulco: they also facilitate an exchange between the productions of the mountains

and the burning plains of the coast. The roads of the table-land running from the S.S.E. to the N.N.W., which from the general configuration of the country we might call *longitudinal*, are very easily kept up. We shall not repeat in this place what we have already stated, relative to the extent and continuity of the high plains of Anahuac, where we find neither fissure nor ravine, and to the progressive fall of the table-land from 8,200 to 2,600 feet of absolute height. Carriages may run from Mexico to Santa Fe, in an extent exceeding the length which the chain of the Alps would have, if prolonged without interruption from Geneva to the shores of the Black Sea. In fact, the central table-land is crossed in all directions in four-wheel carriages, from the capital to Guanaxuato, Durango, Chihuahua, Valladolid, Guadalaxara, and Perote; but in the present bad state of the roads, waggons are not established for the conveyance of goods. The inhabitants give the preference to the employment of beasts of burden; and thousands of horses and mules in long files *(requas)* cover the roads of Mexico. A considerable number of Mestizoes and Indians are employed to conduct these caravans. Preferring a wandering life to any sedentary occupation, they pass the night in the open air, or in sheds, *(tambos,* or *casas de communidad,)* which are constructed in the middle of the villages for the convenience of travellers. The mules feed at liberty in the

D

savannahs; but when the great droughts have
parched up' the grass, the drivers feed them on
maize either in herb *(zacate)*, or in grain.

The introduction of camels would be exceedingly
useful in Mexico. The table-lands over which the
great roads pass are not sufficiently elevated for the
cold to be prejudicial to these animals; and they
would suffer less than horses and mules from the
aridity of the soil, and the want of water and pas-
turage to which the beasts of burden are exposed to
the north of Guanaxuato, especially in the desert by
which New Biscay is separated from New Mexico.

The roads which lead from the interior table-
land to the coasts, and which I call transversal,
are the most difficult, and chiefly deserve the
attention of Government. The roads from Mexico
to Vera Cruz and Acapulco, from Zacatecas to
New Santander, from Guadalaxara to San Blas,
from Valladolid to the port of Colima, and from
Durango to Mazatlan passing by the western
branch of the Sierra Madre, all belong to this class.
The roads by which the capital carries on a communication with the ports of Acapulco and Vera
Cruz, are of course the most frequented. The
value of the precious metals, of the agricultural
productions, and of the goods of Europe and Asia
which flow through these two channels, amounts
to the total sum of nearly 14,000,000*l.* sterling
per annum. These treasures pass along a road
which resembles that of Airolo at the hospital of

Saint Gothard. From the village of Vigas to L'Encero, the road to Vera Cruz is frequently nothing but a narrow and crooked path, and the most difficult, perhaps, in all America, with the exception of that by which the goods of Europe are transported from Honda to Santa Fe de Bogota, and from Guayaquil to Quito.

The productions from the Philippine Islands and Peru, arrive by the road from Mexico to Acapulco. It is carried along a less rapid slope of the Cordilleras, than the road leading from the capital to Vera Cruz. In the European road we remain, from the valley of Mexico to beyond Perote, on the central plain, at an elevation of 7,550 feet above the level of the ocean; and from that village we descend with extreme rapidity to the ravine of the *Plan del Rio*, to the west of Rinconada. On the other hand, on the road from Acapulco, which we designate by the name of the Asiatic Road, the descent begins at a distance of twenty-four miles from Mexico, on the southern slope of the basaltic mountain of Guarda.

The construction and embellishment of a new road from Mexico to the port of Vera Cruz has latterly become the object of the solicitude of Government. A fortunate rivalry is displayed between the new Council of Commerce established at Vera Cruz, under the name of *Real tribunal del consulado*, and the old *Consulado* of the capital; and the latter is gradually beginning to shake off

the inactivity with which it has so long been re-
proached. The merchants of Mexico, having
constructed at their expense an excellent causeway
along the heights of Tiangillo and *las Cruzes*,
which separate the basin of Toluca from that of
Mexico, wish the new road of Vera Cruz to pass
through Orizaba; while the merchants of Vera
Cruz who have country-houses at Xalapa, and who
maintain numerous commercial relations with that
town, insist that the new carriage road *(camino
carretero)* should go by Perote and Xalapa. After
a discussion of several years, the *Consulado* of Vera
Cruz profited by the arrival of the viceroy, Don
Josef de Yvirigarras, who declared himself in favour
of the road by Xalapa as of the greatest utility, and
who gave the direction of it to M. Garcia Conde,
an active and intelligent engineer.

The old road from Mexico to Xalapa and Vera
Cruz passed along the elevated plains of Apa, without touching the great town of Puebla de los Angeles. The indigenous merchandises and productions were then conveyed from Mexico to Perote
and Xalapa, by a very circuitous route. They reckoned by this road, 130 miles from Mexico to Perote,
and 220 from Mexico to Vera Cruz. At last a new
and very short road was opened by the Venta de Chalco, the small chain of porphyritic mountains of Cordova, Tesmelucos, and Ocotlan. The advantages of
these more direct communications between the capital, the city of Puebla, and the fortress of Perote,

will be easily discovered by examining an atlas of New Spain.

The new road from Mexico to Puebla still possesses the inconsiderable difficulty of the passage of the mountains, which separate the basin of Tenochtitlan from that of Cholula. The table-land which extends from the foot of the volcanoes of Mexico to the mountains of Orizaba and the Coffre, is a level plain, covered with sand, fragments of pearled rock, and saline efflorescences. The road from Puebla to Vera Cruz passes through Cocosingo, Acaxete and Perote. We imagine we are travelling over a surface levelled by being long covered with water. When these plains are heated by the solar rays, they exhibit at the height of the passage of Saint Bernard, the same phenomena of suspension and extraordinary refraction, which we generally observe only in the neighbourhood of the ocean.

To the activity of the Consulado of Vera Cruz we owe not only the undertaking of the road of Perote, which in 1803 cost from six to seven thousand pounds per mile, but also the amelioration of the hospitals, and the construction of a beautiful gyratory light-house, executed at London after the plan of the celebrated astronomer *M. Mendoza y Rios.* This light-house consists of a very elevated tower, placed at the extremity of the castle of San Juan d'Ulua, which, with the lantern, cost nearly, 20,000*l.* The lamps, with a current of air, and furnished with reflectors, are fixed on a triangle which turns by means of clock-work ; so that the light disappears whenever the machine presents one of its angles to the entry of the port.  At my departure from Vera Cruz, the Consulado were occupied with two new projects of equal utility,—the supplying the town with potable water, and the construction of a mole, which, advancing in the form of a pier, may resist the shock of the waves.

The magnificent road constructing from Perote to Vera Cruz will rival those of the Simplon and Mount Cenis.  It is broad, solid, and of a very gentle fall.  They have not followed the track of the old road, which was narrow and paved with basaltic porphyry, and which appears to have been constructed towards the middle of the eighteenth century.  Rapid ascents have been carefully avoided ; and the charge which is brought against the engineer, of lengthening the road too much, will be abandoned when wheel carriages shall be substituted for the carriage of goods on the backs of mules.  The construction of this road will probably cost more than 600,000*l.* sterling ; but we hope that so beautiful and useful a work will not suffer any interruption.  It is an object of the highest importance to those parts of Mexico the most remote from the capital, and from the port of Vera Cruz ; for when the road shall be completed, the price of iron, mercury, spirituous liquors, paper, and all the other commodities of Europe, will experience a sensible fall. The Mexican flour, which has hitherto been dearer at the Havannah than the flour of Philadelphia, will be naturally preferred to the latter ; the exportation of the sugars and hides of the country will be more considerable ; and the transportation of goods on waggons will require a much smaller number of mules and horses than are now employed. These changes will produce a double effect on subsistence ; and the scarcities which have hitherto almost periodically desolated Mexico will be more rare ; not only because the consumption of maize will be less, but because the agriculturist, stimulated by the hope of selling his flour at Vera Cruz, will appropriate more of his land to the cultivation of wheat.

During my stay at Xalapa in the month of February 1804, the new road constructed under the direction of Don Garcia Conde, had been commenced on those points which presented the greatest difficulties ; namely, the ravine called the *Plan del Rio*, and the *Cuesta del Soldado*. It is intended to place columns of porphyry along the road, for the purpose of indicating both the distances and the elevation of the surface above the level of the ocean. These inscriptions, which are no where to be met with in Europe, will be particularly interesting to a traveller who is climbing the eastern ascent of the Cordillera ; they will quiet his mind, by announcing to him that he is approaching that fortunate and elevated region, in which the scourge of the *black vomit*, or yellow fever, is no longer to be dreaded.

The old road of Xalapa leads from Rinconada eastward, by the old Vera Cruz vulgarly called *la Antigua*. After passing below this village the river of the same name, 650 feet in breadth, we follow the coast by Punta Gorda and Vergara; or if the tide is high, we take the road of la Manga de Clavo, which does not rejoin the coast till the very port of Vera Cruz. It would be advantageous to construct a bridge over the Rio de la Antigua, near la Ventilla, where the bed of the river is only 350 feet in breadth, by which means the Xalapa road would be shortened more than 18 miles; and without touching old Vera Cruz, it would lead immediately from the Plan del Rio, by the bridge of la Ventilla, Passo de Ovejas, Cienega de Olocuatla, and Loma de San Juan, to Vera Cruz. This change is so much the more desirable, as it is the journey from Encero to the coast which is the most dangerous to the health of the inhabitants of the interior of Mexico, when they descend from the table-land of Perote and the heights of Xalapa.

## CHAPTER II.

*City of Mexico—situation—population—buildings—sur-*
*rounding country—scientific establishments—progress of*
*opinion—distribution of property.*

THE situation of the city of Mexico possesses in-
estimable advantages, if we consider it with relation
to its intercourse with the rest of the civilized world.
Placed on an isthmus, washed by the South Sea
and Atlantic Ocean, Mexico appears destined to
possess a powerful influence over the political events
which agitate the two continents. A king of
Spain resident in the capital might transmit his
orders in five weeks to the Peninsula in Europe,
and in six weeks to the Philippine islands in Asia.
This vast empire, under a careful cultivation, would
alone produce all that commerce collects together
from the rest of the globe,—sugar, cochineal,
cacao, cotton, coffee, wheat, hemp, flax, silk, oils,
and wine. It would furnish every metal, without
even the exception of mercury. The finest timber
and an abundance of iron and copper might favour
the progress of Mexican navigation, although the state
of the coasts and the want of ports oppose obstacles
in this respect which would be difficult to overcome.

Mexico is the most populous city of the new continent. It contains nearly 40,000 inhabitants less

E

than Madrid; and as it forms a great square of
which each side is about 9,000 feet, its population
is spread over a great extent of ground. The streets
being very spacious, in general appear rather de-
serted. They are the less frequented, as, in a climate
considered cold by the inhabitants of the tropics,
people do not expose themselves so much to the
open air, as in the cities at the foot of the Cordillera.
Hence the latter *(ciudades de tierra caliente)* uniformly appear more populous than the cities of the
temperate or cold regions *(ciudades de tierra fria)*

Adorned with numerous teocallis\*, like so many
Mahometan steeples, surrounded with water and
dikes, founded on islands covered with verdure, and
receiving hourly in its streets thousands of boats,
which animated the lake, the ancient Tenochtitlan, according to the accounts of the first conquerors,
must have resembled some of the cities of Holland,
China, or the Delta of Lower Egypt. The capital,
reconstructed by the Spaniards, exhibits, perhaps, a
less lively, though a more august and majestic appearance. Mexico is undoubtedly one of the finest
cities ever built by Europeans in either hemisphere.
With the exception of Petersburg, Berlin, Philadelphia, and some parts of Westminster, there does
not exist a city of the same extent which can be
compared to the capital of New Spain—for the
uniform level of the ground on which it stands, for

---

\* Houses of God.

the regularity and breadth of the streets, and the extent of the public places. The architecture is generally of a very pure style, and there are some edifices of very beautiful structure. The exterior of the houses is not loaded with ornaments. Two sorts of hewn stone, the porous amygdaloid called tetzontli, and especially a porphyry of vitreous feld-spath without any quartz, give to the Mexican buildings an air of solidity, and sometimes even of magnificence. None of those wooden balconies and galleries are to be seen, which so much disfigure all the European cities in both Indies. The balustrades and gates are all of Biscay iron, ornamented with bronze; and the houses, instead of roofs, have ter-races like those in Italy and other southern coun-tries.

Mexico has been very much embellished since the residence of the Abbé Chappe there in 1769. The edifice destined to the School of Mines, for which the richest individuals of the country fur-nished a sum of more than 125,000*l.* sterling, would adorn the principal places of Paris or London. Two great palaces *(hotels)* were recently constructed by Mexican artists, pupils of the Academy of Fine Arts of the capital. One of these palaces, in the quarter *della Traspana*, exhibits in the interior of the court a very beautiful oval peristyle of clustered columns. The traveller admires a vast circumfe-rence paved with porphyry flags, and inclosed with an iron railing, richly ornamented with bronze,

containing an equestrian statue of King Charles
the Fourth, placed on a pedestal of Mexican mar-
ble, in the midst of the *Plaza Major* of Mexico,
opposite the cathedral and the viceroy's palace. It
must however be allowed, that, notwithstanding the
progress of the arts within these last thirty years,
it is much less from the grandeur and beauty of
the monuments, than from the breadth and straight-
ness of the streets, and much less from its edifices,
than from its uniform regularity, its extent and
position, that the capital of New Spain attracts the
admiration of Europeans. From a singular con-
currence of circumstances, I have seen successively,
within a very short space of time, Lima, Mexico,
Philadelphia, Washington, Paris, Rome, Naples,
and the largest cities of Germany. By comparing
together impressions which follow in rapid succes-
sion, we are enabled to rectify any opinion which
we may have too easily adopted. Notwithstanding
these unavoidable comparisons, several of which,
one would think, must have proved disadvantageous to the capital of Mexico, it has left in my
mind a recollection of grandeur, which I principally
attribute to the majestic character of its situation
and the surrounding scenery.

Nothing, indeed, can present a more rich and
varied appearance than the valley, when, in a fine
summer morning, under a sky without a cloud, and
of that deep azure which is peculiar to the dry and
rarefied air of high mountains, we transport our-

selves to the top of one of the towers of the cathedral of Mexico, or ascend the hill of Chapoltepec. A beautiful vegetation surrounds this hill. Old cypress trunks, of more than 50 feet in circumference, raise their naked heads above those of the schinus, which resemble in their appearance the weeping-willows of the East. From the centre of this solitude, the summit of the porphyritical rock of Chapoltepec, the eye sweeps over a vast plain of carefully cultivated fields, which extend to the very feet of the colossal mountains covered with perpetual snow. The city appears as if washed by the waters of the lake of Tezcuco, whose basin, surrounded with villages and hamlets, brings to mind the most beautiful lakes of the mountains of Switzerland. Large avenues of elms and poplars lead in every direction to the capital; and two aqueducts, constructed over arches of very great elevation, cross the plain, and exhibit an appearance equally agreeable and interesting. The magnificent convent of Nuestra Señora de Guadalupe appears joined to the mountains of Tepeyacac, among ravines, which shelter a few date and young yucca trees. Towards the south, the whole tract between San Angel, Tacabaya, and San Augustin de las Cuevas, appears an immense garden of orange, peach, apple, cherry, and other European fruit-trees. This beautiful cultivation forms a singular contrast with the wild appearance of the naked mountains which inclose the valley, among which

the famous volcanos of LaPuebla, Popocatepetl, and
Iztaccihuatl are the most distinguished. The first
of these forms an enormous cone, of which the
crater, continually inflamed and throwing up smoke
and ashes, opens in the midst of eternal snows.

The market of Mexico is richly supplied with
eatables, particularly with roots and fruits of every
sort. It is a most interesting spectacle, which
may be enjoyed every morning at sun-rise, to see
these provisions, and a profusion of flowers, brought
in by Indians in boats descending the canals of
Istacalco and Chalco. The greater part of these
roots are cultivated on the *chinampas*, called by
the Europeans floating gardens. There are two
sorts of them, of which the one is moveable, and
driven about by the winds, and the other fixed and
attached to the shore. The first alone merit the
denomination of floating gardens, but their number
is daily diminishing.

The city of Mexico is also remarkable for its
excellent police. Most of the streets have very
broad pavements; and they are clean and well
lighted. These advantages are the fruits of the
activity of the Count de Revillagigedo, who on his
arrival found the capital extremely dirty.

Water is every where to be had in the soil of
Mexico a very short way below the surface, but it
is brackish, like the water of the lake of Tezcuco.
The two aqueducts already mentioned, by which the
city receives fresh water, are monuments of modern

construction worthy of the traveller's attention. The springs of potable water are situated to the east of the town, one in the insulated hill of Chapoltepec, and the other in the cerros of Santa Fe, near the Cordillera which separates the valley of Tenochtitlan from that of Lerma and Toluca. The arches of the aqueduct of Chapoltepec occupy a length of near 11,000 feet. The water of Chapoltepec enters by the southern part of the city, at the *Salto del Agua*.

The valley of Tenochtitlan offers to the examination of naturalists two sources of mineral water, that of Nuestra Señora de Guadalupe, and that of the Peñon de los Baños. These sources contain carbonic acid, sulfate of lime and soda, and muriate of soda. Baths have been established there in a manner equally salutary and convenient. The Indians manufacture their salt near the Peñon de los Baños.

No city of the new continent, without even excepting those of the United States, can display such great and solid scientific establishments as the capital of Mexico. I shall content myself here with naming the School of Mines, directed by the learned Elhuyar, to which we shall return when we come to speak of the mines ; the Botanic Garden ; and the Academy of Painting and Sculpture. This academy bears the title of *Academia de las Nobles Artes de Mexico.*

The revenues of the Academy of Fine Arts at

Mexico amount to above 5,000*l.* sterling, of which
the Government gives 3,000*l.*, the body of Mexican
Miners 1,000*l.*, the *Consulado,* or association of
merchants of the capital, 1,000*l.* It is impossible not to perceive the influence of this establishment on the taste of the nation. This influence is
particularly visible in the symmetry of the buildings, in the perfection with which the hewing of
stone is conducted, and in the ornaments of the
capitals and stucco relievos. What a number of
beautiful edifices are to be seen at Mexico! nay,
even in provincial towns like Guanaxuato and
Queretaro! These monuments, which frequently
cost from 40,000*l.* to 60,000*l.* sterling, would appear to advantage in the finest streets of Paris,
Berlin, and Petersburg. M. Tolsa, professor of
sculpture at Mexico, has cast an equestrian statue
of King Charles the Fourth, which, with the exception of the Marcus Aurelius at Rome, surpasses
in beauty and purity of style every work of the
kind in Europe. Instruction is communicated
*gratis* at the Academy of Fine Arts. It is not
confined alone to the drawing of landscapes and
figures ; they have had the good sense to employ
other means for exciting the national industry.
The academy labours successfully to introduce
among the artisans a taste for elegance and beautiful forms. Large rooms well lighted by Argand's
lamps, contain every evening some hundreds of
young people, some of whom draw from relievo or

living models, while others copy drawings of furniture, chandeliers, or other ornaments in bronze.
In this assemblage (and this is very remarkable in
the midst of a country where the prejudices of the
nobility against the castes are so inveterate) rank,
colour and race are confounded: we see the Indian
and the Mestizo sitting beside the White, and the
son of a poor artisan entering into competition
with the children of the great lords of the country.
It is a consolation to observe, that under every zone
the cultivation of science and art establishes a certain equality among men, and obliterates, for a time
at least, all those petty passions of which the effects
are so prejudicial to social happiness.

Since the close of the reign of Charles the Third,
and under that of Charles the Fourth, the study of
the physical sciences has made great progress, not
only in Mexico, but in general in all the Spanish
colonies.

The principles of the new chemistry, which is
known in the Spanish colonies by the equivocal ap-
pellation of new philosophy, (*nueva filosofia,*) are
more diffused in Mexico than in many parts of the
peninsula. A European traveller is surprised to
meet in the interior of the country, on the very
borders of California, with young Mexicans who
reason on the decomposition of water in the process of amalgamation with free air. The School
of Mines possesses a chemical laboratory; a geological collection, arranged according to the system

F

of Werner; a physical cabinet, in which we
not only find the valuable instruments of Rams-
den, Adams, Le Noir, and Louis Berthoud, but
also models executed in the capital, with the
greatest precision, and from the finest wood in the
country.   The best mineralogical work in the
Spanish language was printed at Mexico, I mean
the Manual of Oryctognosy, composed by M. del
Rio, according to the principles of the school of
Freyberg, in which the author was formed.   The
first Spanish translation of Lavoisier's Elements of
Chemistry was also published at Mexico.   I cite
these insulated facts, because they give us the measure of the ardour with which the exact sciences
are beginning to be studied in the capital of New
Spain.   This ardour is much greater than that
with which they addict themselves to the study of
languages and ancient literature.

Instruction in mathematics is less carefully attended to in the university of Mexico than in the
School of Mines.   The pupils of this last establishment go further into analysis; they are instructed
in the integral and differential calculi.   On the
return of peace and free intercourse with Europe,
when astronomical instruments (chronometers, sex-
tants, and the repeating circles of Borda) shall become more common, young men will be found in
the most remote parts of the kingdom capable of
making observations, and calculating them after the
most recent methods.

Within these twenty years, the Spanish and
Portuguese settlements of the New Continent have
experienced considerable changes in their moral
and political state; and the want of education and
knowledge has begun to be felt with the increasing
population and prosperity. The free trade with
neutrals, which the Court of Madrid, yielding to
imperious circumstances, has from time to time
granted to the island of Cuba, the coast of Caraccas, the ports of Vera Cruz and Monte Video, has
brought the colonists into contact with the Anglo-
Americans, the French, the English, and the
Danes; the colonists have formed the most correct
ideas respecting the state of Spain, compared with
the other powers of Europe; and the American
youth, sacrificing part of their national prejudices,
have formed a marked predilection for those nations
whose cultivation is further advanced than that of
the European Spaniards. In these circumstances,
we are not to be astonished, that the political
movements which have taken place in Europe since
1789, have excited the liveliest interest among a
people who have long been aspiring to rights, the
privation of which is both an obstacle to the public
prosperity, and a source of resentment against the
Mother Country.

Mexico is the country of inequality. No where
does there exist such a fearful difference in the
distribution of fortune, civilization, cultivation of
the soil, and population. The interior of the

country contains four cities, which are not more
than one or two days' journey distant from one another, and possess a population of 35,000, 67,000,
70,000, and 135,000 souls. The central table-
land from La Puebla to Mexico, and from thence
to Salamanca and Zelaya, is covered with villages
and hamlets like the most cultivated parts of Lom-
bardy. To the east and west of this narrow strip
succeed tracts of uncultivated ground, on which
we scarcely find above one person to the square
mile. The capital and several other cities have
scientific establishments, which will bear a comparison with those of Europe. The architecture
of the public and private edifices, the elegance of
the furniture, the equipages, the luxury and dress
of the women, the tone of society, all announce a
refinement to which the nakedness, ignorance, and
vulgarity of the lower people form the most striking
contrast. This immense inequality of fortune does
not only exist among the caste of Whites (Europeans or Creoles), it is even discoverable among the
Indians.

If, in the present state of things, the caste of
Whites is the only one in which we find any
thing like intellectual cultivation, it is also the
only one which possesses great wealth. This
wealth is unfortunately still more unequally distributed in Mexico than in the *capitania general*
of Caraccas, the Havannah, and especially Peru.
At Caraccas, the heads of the richest families

possess an income of about 8,000*l*.   In the
island of Cuba we find incomes of from 25,000*l*.
to 30,000*l*.   In these two industrious colonies
agriculture has founded more considerable fortunes
than have been accumulated by the working of the
mines in Peru.   At Lima an annual income of
30,000*l*. is very rare.   I know in reality of no
Peruvian family in the possession of a fixed and
sure revenue of 50,000*l*.   But in New Spain there
are individuals who possess no mines, whose income amounts to 40,000*l*.   The family of the
Count de la Valenciana, for example, possesses
alone, on the ridge of the Cordillera, a property
worth more than a million sterling, without including the mine of Valenciana near Guanaxuato,
which, *communibus annis*, yields a net revenue of
60,000*l*.   This family, of which the present head,
the young Count de la Valenciana, is distinguished
for a generous character and a noble desire of instruction, is divided into only three branches ; and
they possess all together, even in years when the
mine is not very lucrative, a revenue of more than
90,000*l*.   The Count de *Regla*, whose youngest
son, the Marquis de San Christobal*, distinguished
himself at Paris for his physical and physiological
knowledge, constructed at the Havannah, at his

* M. Terreros (this is the name by which this modest
savant is known in France) preferred for a long time the instruction which his abode at Paris enabled him to procure, to
the great fortune which he could only enjoy living in Mexico.

own expense, of acajou and cedar *(cedrella)* wood, two vessels of the line of the largest size, which he presented to his sovereign.  It was the vein of la Biscaina, near Pachuca, which laid the foundation of the fortune of the house of Regla.  The family of *Fagoaga,* well known for its beneficence, intelligence, and zeal for the public good, exhibits the example of the greatest wealth which was ever derived from a mine.  A single vein which the family of the Marquis of Fagoaga possesses in the district of Sombrerete, left, in five or six months, all charges deducted, a net profit of upwards of 800,000*l.*

From these data one would suppose there existed capitals in the Mexican families infinitely greater than what are really observed.  The deceased Count de la Valenciana, the first of the title, sometimes drew from his mine alone, in one year, a net revenue of no less than 250,000*l.*  This annual income, during the last twenty-five years of his life, was never below from 80,000*l.* to 125,000*l.* ; and yet this extraordinary man, who came without any fortune to America, and who continued to live with great simplicity, left behind him at his death, besides his mine, which is the richest in the world, in property and capital, only about 400,000*l.*  This fact, which may be relied on, will not surprise those who are acquainted with the internal management of the great Mexican houses.  Money rapidly gained is as rapidly spent.  The working of mines

becomes a game, in which they embark with un-
bounded passion. The rich proprietors of mines
lavish immense sums on quacks, who engage them
in new undertakings in the most remote provinces.
In a country where the works are conducted on
such an extravagant scale, that the shaft of a mine
frequently requires 80,000*l.* to pierce, the bad success of a rash project may, in a few years, absorb all
that was gained in working the richest veins. We
must add, that from the internal disorder which
prevails in most of the great houses of both Old
and New Spain, the head of a family is not un-
frequently straitened with a revenue of 20,000*l.*,
though he display no other luxury than that of
numerous yokes of mules.

The mines have undoubtedly been the principal
sources of the great fortunes of Mexico. Many
miners have laid out their wealth in purchasing
land, and have devoted themselves with great zeal
to agriculture. But there is also a considerable
number of powerful families who have never had
the working of any very lucrative mines. Such
are the rich descendants of Cortez, or the *Marquis
del Valle*. The Duke of Monteleone, a Neapolitan
nobleman, who is now the head of the house of
Cortez, possesses magnificent estates in the province
of Oaxaca, near Toluca, and at Cuernavaca. The
net produce of his rents is now no more than
23,000*l.*, the king having deprived the duke of the
collection of the *alcavalus* and the duties on tobacco.

The ordinary expenses of the management of his property amount to more than 5000*l.* per annum. Several governors of the *marquesado* have however become extremely wealthy. If the descendants of the great *conquistador* would only live in Mexico, their revenue would immediately rise to more than 60,000*l.*

As a further proof of the immense wealth centred in the hands of a few individuals in New Spain, which may compete with any thing in Great Britain, or the European possessions in Hindostan, I must mention the pecuniary sacrifices annually made by the body of Miners (*Cuerpo de mineria*) for the improvement of mining. This body, formed by a union of the proprietors of mines, and represented by deputies who sit in the *Tribunal de Mineria,* advanced in three years, between 1784 and 1787, more than 160,000*l.* to individuals who were in want of the necessary funds to carry on great works. It is believed in the country that this money has not been very usefully employed (*para habilitar*); but its distribution proves the generosity and opulence of those who are able to make such donations. A European reader will be still more astonished when I inform him of the extraordinary fact, that the respectable family of Fagoagas lent, a few years ago, without interest, nearly 150,000*l.* to a friend, whose fortune they believed would be permanently secured by it. This sum was irrevocably lost in an unsuccessful new mining undertaking. The architectural works which are carried on in the capital of Mexico for the embellishment of the city are so expensive, that, notwithstanding the low rate of wages, the superb edifice constructed by order of the *Tribunal de Mineria* for the School of Mines will cost at least 125,000*l.*, of which 80,000*l.* were in readiness before the foundation was laid. To hasten the construction, and particularly to furnish the students immediately with a proper laboratory for metallic experiments on the amalgamation of great masses of minerals (*beneficio de patio*), the body of Mexican Miners contributed monthly, in the year 1803 alone, the sum of 2000*l.* Such is the facility with which vast projects are executed in a country where wealth is divided among a small number of individuals.

# 42

## CHAPTER III.

*Climate—variety under the same latitude—rains—general salubrity—fertility of the soil—corn, fruits—cattle—general improvement in agriculture—influence of mines on agriculture—habits of Indian cultivators.*

HAVING traced the physical outline of the country, and described the inequalities of its surface, we shall proceed to point out the effect of these inequalities upon its climate, and to give some account of the state of cultivation. We shall confine ourselves to a few general and important facts. Details of natural history do not fall within the compass or the purpose of this work; but it is impossible to form an exact idea of the territorial riches of a country without knowing the form of the mountains, the height of the great plains of the interior, and the temperature of the regions in which there are (if we may so express ourselves) successive strata of climate.

If we take a general view of the whole surface of the kingdom of Mexico, we shall see that two-thirds are situated under the temperate, and one under the torrid zone. The former part contains 738,000 square miles, and includes the *Provincias Internas de la Commendancia-general*, a district thinly peopled. The latter, containing 324,000 square miles, enjoys a climate which is cool or temperate, rather than sultry. It is well known that the climate of a country depends, not only on its distance from the pole, but also on its elevation above the level of the sea, proximity to the ocean, configuration, and many other local circumstances. The interior of the viceroyalty of Mexico forms an immense plain, elevated from 6000 to 8200 feet above the level of the sea. The country lying between the capital of Mexico and the port of Vera Cruz may be divided into three districts or zones, the climate of which depends on their elevation. The first of these, called by the natives *terras calientes*, comprehends all the country on the coast, nearly the whole intendancy of Vera Cruz, the southern regions of the intendancies of Mexico, Valladolid, and La Puebla. It is all flat country, intersected by inconsiderable hills. The mean temperature of these plains is about 77° of Fahrenheit's thermometer, that is to say, 15° or 16° higher than the temperature of Naples. They produce sugar, indigo, cotton, and bananas, in abundance, but are extremely unhealthy. They are liable to great and sudden changes of temperature, and are frequently visited by yellow fever.

The next region, called *terras templadas*, lies on the declivity of the Cordilleras, at the height of from 4000 to 5000 feet, and enjoys a perpetual spring. The temperature is soft and equal, never varying

more than 4° or 5° : the mean heat of the whole
year is from 68° to 70°. This region is, however,
extremely liable to fogs from the sea.

The third zone, the *terras frias*, comprehends
the table-lands, which are elevated more than 7200
feet above the level of the sea. Although they are
known under the name of *terras frias*, the thermometer has very rarely been known to be down to
the freezing point : in the coldest season the mean
heat of the day is from 55° to 60°. In summer the
thermometer in the shade does not rise above 75°.
The general mean temperature of the whole vast
table-land of Mexico is 62°. It is equal to the
temperature of Rome. This is a sufficient proof
that the words hot and cold have no positive value.
The table-lands higher than that of Mexico have a
very rough and disagreeable climate, even to the
feelings of a native of a northern latitude. The
winters are not severe, but there is a total absence
of that transient summer which has a peculiar
beauty in high latitudes.

These general considerations on the physical division of New Spain are extremely interesting in a
political point of view. In France, and even in
the greatest part of Europe, the cultivation of
the soil depends almost entirely on geographical
latitude; but in the equinoctial regions of Peru,
New Grenada, and Mexico, the climate, productions, and aspect of the country, are solely
modified by the elevation of the soil above the level

of the sea. The influence of geographical position is absorbed in the effect of this elevation.

There are only two seasons known in the equinoctial region of Mexico even as far as the 28th degree of N. latitude ; the rainy season (*estacion de las aguas*), which begins in the month of June or July, and ends in the month of September or October, and the dry season (*el estio*), which lasts eight months, from October to the end of May. The first rains generally commence on the eastern declivity of the Cordillera. The formation of the clouds, and the precipitation of the water dissolved in the air, commence on the coast of Vera Cruz. These phenomena are accompanied with strong electrical explosions, which take place successively at Mexico, Guadalaxara, and on the western coast. The chemical action is propagated from east to west in the direction of the trade winds, and the rains begin fifteen or twenty days sooner at Vera Cruz than on the central table-land. Sometimes we see in the mountain, even below 6600 feet of absolute height, rain mixed with hail (*gresil*) and snow in the months of November, December, and January ; but these rains are very short, and only last from four to five days ; and, however cold they may be, they are considered as very beneficial to the wheat and pasture lands. In Mexico, as in Europe, the rains are most frequent in the mountainous regions, especially in that part of the Cordilleras which extends from the Pic d'Orizaba by Guanaxuato,

Sierra de Pinos, Zacatecas, and Bolaños, to the mines of Guarisamey and the Rosario.

To the north of 20°, from the 22d to the 30th degree of latitude, the rains, which fall only in the months of June, July, August, and September, are very unfrequent in the interior of the country.

The aridity of the central plain, the want of trees, occasioned, perhaps, in a good measure by the length of time the great valleys have remained covered with water, obstruct very much the working of the mines. These disadvantages have augmented since the arrival of Europeans in Mexico, who have not only destroyed without planting, but in draining great tracts of land have occasioned another more important evil. Muriate of soda and lime, nitrate of potash, and other saline substances, cover the surface of the soil, and spread with a rapidity very difficult to be explained. Through this abundance of salt, and these efflorescences, hostile to cultivation, the table-land of Mexico bears a great resemblance in many places to Thibet and the saline steppes of central Asia. In the valley of Tenochtitlan particularly, the sterility and want of vigorous vegetation have been sensibly augmenting since the Spanish conquest; for this valley was adorned with beautiful verdure when the lake occupied more ground, and the clayey soil was washed by more frequent inundations.

Happily, however, this aridity of soil, of which we have been indicating the principal physical causes, is only to be found in the most elevated plains. A great part of the vast kingdom of New Spain may be ranked among the most fertile regions of the earth. The declivity of the Cordillera is exposed to humid winds and frequent fogs; and the vegetation nourished by these aqueous vapours exhibits an uncommon beauty and strength. The humidity of the coasts, assisting the putrefaction of a great mass of organic substances, gives rise to maladies, to which Europeans and others not seasoned to the climate are alone exposed ; for under the burning sun of the tropics the unhealthiness of the air almost always indicates extraordinary fertility of soil. Thus at Vera Cruz the quantity of rain in a year amounts to 63 inches, while in France it scarcely amounts to 31 inches. Yet with the exception of a few sea-ports and deep valleys, where the natives suffer from intermittent fevers, New Spain must be considered as a remarkably healthy country.

In hot but dry climates the human species enjoys a longevity perhaps greater than what we observe in the temperate zones. This is especially the case whenever the temperature and climate are very variable. The Europeans who settle in the equinoctial part of the Spanish colonies at an advanced period of life, generally live and enjoy health to a great age. At Vera Cruz, in the midst of the epidemical *black vomit*, the natives and strangers seasoned for several years to the climate enjoy the most perfect health.

In general, the coasts and arid plains of equato

rial America, must be regarded as healthy, notwithstanding the excessive heat of the sun, whose perpendicular rays are reflected by the soil. Individuals arrived at maturity, particularly those who approach to old age, have little to fear from these regions, the unhealthiness of which has been unjus-
tifiably exaggerated. The chief mortality is among
the children and young people, particularly in those
parts where the climate is at once hot and moist.

The inhabitants of Mexico are less disturbed by
earthquakes and volcanic eruptions than those of
Quito and the provinces of Guatimala and Cumana.
There are only five burning volcanoes in all New
Spain, Orizaba, Popocatepetl, and the mountains
of Tustla, Jorullo, and Colimà. Earthquakes, however, are by no means rare on the coast of the Pacific Ocean, and in the environs of the capital, but
they never produce such desolating effects as have
been experienced in the more southern provinces.

A very serious inconvenience is common to the
eastern coast, and to the coast washed by the great
ocean falsely called the Pacific Ocean. They are
rendered inaccessible for several months by violent tempests, which effectually prevent all navigation. The north-west winds (*los nortes*) blow
in the Gulf of Mexico from the autumnal to
the spring equinox. These winds are generally
moderate in the months of September and October; their greatest fury is in the month of
March, and they sometimes last into April. Navi-
gators who have long frequented the port of Vera

Cruz, know the symptoms which always foretell the approach of the tempest.

An empire extending from the sixteenth to the thirty-seventh degree of latltude affords us, from its geometrical position, all the modifications of climate to be found on transporting ourselves from the banks of the Senegal to Spain, or from the Malabar coast to the steppes of the Great Bucharia. This variety of climate is also augmented by the geological constitution of the country, by the mass and extraordinary form of the Mexican mountains, which we have already described. On the ridge and declivity of the Cordilleras the temperature of each table-land varies as it is more or less elevated ; not merely insulated peaks, the summits of which approach the region of perpetual snow, are covered with oaks and pines, but whole provinces spontaneously produce alpine plants ; and the cultivator inhabiting the torrid zone frequently loses the hopes of his harvest from the effects of frost or from the abundance of snow.

Geographical position alone does not determine the nature of the productions of these fine regions. The union of several physical causes alluded to above, gives to a part of the equinoctial regions a temperature adapted to the cultivation of the wheat and fruit-trees of Europe. Latitude has small influence on the fertility of a country, where, on the summit and declivity of the mountains, nature exhibits an union of every climate.

H

We may conceive that, in a country like Mexico, the variety of indigenous productions must be immense, and that there hardly exists a plant on the rest of the globe which is not capable of being cultivated in some part of New Spain.

In general, in the equinoctial regions of New Spain, the soil, climate, physiognomy of vegetables, all assume the character of the temperate zones.

The riches of the harvests are surprising in lands carefully cultivated, especially in those which are watered, or properly separated by different courses of labour. The most fertile part of the table-land is that which extends from Queretaro to the town of Leon. These elevated plains are 90 miles in length by 20 or 30 in breadth. The wheat harvest is 35 and 40 for 1, and several great farms can even reckon on 50 or 60 to 1. I found the same fertility in the fields which extend from the village of Santiago to Yurirapundaro in the intendancy of Valladolid. In the environs of Puebla, Atlisco, and Zelaya, in a great part of the bishopricks of Michoacan and Guadalaxara, the produce is from 20 to 30 for 1. A field is considered there as far from fertile when a fanega* of wheat yields only, *communibus annis*, 16 fanegas. At Cholula the common harvest is from 30 to 40, but it frequently exceeds from 70 to 80 for 1. In the valley of Mexico the maize yields 200 and the wheat 18 or 20.

* About a hundred weight.

In good years the kingdom of New Spain produces much more maize than it can consume. As
the country unites in a small space a great variety
of climates, and as maize rarely succeeds at the
same time in the warm region (*tierras calientas*)
and on the central table-land in the *terras frias*,
the interior commerce is greatly animated by the
transport of this grain. Maize compared with European grain has the disadvantage of containing a
smaller quantity of nutritive substance in a greater
volume. This circumstance, and the difficulty of
the roads on the declivities of the mountains, present obstacles to its exportation, which will be in
a great degree removed by the construction of the
fine causeway from Vera Cruz to Xalapa and Perote.

The Mexican wheat is of the very best quality ;
it may be compared with the finest Andalusian
grain. The grain is very large, white, and nutritive, especially in farms where watering is employed.

The interior of New Spain is infinitely productive in nutritive gramina, wherever the industry of
man has corrected the natural dryness of the soil and
the air. No where does the proprietor of a large farm
more frequently feel the necessity of employing engineers skilled in surveying ground and in the principles of hydraulic constructions. At Mexico however, as elsewhere, those arts which please the imagination have been preferred to those which are indispensable to the wants of domestic life. They possess architects, who judge scientifically of the beauty

and symmetry of an edifice ; but nothing is still so
rare there, as to find persons capable of constructing machines, dikes, and canals. Fortunately, the
feeling of their want has excited the national industry ; and a certian sagacity peculiar to all mountainous people supplies in some degree the want of
instruction.

Mexico is extremely rich in vegetables with nutritive roots. The plants which are cultivated in the
highest and coldest part of the Andes and Mexican
Cordilleras are the potatoe, the *tropæolum esculen-
tum,* and the *chenopodium quinoa,* the grain of
which is an aliment equally agreeable and healthy.
In New Spain the first of these becomes an object of
cultivation, of so much the greater importance and
extent, as it does not require any great humidity
of soil. The Mexicans, like the Peruvians, can
preserve potatoes for years by exposing them to
the frost and drying them in the sun.

The Mexicans now possess all the garden-stuffs
and fruit-trees of Europe. The central table-land
of New Spain produces in the greatest abundance
cherries, plums, peaches, apricots, figs, grapes, me-
lons, apples, and pears. In the environs of Mexico,
the villages of San Augustin de las Cuevas and Tacubaya, the famous garden of the Convent of Carmelites at San Angel, and that of the family of Fagoaga at Tanepantla, yield in the months of June,
July, and August, an immense quantity of fruit,
for the most part of an exquisite taste, although

the trees are in general very ill taken care of. The traveller is astonished to see in Mexico, Peru, and New Grenada, the tables of the wealthy inhabitants loaded at once with the fruits of temperate Europe, ananas, different species of *passiflora* and *tacsonia*, sapotes, mameis, goyavas, anonas, chilimoyas, and other valuable productions of the torrid zone.

There is a great abundance of horned cattle all along the eastern coast of Mexico, especially at the mouths of the rivers of Alvarado, Guasacualco, and Panuco, where numerous flocks feed on pastures of perpetual verdure. Since the middle of the sixteenth century, the most useful animals of the old continent, oxen, horses, sheep, and hogs, have multiplied surprisingly in all parts of New Spain, and especially in the vast plains of the *Provincias Internas.*

The horses of the northern provinces, and particularly those of New Mexico, are as celebrated for their excellent qualities as the horses of Chili; both descend, as it is pretended, from the Arab race; they wander wild in herds, in the savannahs of the *Provincias Internas.* The exportation of these horses to Natchez and New Orleans, becomes every year of greater importance. Many Mexican families possess in their *Hatos de ganado,* from thirty to forty thousand head of horses and oxen. The mules would be still more numerous, if so many of them did not perish on the highways from the excessive fatigues of journeys of several months. It is reckoned that the commerce of Vera Cruz

alone, employs annually nearly 70,000 mules.
More than 5,000 are employed for purposes of luxury in the carriages of the city of Mexico.

The cultivation of the soil, notwithstanding the
fetters with which it is every where shackled, has
lately made a more considerable progress, on account of the immense capitals laid out in land, by
families enriched either by the commerce of Vera
Cruz and Acapulco, or by the working of the
mines.

Those who only know the interior of the Spanish
colonies from the vague and uncertain notions hitherto published, will have some difficulty in be-
lieving that the principal sources of the Mexican
riches are by no means the mines, but an agriculture which has been gradually ameliorating since
the end of the last century. Without reflecting on
the immense extent of the country, and especially
the great number of provinces which appear totally
destitute of precious metals, we generally imagine
that all the activity of the Mexican population is
directed to the working of mines.

The best cultivated fields of Mexico, those which
recall to the mind of the traveller the beautiful
plains of France, are those which extend from Salamanca towards Silao, Guanaxuato, and the Villa
de Leon, and which surround the richest mines of
the known world. Wherever metallic veins have
been discovered in the most uncultivated parts of
the Cordilleras, on the insulated and desert table-

lands, the working of mines, far from impeding the cultivation of the soil, as it is generally imagined, has been singularly favourable to it. Travelling along the ridge of the Andes, or the mountainous part of Mexico, we every where see the most striking examples of the beneficial influence of the mines on agriculture. Were it not for the establishments formed for the working of the mines, how many places would have remained desert! how many districts uncultivated in the four intendancies of Guanaxuato, Zacatecas, San Luis Potosi, and Durango, between the parallels of 21° and 25°, where the most considerable metallic wealth of New Spain is to be found! If the town is placed on the arid side or the crest of the Cordilleras, the new colonists can only draw from a distance means for their subsistence, and for the maintenance of the great number of cattle employed in drawing off the water, and raising and amalgamating the mineral produce. Want soon awakens industry. The soil begins to be cultivated in the ravines and declivities of the neighbouring mountains, wherever the rock is covered with earth. Farms are established in the neighbourhood of the mine. The high price of provision, from the competition of the purchasers, indemnifies the cultivator for the privations to which he is exposed from the hard life of the mountains. Thus from the hope of gain, and the motives of mutual interest, —the most powerful bonds of society,—and without any interference on the part of the Government to promote colonization, a mine which at first appeared insulated in the midst of wild and desert mountains, becomes in a short time connected with the lands which have long been under cultivation.

Moreover, this influence of the mines on the progressive cultivation of the country is more durable than they are themselves. When the veins are exhausted, and the subterraneous operations are abandoned, the population of the canton undoubtedly diminishes, because the miners emigrate elsewhere; but the colonist is retained by his attachment for the spot where he received his birth, and which his fathers cultivated with their hands. The more lonely the cottage is, the more charms has it for the inhabitant of the mountains. It is with the beginning of civilization as with its decline : man appears to repent of the constraint which he has imposed on himself by entering into society; and he loves solitude because it restores to him his former freedom. This desire for solitude is particularly manifested by the copper-coloured natives, whom a long and sad experience has disgusted with social life, and more especially with the neighbourhood of the Whites. Like the Arcadians, the Aztec people love to inhabit the summits and brows of the steepest mountains. This peculiar trait in their disposition contributes very much to extend population in the mountainous regions of Mexico.

What a pleasure is it for the traveller to follow these peaceful conquests of agriculture, to contemplate the numerous Indian cottages dispersed in the wildest ravines, and necks of cultivated ground advancing into a desert country between naked and arid rocks!

The Indian cultivator is poor, but he is free. His state is even greatly preferable to that of the peasantry in a great part of the north of Europe. There are neither *corvées* nor villenage in New Spain; and the number of slaves is next to nothing. Sugar is chiefly the produce of free hands. There the principal objects of agriculture are not the productions to which European luxury has assigned a variable and arbitrary value, but cereal gramina, nutritive roots, and the agave, the vine of the Indians. The appearance of the country proclaims to the traveller that the soil nourishes him who cultivates it, and that the true prosperity of the Mexican people neither depends on the accidents of foreign commerce, nor on the unsettled politics of Europe.

We have thus examined the true national wealth of Mexico; for the produce of the earth is, in fact, the sole basis of permanent opulence. It is consolatory to see that the labour of man, for half a century, has been more directed towards this fertile and inexhaustible source, than towards the working of mines, of which the wealth has not so direct an influence on the public prosperity, and

I

merely changes the nominal value of the annual produce of the earth. The territorial impost levied by the clergy, under the name of tenth, or tithe, measures the quantity of that produce, and indicates with precision the progress of agricultural industry, if we compare the periods, in the intervals of which the price of commodities has undergone no sensible variation.

The result of such a comparison made from the most exact data is, that the total augmentation has been, in the last ten years, 1,062,500*l.*, or two-fifths of the total produce. The same data also indicate the rapidity of the progress of agriculture, in the intendancies of Mexico, Guadalaxara, Puebla, and Valladolid, compared with the provinces of Oaxaca and New Biscay. The tithes have been nearly doubled in the archbishoprick of Mexico; for those which were levied during the ten years anterior to 1780, were to those levied ten years afterwards in the proportion of 10 to 17. In the intendancy of Durango or New Biscay, this augmentation has been only in the proportion of 10 to 11.

## CHAPTER IV.

*Population—numbers and character of native Indians—*
*comparison between the population of Mexico and that*
*of the United States—small number of Negro slaves—*
*increase of population—census of* 1794.

THE Mexican population is composed of the same
elements as the other Spanish colonies. They
reckon seven races : 1. The individuals born in Europe, vulgarly called *Gachupines;* 2. The Spanish
Creoles, or Whites of European extraction born in
America ; 3. the *Mestizos,* descendants of Whites
and Indians; 4. the Mulattos, descendants of Whites
and Negros; 5. the *Zambos,* descendants of Negros
and Indians; 6. the Indians, or copper-coloured indigenous race; and 7. the African Negros. Abstracting the subdivisions, there are four castes : the
Whites comprehended under the general name of
Spaniards, the Negros, the Indians, and the men of
mixed extraction from Europeans, Africans, American Indians, and Malays ; for from the frequent
communication between Acapulco and the Philippine islands, many individuals of Asiatic origin,
both Chinese and Malays, have settled in New
Spain.

A very general prejudice exists in Europe, that
an exceeding small number of the copper-coloured
race, or descendants of the ancient Mexicans, re-

I 2

main at this day. The cruelty of the Europeans has entirely extirpated the old inhabitants of the West Indies; the continent of America, however, has witnessed no such horrible result. The number of Indians in New Spain exceeds two millions and a half, including those only who have no mixture of European or African blood. It is still more consolatory, that the indigenous population, far from declining, has been considerably on the increase for the last fifty years, as is proved by the registers of capitation or tribute.

The Indians appear to form two-fifths of the whole population of Mexico. In the four intendancies of Guanaxuato, Valladolid, Oaxaca, and La Puebla, this population amounts even to three-fifths. The census of 1793 gave the following result.

| Names of intendancies. | Total population. | Number of Indians. |
|---|---|---|
| Guanaxuato . | 398,000 | . 175,000 |
| Valladolid . . | 290,000 | . 119,000 |
| Puebla . . . | 638,000 | . 416,000 |
| Oaxaca . . . | 411,000 | . 363,000 |

To give an accurate idea of the indigenous inhabitants of New Spain, it is not enough to paint them in their present state of degradation and misery; we must go back to a remote period, when, governed by its own laws, the nation could display its native energy; and we must consult the hieroglyphical paintings, buildings of hewn stone, and works of sculpture still in preservation, which though they attest the infancy of the arts, yet bear a striking analogy to several monuments of the most civilized people. The nature of this work does not permit us to enter into such details, however interesting they may be, both for the history and the psychological study of our species. We shall merely point out here a few of the most prominent features of the immense picture of American indigenous population.

The Indians of New Spain bear a general resemblance to those who inhabit Canada, Florida, Peru, and Brasil. They have the same swarthy and copper colour, flat and smooth hair, small beard, squat body, long eye, with the corner directed upwards towards the temples, prominent cheek bones, thick lips, and an expression of gentleness in the mouth, strongly contrasted with a gloomy and severe expression of eye. The American race, after the hyperborean race, is the least numerous; but it occupies the greatest space on the globe.

Intellectual cultivation is what contributes the most to diversify the features. In barbarous nations there is rather a physiognomy peculiar to the tribe or horde, than to any individual. When we compare our domestic animals with those which inhabit our forests, we make the same observation. But an European, when he decides on the strong resemblance among the copper-coloured races, is subject to a particular illusion.  He is struck with a complexion so different from our own, and the uniformity of this complexion conceals for a long time from him the diversity of individual features. The new colonist at first can hardly distinguish the natives, because his eyes are less fixed on the gentle, melancholy, or ferocious expression of the countenance, than on the red coppery colour, and black coarse hair, so straight and glossy that it always appears wet.

As to the moral faculties of the Indians, it is difficult to appreciate them with justice, if we only consider this long oppressed caste in their present state of degradation.  The better sort of Indians, among whom a certain degree of intellectual culture might be expected, perished in great numbers, at the commencement of the Spanish conquest, the victims of European ferocity.  The Christian fanaticism was particularly directed against the Aztec priests ; and the Teopixqui, or ministers of the divinity, and all those who inhabited the Teocalli, or houses of God, who might be considered as the depositories of the historical, mythological, and astronomical knowledge of the country, were exterminated ; the priests observed the meridian shades in the gnomons, and regulated the calendar. The monks burned the hieroglyphical paintings, by which every kind of knowledge was transmitted from generation to generation.  The people, deprived of these means of instruction, were plunged

in an ignorance so much the deeper, as the Missionaries were unskilled in the Mexican languages,
and could substitute few new ideas in the place of
the old.  The remaining natives then consisted
only of the most indigent race, poor cultivators,
artisans, among whom were a great number of
weavers, porters, who were used like beasts of burden, and especially of those dregs of the people,
those crowds of beggars, who bore witness to the
imperfection of the social institutions, and the existence of feudal oppression, and who filled, in the
time of Cortez, the streets of all the great cities of
the Mexican empire.  How shall we judge, then,
from these miserable remains of a powerful people,
of the degree of cultivation to which it had risen
from the twelfth to the sixteenth century, and of
the intellectual development of which it is susceptible ?  If all that remained of the French or
German nation were a few poor agriculturists,
could we read in their features that they belonged
to nations which had produced a Descartes and
Clairaut, a Kepler and a Leibnitz ?

How is it possible to doubt that a part of the
Mexican nation had arrived at a certain degree of
cultivation, when we reflect on the care with which
their hieroglyphical books were composed, and
when we recollect that a citizen of Tlascala, in the
midst of the tumults of war, took advantage of
the facility offered him by our Roman alphabet to
write in his own language five large volumes on the

history of a country of which he deplored the sub-
jection ?

In the portrait which we draw of the different
races of men composing the population of New
Spain, we shall merely consider the Mexican
Indian in his actual state. We perceive in him
neither that mobility of sensation, gesture, or feature, nor that activity of mind, for which several
nations of the equinoctial regions of Africa are so
advantageously distinguished. There cannot exist
a more marked contrast than that between the
impetuous vivacity of the Congo negro, and the
apparent phlegm of the Indian. From a feeling
of this contrast, the Indian women not only prefer
the negros to the men of their own race, but also
to the Europeans. The Mexican Indian is grave,
melancholy, and silent, so long as he is not under
the influence of intoxicating liquors. This gravity
is peculiarly remarkable in Indian children, who
at the age of four or five display much more intelligence and maturity than White children. The
Mexican loves to throw a mysterious air over the
most indifferent actions. The most violent passions are never painted in his features ; and there
is something frightful in seeing him pass all at once
from absolute repose to a state of violent and un-
restrained agitation. The Peruvian Indian possesses more gentleness of manners ; the energy of
the Mexican degenerates into harshness. These
differences may have their origin in the different

religions and different governments of the two countries in former times. This energy is displayed particularly by the inhabitants of Tlascala. In the midst of their present degradation, the descendants of the citizens of that republic are still to be distinguished by a certain haughtiness of character, inspired by the memory of their former grandeur.

The Americans, like the Hindoos and other nations who have long groaned under a civil and military despotism, adhere to their customs, manners, and opinions, with extraordinary obstinacy*. I say opinions; for the introduction of Christianity has produced little other effect on the Indians of

* It is of the utmost importance to the prosperity and security of the great undertaking which now occupies so large a share of the public attention, that all the Officers and Servants sent out by the Mining Companies of England should observe the most inviolable respect for the religious opinions and institutions of the natives. The Protestant opinions of Englishmen are sufficiently obnoxious, without being called into notice by any injudicious and absurd and fruitless attempts at conversion. How totally these attempts have failed to produce any thing but disgust among the Hindoos, to whom the Baron de Humboldt here compares the Mexican Indians, is well known to every calm and well-informed man in our Eastern possessions. If the utility and policy of agitating such a source of discord, where we are undisputed masters, may be questioned, we presume it will be admitted by all but fanatics, that it would be little short of insanity to do it in a country where our establishments will stand in need of the countenance and protection of all classes. We have pressed this subject the more warmly

K

Mexico than to substitute new ceremonies, the symbols of a gentle and humane religion, to the ceremonies of a sanguinary worship. This change from old to new rites was the effect of constraint, and not of persuasion, and was produced by political events alone. In the new continent, as well as in the old, half-civilized nations were accustomed to receive from the hands of the conqueror new laws and new divinities; and the vanquished Indian gods appeared to them to yield to the gods of the strangers.

Accustomed to a long slavery, as well under the domination of their own sovereigns as under that of the first conquerors, the natives of Mexico patiently suffer the vexations to which they are frequently exposed from the Whites. They oppose to them only cunning, veiled under the most deceitful appearances of apathy and stupidity. As the Indian can very rarely revenge himself on the Spaniards, he delights in making common cause with them for the oppression of his own fellow citizens. Oppressed for ages, and compelled to a blind obedience, he wishes to tyrannize in his turn. The Indian villages are governed by magistrates of

---

upon our readers, as we know that among many of the inferior Officers, the motive to the course of action so earnestly deprecated will be found in peculiar force. However we may respect the disinterestedness of this motive, we are bound to repeat, that the safety of our establishments is absolutely dependant on caution and forbearance on this point.

the copper-coloured race; and an Indian alcade exercises his power with so much the greater severity, because he is sure of being supported by the priest or the *Spanish subdelegado* Oppression produces every where the same effects; it every where corrupts the morals.

As the Indians almost all of them belong to the class of peasantry and labourers, it is not easy to judge of their aptitude for the arts which embellish life. I know no race of men who appear more destitute of imagination. When an Indian attains a certain degree of civilization, he displays a great facility of apprehension, a judicious mind, a natural logic, and a particular disposition to subtilize or seize the finest differences in the comparison of objects. He reasons coolly and methodically; but he never manifests that versatility of imagination, that glow of sentiment, and that creative and animating spirit, which characterize the nations of the south of Europe, and several tribes of African Negros. I deliver this opinion, however, with great diffidence. We cannot be too circumspect, in pronouncing on the moral or intellectual dispositions of nations from which we are separated by the multiplied obstacles resulting from a difference in language, and in manners and customs.

The Indians of New Spain, those at least subject to the European domination, generally attain to a pretty advanced age. As peaceable cultivators, and inhabitants of villages, they are not exposed to the accidents attending the wandering life of the hunters and warriors of the Mississippi and the savannas of the Rio Gila. Accustomed to uniform nourishment of an almost entirely vegetable nature, that of their maize and cereal gramina, the Indians would undoubtedly attain very great longevity if their constitutions were not weakened by drunkenness. Their intoxicating liquors are rum, a fermentation of maize and the root of the jatropha, and especially the wine of the country, made of the juice of the agave americana, called *pulque.* This last liquor is nutritive, on account of the undecomposed sugar which it contains. Many Indians addicted to *pulque* take, for a long time, very little solid nourishment. When used with moderation it is very salutary, and, by fortifying the stomach, assists the functions of the gastric system.

The vice of drunkenness is, however, less general among the Indians than is generally believed. There are several Indian tribes very sober, whose fermented beverages are too weak to intoxicate. In New Spain drunkenness is most common among the Indians who inhabit the valley of Mexico, and the environs of Puebla and Tlascala, wherever the maguey or agave is cultivated on a great scale. The police in the city of Mexico sends round tumbrils, to collect the drunkards to be found stretched out in the streets. These Indians, who are treated like dead bodies, are carried to the principal guard-house. In the morning an iron ring is put round their ancles, and they are made to clear the streets for three days. On letting them go on the fourth day, they are sure to find several of them in the course of the week. It is to be hoped that this evil will diminish, as civilization advances.

We are tempted to compare together the extent and population of Mexico, and that of two empires with which this fine colony is in relations of union and of rivalry. Spain is five times smaller than Mexico. Should no unforeseen misfortunes occur, we may reckon that in less than a century the population of New Spain will equal that of the mother country. The United States of North America since the cession of Louisiana, and since they recognise no other boundary than the *Rio-Bravo del Norte*, contain 2,160,000 square miles. Their population is not much greater than that of Mexico, as we shall see on examining the population and the area of New Spain.

If the political force of two states depended solely on the space which they occupy on the globe, and on the number of their inhabitants; if the nature of the soil, the configuration of the coast, and if the climate, the energy of the nation, and above all the degree of perfection of its social institutions, were not the principal elements of this grand dynamical calculation, the kingdom of New

Spain might now be placed in competition with the confederation of the American republics. Both labour under the inconvenience of an unequally distributed population; but that of the United States, though in a soil and climate less favoured by nature, augments with an infinitely greater rapidity. Neither does it comprehend, like the Mexican population, nearly two millions and a half of aborigines, degraded by the despotism of their ancient *Aztec* sovereigns, and by the vexations of the first conquerors. The kingdom of New Spain has, however, one decided advantage over the United States. The number of slaves there, either of African or of mixed race, is almost nothing; an advantage which the European colonists have only begun rightly to appreciate since the tragical events of the revolution of St. Domingo.

The kingdom of New Spain is, of all the European colonies under the torrid zone, that in which there are the fewest Negros. We may almost say that there are no slaves. We may go through the whole city of Mexico without seeing a black countenance. The service of no house is carried on by slaves. In this point of view especially, Mexico presents a singular contrast to the Havannah, Lima, and Caraccas. From exact information procured by those employed in the enumeration of 1793, it appears that in all New Spain there are not six thousand Negros, and not more than nine or ten thousand slaves, of whom the greatest number belong to the ports of Acapulco and Vera Cruz, or the warm regions of the coasts (*tierras calientes*).

The slaves, who fortunately are in very small numbers in Mexico, are there, as in all the other Spanish possessions, somewhat more under the protection of the laws than the Negros of the other European colonies. These laws are always interpreted in favour of liberty. The Government wishes to see the number of freemen increased. A slave, who by his industry has procured a little money, may compel his master to give him his liberty on paying the moderate sum of 60*l.* or 80*l.* Liberty cannot be refused to a Negro on the pretext that he cost triple that sum, or that he possesses a peculiar talent for some lucrative employment. A slave who has been cruelly treated acquires, on that account, his freedom by the law, if the judge do justice to the cause of the oppressed ; but it may be easily conceived that this beneficent law is frequently eluded.

Politico-economical investigations have been so rare in Spain, that it excites no surprise that the archives of the viceroyalty of Mexico contain no census of the population before 1794, when the Count of Villagegido, one of the wisest and most active of administrators, had resolution enough to undertake it. Those who know the difficulty of obtaining an exact census in the most cultivated

countries of Europe, will easily imagine what powerful obstacles opposed themselves to his researches.
He was indeed unable to terminate his undertaking.

The following is however a statement of the population of New Spain, from the notices transmitted by the intendants and governors of provinces
to the viceroy, previous to the 12th May, 1794:

| Names of the intendancies and governments in which the enumeration was completed in 1793. | POPULATION | |
|---|---|---|
| | Of the intendancies and governments. | Of the capitals. |
| Mexico . . . . . | 1,162,886 | 112,926 |
| Puebla . . . . . | 566,443 | 52,717 |
| Tlascala . . . . | 59,177 | 3,357 |
| Oaxaca . . . . . | 411,366 | 19,069 |
| Valladolid . . . . | 289,314 | 17,093 |
| Guanaxuato . . . . | 397,924 | 32,098 |
| San Luis Potosi . . . . | 242,280 | 8,571 |
| Zacatecas . . . . | 118,027 | 25,495 |
| Durango . . . . | 122,806 | 11,027 |
| Sonora . . . . | 93,396 | |
| Nuevo Mexico . . . . | 30,953 | |
| The two Californias . . | 12,666 | |
| Yucatan . . . . . | 358,261 | 28,392 |
| Total population of New Spain deduced from the census of 1793 . . . . . | 3,865,529 | |
| In a Report to the King, Count de Revillagigedo estimated the intendancy of Guadalaxara at 485,000 ⎫ Intendancy of Vera Cruz at 120,000 ⎬ Province of Cohahuila at 13,000 ⎭ *Inhabitants.* | 618,000 | |
| Approximative result of the enumeration in 1793 . . . | 4,483,529 | inhabitants. |

The viceroys who succeeded to the Count de Revillagigedo have never renewed the enumeration;

and since that time the Government has paid very
little attention to statistical researches. Several me-
moirs, drawn up by intendants on the actual state
of the country confided to their care, contain exactly the same numbers as the table of 1793, as if
the population could have remained the same for
ten years. It is certain, however, that this population has made the most extraordinary progress.
The augmentation of tithes and of the Indian capitation, and of all the duties on consumption,
the progress of agriculture and civilization, the
aspect of a country covered with newly constructed
houses, announce a rapid increase in every part of
the kingdom.

The only true sign of a real and permanent increase of population, is an increase in the means of
subsistence. This increase, this augmentation of
the produce of agriculture, is evident in Mexico ;
and appears even to indicate a much more rapid
progress of population than has been supposed, in
deducing the population of 1803 from the imperfect census of 1793. In a catholic country, the
ecclesiastical tithes are, as it were, the thermometer
by which we may judge of the state of agriculture ;
and these tithes have doubled in less than 24 years.

In speaking of the progress of the Mexican
population, we must briefly advert to its supposed
increase by the arrival of European colonists, and
to its diminution by the yellow fever or *black
vomit*. It is sufficient to observe that Europe does

not send more than 800 annually to Mexico. Political writers have always exaggerated what they call the depopulation of the old continent by the new. M. Page, for instance, asserts in his work on the Commerce of St. Domingo, that the emigrations from Europe supply annually more than 100,000 individuals to the United States. This estimate is twenty times higher than the truth; for in 1784 and 1792, when the United States received the greatest number of European colonists, their number did not exceed 5000. The progress of population in Mexico and North America is derived solely from an increase of internal prosperity. As for the *vomito prieto*, it is never felt but on the coast, nor does it carry off annually more than from two to three thousand persons.

## CHAPTER V.

*Manufactures—powder manufactory—goldsmiths—mint—
interior commerce—foreign commerce—smuggling—average value of exports and imports.*

If we consider the small progress of manufactures
in Spain, notwithstanding the numerous encou-
ragements which they have received, since the Ministry of the Marquis de la Ensenada, we shall not
be surprised that whatever relates to manufactures
and manufacturing industry is still less advanced in
Mexico. The restless and suspicious policy of the
nations of Europe, the legislation and colonial policy of the moderns, which bear very little resemblance to those of the Phœnicians and Greeks, have
thrown insurmountable obstacles in the way of the
prosperity of their distant possessions.

Notwithstandig all these obstacles, the manufactures have made some progress in three centuries, during which time Biscayans, Catalonians,
Asturians, and Valencians, have settled in the New
World, and carried there the industry of their native provinces. The manufacture of coarse stuffs
can every where be carried on at a low rate, when
raw materials are found in abundance, and when
the price of the goods of Europe and Oriental Asia
is so much increased by carriage. In time of war,

the want of communication with the mother country, and the regulations prohibiting commerce with neutrals, have favoured the establishment of manufactures of calicoes, fine cloth, and whatever is connected with the refinements of luxury.

The value of the produce of the manufacturing industry of New Spain is estimated at about 1,600,000*l.* per annum. From the quantity and quality of the cotton which the low-lands of New Spain are so well adapted to produce, native manufactures of that material appear to hold the first place in importance. Those of the intendancy of Puebla furnish annually, in time of peace, for the interior commerce, a produce to the value of 325,000*l.* The weavers of cottons of all sorts in Puebla were computed in 1802 at more than 1200. In this town, as well as in Mexico, the printing of calicoes, both those imported from Manilla and those manufactured in New Spain, has made considerable progress within these few years.

The oldest cloth manufactories of Mexico are those of Tezcuco. They were in great part established in 1592 by the viceroy Don Louis de Velasco II., the son of the celebrated constable of Castille, who was second viceroy of New Spain. By degrees, this branch of national industry passed entirely into the hands of the Indians and Mestizoes. The value of the cloths and woollen stuffs manufactured in Queretaro at present amounts to more than 135,000*l.*

With the exception of a few stuffs of cotton mixed with silk, the manufacture of silks is at present next to nothing.

New Spain has no flax or hemp manufactories, and the manufacture of paper is also unknown in it. The manufacture of tobacco is a royal right.

The manufacture of hard soap is a considerable object of commerce at Puebla, Mexico, and Guadalaxara. The first of these towns produces nearly 2143 tons per annum ; and in the intendancy of Guadalaxara, the quantity manufactured is computed at 54,000*l.* The abundance of soda which we find almost every where at elevations of 6000 to 8000 feet, in the interior table land of Mexico, is highly favourable to this manufacture.

The town of Puebla was formerly celebrated for its fine manufactories of delft ware (*loza*) and hats. We have already observed, that, till the commencement of the eighteenth century, these two branches of industry enlivened the commerce between Acapulco and Peru. At present there is little or no communication between Puebla and Lima; and the delft manufactories have fallen off so much, on account of the low price of the stoneware and porcelain of Europe imported at Vera Cruz, that of 46 manufactories which were still existing in 1793, there were in 1802 only sixteen remaining of delft ware, and two of glass.

In New Spain, as well as in the greatest number of countries in Europe, the manufacture of powder is a royal monopoly. To form an idea of the enormous quantity of powder manufactured and sold in contraband, we have only to bear in mind, that notwithstanding the flourishing state of the Mexican mines, the King has never sold to the miners more than 300,000 or 400,000lbs. of powder per annum ; while a single mine, that of Valenciana, requires from 150,000 to 160,000lbs.    It appears from the researches I have made, that the quantity of powder manufactured at the expense of the King, is, to that sold fraudulently, in the proportion of 1 to 4. As, in the interior of New Spain, the nitrate of potash and sulphur are every where to be had in abundance, and the contraband manufacturer can afford to sell powder to the miner at nine pence the pound, the Government ought either to diminish the price of the produce of the manufactory, or to throw the trade in powder entirely open. How is it possible to prevent fraud in a country of an immense extent, in mines at a distance from towns, and dispersed on the ridge of the Cordilleras, in the midst of the wildest and most solitary situations ?

The royal manufactory of powder, the only one in Mexico, is situated near Santa Fe, in the valley of Mexico, about nine miles from the capital. The buildings, which are very beautiful, were constructed in 1780 from the plans of M. Costanzo, the head of the corps of engineers, in a narrow valley which supplies in abundance the necessary water for setting

hydraulic wheels in motion, and through which the
aqueduct of Santa Fe passes. All the parts of the machines, and chiefly the wheels, are disposed with great
skill. It is to be wished, however, that the sieves
necessary to make the *grain*, were either moved by
water or by horses. Eighty Mestizo boys, paid at
the rate of 1*s*. 1*d*. per day, are employed in this
work. Sulphur, which abounds in the volcanoes of
Orizaba and Puebla, in the province of San Luis
near Colima, and especially in the intendancy of
Guadalaxara, where the rivers bring down considerable masses of it, mixed with fragments of pumice-
stone, comes perfectly purified from the town of
San Luis Potosi. There were made, in the royal
powder manufactory of Santa Fe in 1801, more
than 786,000 pounds, of which part is exported for
the Havannah. It is to be regretted that this fine
edifice, where in general more than half a million
of pounds of powder are preserved, is not provided
with an electrical conductor. During my stay in
New Spain, there were only two conductors in that
vast country, which were constructed at La Puebla,
by the order of an enlightened administrator, the
Count de la Cadena, notwithstanding the imprecations of the Indians, and a parcel of ignorant
monks.

We shall conclude the article of the manufactures of New Spain with mentioning the working
of gold and the coining of money, which, considered
merely with relation to industry and mechanical

improvement, are objects every way worthy of attention. There are few countries in which a more considerable number of large pieces of wrought plate, vases, and church ornaments, are annually executed than in Mexico. The smallest towns have gold- and silver-smiths, in whose shops workmen of all castes, Whites, Mestizoes, and Indians, are employed. The academy of fine arts, and the schools for drawing in Mexico and Xalapa, have very much contributed to diffuse a taste for beautiful antique forms. Services of plate, to the value of from six to eight thousand pounds, have been lately manufactured at Mexico, which for elegance of workmanship may rival the finest works of the kind ever executed in the most civilized parts of Europe. The quantity of precious metals which between 1798 and 1802 was converted into plate at Mexico, amounted on an average to 180lbs. of gold, and 12,564 lbs. of silver per annum.

The Mint of Mexico, which is the largest and richest in the whole world, is a building of very simple architecture, belonging to the palace of the viceroys. This establishment contains little or nothing remarkable with respect to the improvement of the machinery or chemical processes; but it well deserves to engage the attention of travellers, from the order, activity and economy which prevail in all the operations of coining. This interest is enhanced by other considerations which are even

those who do not turn their attention to speculations of political administration. In fact, it is impossible to go over this small building without re-
collecting that more than 416,000,000*l.* sterling,
has issued from it in less than three hundred years,
and without reflecting on the powerful influence of
these treasures on the destinies of the nations of
Europe.

The mint of Mexico was established fourteen
years after the destruction of old Tenochtitlan under the first viceroy of New Spain, Antonio de
Mendoza, by a royal *cedula* of the 11th May 1535.

The number of workmen employed in this mint
amounts to 350 or 400; and the number of machines is so great, that it is possible to coin in the
space of a year, without displaying an extraordinary
activity, more than thirty millions of dollars, that
is to say, nearly three times as much as is generally performed in the sixteen mints which exist
in France.

The works of the mint of Mexico contain ten
rollers *(laminoirs)*, moved by sixty mules, fifty-two
cutters *(coupoirs)*, nine adjusting tables *(bancs
d'ajustage)*, twenty machines for marking the edges
*(à creneler)*, twenty stamping presses *(balanciers)*,
and five mills for amalgamating the washings and
filings called *mermas*. As one stamping press can
strike in ten hours more than 15,000 dollars, we
are not to be astonished that with so great a number of machines they are able to manufacture daily
from six to eight thousand pounds weight of silver.

M

The ordinary work, however, does not exceed from five thousand to five thousand six hundred pounds. From these data, which are founded on official papers, it appears that the silver produced in all the mines of Europe together would not suffice to employ the mint of Mexico more than fifteen days.

The parting house *(casa del apartado)*, in which is carried on the separation of the gold and silver proceeding from the ingots of auriferous silver, formerly belonged to the family of the Marquis de Fagoaga. This important establishment was only annexed to the Crown in 1779. The building is very small and very old.

The *casa del apartado* contains three sorts of works, which are destined, 1st, to the manufacture of glass ; 2nd, to the preparation of nitrous acid ; and 3rd, to the separation of the gold and silver. The processes used in these different works, are as imperfect as the construction of the glass-work furnaces used for the manufacture of retorts and the distillation of aqua-fortis.

It is surprising that none of the pupils of the School of Mines are employed either in the mint or in the *casa del apartado* ; and yet these great establishments might expect useful reforms, from availing themselves of mechanical and chemical knowledge. The mint is also situated in a quarter of the town where running water might be easily procured to put in motion hydraulic wheels. The machinery is yet very far from the perfection which it has recently attained in England and in France. The improvements will be the more important, as the manufacture embraces a prodigious quantity of gold and silver; for the dollars coined at Mexico may be considered as the matter which maintains the activity of the greatest number of the mints of Europe.

Not only has the working of gold and silver been improved in Mexico, but very considerable progress has also been made in other branches of industry dependent on luxury and wealth. Chandeliers, and other ornaments of great value, were recently executed in gilt bronze, for the new cathedral of Puebla, the bishop of which possesses an income of nearly 23,900l. Although the most elegant carriages driven through the streets of Mexico and Santa Fe de Bogota, at from 9,000 to 11,000 feet above the surface of the ocean, come from London, very handsome ones are also made in New Spain. The cabinet-makers execute articles of furniture, remarkable for their form, and for the colour and polish of the wood, which is procured from the equinoctial region adjoining the coast, especially from the forests of Orizaba, San Blas, and Colima. It is impossible to read without interest in the Gazette of Mexico, that even in the *provincias internas*, for example at Durango, 600 miles north of the capital, harpsichords and piano-fortes are manufactured. The Indians display indefatigable patience in the manufacture of small toys, in wood,

bone, and wax. In a country where the vegetation affords the most precious productions*, and
where the workman may choose at will the accidents of colour and form among the roots, the me-
dullary prolongations of the wood, and the kernels
of fruits, these toys of the Indians may one day become an important article of exportation for Europe. We know what large sums of money this
species of industry brings to the inhabitants of Nu-
remberg, and to the mountaineers of Berchtolsga-
den and the Tyrol, who however can only use in
the manufacture of boxes, spoons, and children's
toys, pine, cherry, and walnut-tree wood. The
Americans of the United States send to the island
of Cuba, and the other West India Islands, large
cargoes of furniture, for which they get the wood
chiefly from the Spanish colonies. This branch of
industry will pass into the hands of the Mexicans,
whenever they shall begin to derive advantage from
the productions of their own soil.

Having given a general view of the state of agriculture, and of the manufactures, it remains for
us to speak of the exchanges which are carried on
with the interior, the mother country, and with
other parts of the New Continent. We shall not
repeat the just complaints respecting the restrictions
on commerce, and the prohibitory system, which

* Swietenia Cedrela and Cæsalpinia wood ; trunks of Des-
manthus and Mimosa, of which the heart is a red approaching
to black.

serve as a basis to the colonial legislation of Europe. It would be difficult to add to what has been already said on that subject, at a time when the great problems of political economy occupy the mind of every man. Instead of attacking principles, whose falsity and injustice are universally acknowledged, we shall confine ourselves to the collection of facts, and to the proving of what importance the commercial relations of Mexico with Europe may become, when they shall be freed from the fetters of an odious monopoly, disadvantageous even to the mother country.

The *internal commerce* comprehends both the carriage of produce and goods into the interior of the country, and the coasting along the shore of the Atlantic and Pacific Oceans. This commerce is not enlivened by an internal navigation on rivers or artificial canals ; for, like Persia, the greatest part of New Spain is in want of navigable rivers. The Rio del Norte, which from its breadth hardly yields to the Mississippi, flows through regions susceptible of the highest cultivation, but which in their present state exhibit nothing but a vast desert. This vast river has no greater influence on the activity of the inland trade, than the Missouri, the Cassiquiare, and the Ucayale, which run through the savannahs and uninhabited forests of North America. In Mexico, between the 16th and 23d degrees of latitude, the part of the country where the population is most concentrated, the Rio de Santiago alone can be rendered navigable at a moderate expense. The length of its course equals that of the Elbe and the Rhone. It fertilizes the table-lands of Lerma, Salamanca, and Selaya, and might serve for the conveyance of flour from the intendancies of Mexico and Guanaxuato towards the western coast. We are of opinion, that it would be very easy to cut canals in the valley of Mexico, from the northern point, the village of Huehuetoca, to the southern extremity, the small town of Chalco.

The principal objects of the internal commerce of New Spain are, 1st, The productions and goods imported and exported at the two ports of Vera Cruz and Acapulco; 2d, The exchange which is carried on between the different provinces, and particularly between Mexico Proper and the *Provincias Internas;* 3d, Several productions of Peru, Quito, and Guatimala, which are conveyed through the country to be exported at Vera Cruz for Europe. Were it not for the great consumption of commodities in the mines, the commerce between provinces which enjoy, in a great measure, the same climate, and which consequently possess the same productions, could not have any great activity. The elevation of the soil gives the southern regions of Mexico, that middle temperature which is necessary for the cultivation of European plants. The same latitude produces the banana, the apple, the sugar-cane, wheat, the manioc, and the potatoe. The nutritive gramina, which vegetate among the

ices of Norway and Siberia, cover the Mexican fields
of the torrid zone. Hence, the provinces situated
under the 17th and 20th degree of latitude very seldom require the flour of New Biscay. The commerce
of maize is of great importance to the provinces of
Guadalaxara, Valladolid, Guanaxuato, Mexico, San
Luis Potosi, Vera Cruz, Puebla, and Oaxaca.

Thousands of mules, arriving every week from
Chihuahua and Durango at Mexico, carry, besides
bars of silver, hides, tallow, some wine of Passo del
Norte, and flour; and they take in return woollen
cloth of the manufacture of Puebla and Queretaro,
goods from Europe and the Philippine Islands,
iron, steel, and mercury.

The communications with Europe and Asia
being carried on only from the two ports of Vera
Cruz and Acapulco, all the objects of exportation
and importation necessarily pass through the capital,
which has become through that means the central
point of the interior commerce. Mexico, situated
on the ridge of the Cordilleras, commanding as it
were the two seas, is distant in a straight line from
Vera Cruz 207 miles, from Acapulco 198, from
Oaxaca 237, and 1320 from Santa Fe of New
Mexico. From this position of the capital, the
most frequented roads, and the most important
for commerce, are, 1st, the road from Mexico to
Vera Cruz, by Puebla and Xalapa; 2d, the road
from Mexico to Acapulco, by Chilpanzingo; 3d,
the road from Mexico to Guatimala, by Oaxaca;

4th, the road from Mexico to Durango and Santa Fe of New Mexico, vulgarly called *el camino de tierra dentro*. We may consider the roads which lead from Mexico, either to San Luis Potosi and Monterey, or to Valladolid and Guadalaxara, as ramifications of the great road of the *provincias internas*.

The state of the external commerce of New Spain has changed very much within these twelve or fifteen years. The quantity of foreign goods imported fraudulently into the east and west coasts of Mexico, has increased not in volume but in intrinsic value. A greater number of vessels are not employed in the smuggling trade with Jamaica, but the objects of importation have changed with the increase of luxury and national wealth. Mexico now requires finer cloths, a greater quantity of muslins, gauzes, silks, wines, and liquors, than previous to 1791. If on the one hand the increase of luxury has rendered Mexico within the last fifteen or twenty years more dependent on Europe and Asia than formerly, on the other hand the produce of the mines has considerably increased. According to the accounts of the *Consulado*, the importation of Vera Cruz, calculating only from the registers of the customs, amounted before 1791 to 2,335,000*l.*; and it now amounts, at an average, to more than 3,070,000*l.* annually. In the ten years preceding 1791, the mean produce of the mines of New Spain amounted to 4,115,000*l.* per annum, while from

1791 to 1801 the produce amounted to 5,000,000*l.*
annually. In this last period the indigenous manufactures have been exceedingly prosperous ; but at
the same time, as the Indians and people of colour
are better clothed, this progress of the Mexican
manufactures has had no sensible effect on the importation of Europe—cloth, Indian cottons, and
other goods of foreign manufacture. The produce
of agriculture has increased in a greater proportion
than the manufacturing industry.

Bringing together into one point of view the data
collected by me respecting the trade of Acapulco
and Vera Cruz, we find that in the beginning of
the nineteenth century,

The *importation* of foreign goods and produce into
the kingdom of New Spain, including the contraband on the eastern and western coasts,
amounts to 4,333,000*l.*

The *exportation* from New Spain of the produce
of its agriculture and manufacturing industry
amounts to 1,260,000*l.*

Now the mines produce 5,000,000*l.*, of which
about 1,750,000*l.* are exported on account of the
King, either for Spain, or the other Spanish colonies:
consequently, if we deduct from the 3,250,000*l.*
remaining, 3,070,000*l.* to liquidate the excess of the
importation over the exportation, we find hardly

N

180,000*l.* The national wealth, or rather the specie, of Mexico is then annually on the increase.

This calculation, founded on exact data, explains the reason why the country, whose mines are the richest and most constant in their produce, does not possess a great mass of specie, and why the price of labour still remains very low there. Enormous sums are accumulated in the hands of a few individuals ; but the indigence of the people is very striking to Europeans who travel through the country and the towns of the interior of Mexico. I am tempted to believe that of the 19,770,000*l.* which are supposed to exist in specie among the thirteen or fourteen millions of inhabitants of the Spanish colonies of continental America, 12,000,000*l.* or 13,000,000*l.* are to be found in Mexico. Although the population of this kingdom is not in the proportion of one to two to the population of the other continental colonies, its national wealth is to that of the other colonies nearly in the proportion of two to three. The estimate of 13,000,000*l.* gives only 2*l.* 3*s.* 4*d.* per head ; but this sum must appear too great, when we reflect, that in Spain 1*l.* 10*s.* 4*d.*, and in France 3*l.* 0*s.* 8*d.*, are allowed for each inhabitant.

If, in consequence of those events, of which we have examples in the history of every age, the colonies had separated from the mother country, Mexico would have lost 1,933,000*l.* of specie less annually, which were partly paid into the royal treasury of Madrid, and partly, under the improper denomination of *situados*, paid into the provincial treasuries of the Havannah, Porto Rico, Pensacola, and Manilla. By allowing a free course to the national industry, by encouraging agriculture and manufactures, the importation will diminish of itself; and it will then be easy for the Mexicans to pay the value of foreign commodities with the productions of their own soil. The free cultivation of the vine and the olive on the table-land of New Spain; the free distillation of spirits from rum, rice, and the grape; the exportation of flour favoured by the making of new roads; the increase of plantations of sugar-cane, cotton, and tobacco; the working of the iron and mercury mines; and the manufacture of steel, will perhaps one day become more inexhaustible sources of wealth than all the veins of gold and silver united. Under more favourable external circumstances, the balance of trade may be favourable to New Spain, without paying the account, which has been opened for centuries between the two continents, entirely with Mexican dollars.

In the present state of the trade of Vera Cruz and Acapulco, the total value of exported agricultural produce scarcely equals the value of the sugar furnished by the island of Cuba, which amounts to 1,254,000*l*. But the importation of Mexico, which we calculate on an average at 4,333,000*l*. annually, is an object of the very highest import-

ance for the commercial nations of Europe, who
want an outlet for their manufactures.   We shall
call to mind on this occasion, 1st, That the United
States of North America, whose exportation in 1802
amounted to 15,570,328*l.*, exported in 1791 only
to the value of 4,115,000*l.*; 2nd, That England,
at the period of the greatest activity of its trade
with France in 1790, only imported into that
country goods to the value of 1,235,000*l.*; and 3rd,
That the exportation from England to Portugal
and Germany in 1790 did not exceed, to the former
country 1,647,000*l.*, and to the latter 2,687,000*l.*
These data are sufficient to explain, why towards
the end of the last century Great Britain made so
many efforts to procure a share of the trade between the Peninsula and Mexico.

The *foreign commerce* of New Spain, from the
position of the coasts, is naturally composed of
the commerce of the South Sea and that of the
Atlantic Ocean.   The ports on the eastern coast
are Campeche, Huasacualco, Vera Cruz, Tampico,
and Nuevo Santander; if we may give the name
of ports to roads surrounded with shallows, or
mouths of rivers shut by bars, and presenting a
very slight shelter from the fury of the north winds.
All the endeavours which have been made, since
1524, to discover a safer port than Vera Cruz have
been fruitless.   The vast shore which stretches from
Nuevo Santander to the north and north-west is
still very little known; and we may repeat in our

days, what Cortez wrote to the Emperor Charles
the Fifth, three years after the taking of Tenochtitlan, " that the secret of the coast which extends
from the Rio de Panuco to Florida remains to be
discovered."

For centuries, almost all the maritime commerce of New Spain has been concentrated at
Vera Cruz. When we bestow a glance on the
chart of that port, we see that the pilots of Cortez's
squadron were right in comparing the port of Vera
Cruz to a pierced bag. The good anchorage in
the port of Vera Cruz is between the castle of Ulua,
the town, and the sand banks of La Lavandera.
Near the castle we find six fathoms water; but the
channel by which the port is entered is hardly
four fathoms in depth, and 1260 feet in breadth.

The principal objects of exportation at Vera Cruz
are, gold and silver in ingots, or converted into
coin or wrought plate, cochineal, sugar, flour,
Mexican indigo, salted meat and other eatables,
tanned hides, sarsaparilla, vanilla, jalap, soap,
Campeche wood, and pimento. Their annual
amount, according to the declarations at the Customs, taking an average of several years of peace,
is 4,770,000*l.* We have not mentioned the indigo
of Guatimala or the cocoa of Guayaquil, which in
time of war are very important articles in the trade
of Vera Cruz, because we wished to confine ourselves to the indigenous productions of New Spain.

The importation of Vera Cruz includes the

following articles : linen and cotton and woollen cloth, silks, paper, brandy, cocoa, mercury, iron, steel, wine, and wax. Their average annual value is 3,250,000*l.*—Commercial circulation, 8,020,000*l.*

95

## CHAPTER VI.

*Intendancy of Vera Cruz—situation—physical aspect— climate—productions—road from the capital to Vera Cruz port—yellow fever.*

| Extent in North Latitude. | Extent in West Longitude. | Population in 1803. | Extent of Surface in square Miles. | No. of Inhabitants to the square Mile. |
|---|---|---|---|---|
| From 20° 0′ to 21° 15′ | From 99° 0′ to 101° 5′ | 156,000 | 37,269 | 4 to 5 |

BEFORE entering on the subject of the Mines, which we shall treat in considerable detail, we shall subjoin to our brief account of the Commerce of Mexico some description of the Province, through which lies all communication between the interior and Europe.

N.B.—The province of Vera Cruz, situated under the burning sun of the tropics, extends along the Mexican Gulf, from the Rio Baraderas (or *de los Lagartos*) to the great river of Panuco, which rises in the metalliferous mountains of San Luis Potosi. Hence this intendancy includes a very considerable part of the eastern coast of New Spain. Its length, from the bay of Terminos near the island of Carmen to the small port of Tampico, is 630 miles, while its

breadth is only in general from 70 to 80 miles.    It
is bounded on the east by the peninsula of Merida ;
on the west, by the intendancies of Oaxaca, Puebla,
and Mexico ; and on the north, by the colony of
New Santander.

There are few regions in the new continent where
the traveller is more struck with the assemblage of
the most opposite climates    All the western part
of the intendancy of Vera Cruz forms the declivity
of the Cordilleras of Anahuac.    In the space of a
day, the inhabitants descend from the regions of
eternal snow to the plains in the vicinity of the sea,
where the most suffocating heat prevails.    The ad-
mirable order with which different tribes of vegetables rise above one another by strata, as it were,
is no where more perceptible than in ascending
from the port of Vera Cruz to the table-land of
Perote.    We see there the physiognomy of the
country, the aspect of the sky, the form of plants,
the figures of animals, the manners of the inhabitants, and the kind of cultivation followed by them,
assume a different appearance at every step of our
progress.

As we ascend, nature appears gradually less animated, the beauty of the vegetable forms diminishes,
the shoots become less succulent, and the flowers
less coloured.    The aspect of the Mexican oak
quiets the alarms of travellers newly landed at Vera
Cruz.    Its presence demonstrates to him that he
has left behind him the zone so justly dreaded by
the people of the north, under which the yellow fe-

ver exercises its ravages in New Spain. This lower
range of oaks warns the colonist who inhabits the
central table-land, how far he may descend towards
the coast without dread of the mortal disease the
*vomito.* Forests of liquid amber, near Xalapa,
show by the freshness of their verdure that this is
the elevation at which the clouds suspended over
the ocean come in contact with the basaltic summits
of the Cordillera. A little higher, near La Blande-
rilla, the nutritive fruit of the banana tree no longer comes to maturity. In this foggy and cold region, therefore, want spurs on the Indian to labour,
and excites his industry. At the height of San
Miguel, pines begin to mingle with the oaks which
are found by the traveller as high as the elevated
plains of Perote, where he beholds the delightful
aspect of fields sown with wheat. About 2000 feet
higher the coldness of the climate will no longer
admit of the vegetation of oaks; and pines alone
cover the rocks, whose summits enter the zone of
eternal snow. Thus in a few hours the naturalist,
in this miraculous country, ascends the whole scale
of vegetation from the heliconia and the banana
plant, whose glossy leaves swell out into extraordinary dimensions, to the stunted parenchyma of the
resinous trees.

The province of Vera Cruz is enriched by nature
with the most precious productions. At the foot
of the Cordillera, in the ever-green forests of Pa-
pantla, Nautla, and S. Andre Tuxtla, grows the
*epidendrum vanilla,* the odoriferous fruit of which

o

is employed for perfuming chocolate. Near the Indian villages of Colipa and Misantla grows the beautiful *convolvulus jalapæ*, whose tuberose root furnishes the jalap, one of the most energetic and beneficent purgatives. The myrtle (*myrtus pimenta*), whose grain forms an agreeable spice, well known in trade by the name of *pimienta de Tabasco*, is produced in the forests which extend towards the river of Baraderas, in the eastern part of the intendancy of Vera Cruz. The cocoa of Acayucan would be in request, if the natives were to apply themselves more assiduously to the cultivation of cocoa trees. On the eastern and southern declivities of the Pic d'Orizaba, in the valleys which extend towards the small town of Cordoba, tobacco of an excellent quality is cultivated, which yields an annual revenue to the crown of more than 750,000*l*. sterling. The *similax*, the root of which is the true salsaparilla, grows in the humid and umbrageous ravines of the Cordillera. The cotton of the coast of Vera Cruz is celebrated for its fineness and whiteness. The sugar-cane yields nearly as much sugar as in the island of Cuba, and more than in the plantations of St. Domingo.

This intendancy alone would keep alive the commerce of the port of Vera Cruz, if the number of colonists were greater, and if their laziness, the effect of the bounty of nature, and the facility of providing without effort for the most urgent wants of life, did not impede the progress of industry. The old population of Mexico was concentrated in the interior of the country on the table-land. The Mexican tribes who came from northern countries, gave the preference in their migrations to the ridges of the Cordilleras, because they found on them a climate analogous to that of their native country. No doubt, on the first arrival of the Spaniards on the coast of Chalchihucuecan (Vera Cruz), all the country from the river of Papaloapan (Alvarado to Huaxtecapan) was better inhabited and better cultivated than it now is. The conquerors, however, found, as they ascended the table-land, the villages closer together, the fields divided into smaller portions, and the people more polished. The Spaniards, who imagined they founded new cities when they gave European names to Aztec cities, followed the traces of the indigenous civilization. They had very powerful motives for inhabiting the table-land of Anahuac. They dreaded the heat, and the diseases which prevail in the plains. The search after the precious metals, the cultivation of European grain and fruit, the analogy of the climate with that of the Castilles, and other causes, all concurred to fix them on the ridge of the Cordillera. So long as the *Encomenderos*, abusing the rights which they derived from the laws, treated the Indians as serfs, a great number of them were transported from the regions of the coast to the table-land in the interior, either to work in the mines, or merely that they might be near the habitation of their masters. For two centuries the trade in indigo, sugar, and cotton was next to nothing. The

Whites could by no means be induced to settle in the plains, where the true Indian climate prevails, and it appeared that the Europeans came under the tropics merely to inhabit the temperate zone.

Hitherto the Government has neglected every means for increasing the population of this desert coast. From this state of things result a great want of hands, and a scarcity of provisions, singular enough in a country of such great fertility. The wages of an ordinary workman at Vera Cruz are from 4 to 5 shillings per day. A master mason, and every man who follows a particular trade, gains from 10 to 16 shillings per day, that is to say, three times as much as on the central table-land.

Taking our direction from the capital of Mexico towards the east in the road to Vera Cruz, we must advance 180 miles, before arriving at a valley the bottom of which is less than 3000 feet higher than the level of the sea, and in which, consequently, oaks cease to grow.

We have already said that the configuration of the soil in the interior is most favourable for the transport of goods, for navigation, and even for the construction of canals. Great difficulties are, however, opposed by nature to the communication between the interior of the kingdom and the coast. There is an enormous difference of level and temperature, while from Mexico to New Biscay the plain preserves an equal elevation, and consequently a climate rather cold than temperate. From the capital of Mexico to Vera Cruz, the descent is

shorter and more rapid than from the same point
to Acapulco.

Of the 250 miles from the capital to the port
of Vera Cruz, upwards of 160 belong to the great
plain of Anahuac.  The rest of the road is a
laborious and continued descent, particularly from
the small fortress of Perote to the city of Xalapa,
and from this site, one of the most beautiful and
picturesque in the known world, to La Rinconada.
It is the difficulty of this descent which raises the
carriage of flour from Mexico to Vera Cruz, and
prevents it to this day from competing in Europe
with the flour of Philadelphia.   We have already
mentioned the superb causeway which is constructing along this eastern descent of the Cordillera.
This work, due to the great and praiseworthy
activity of the merchants of Vera Cruz, will have
the most decided influence on the prosperity of the
inhabitants of the whole kingdom of New Spain.
The place of thousands of mules will be supplied
by carriages fit to transport merchandise from sea
to sea, which will connect the Asiatic commerce
of Acapulco with the European commerce of Vera
Cruz.

The inhabitants of Mexico, discontented with
the port of Vera Cruz, if we may give the name
of port to the most dangerous of all anchorages,
entertain the hope of finding out surer channels for
the commerce with the mother country.   I shall
merely name the mouths of the rivers Alvarado

and Guasacualco to the south of Vera Cruz; and to the north of that city the Rio Tampico, and especially the village of Sotto la Marina, near the bar of Santander. These four points have long fixed the attention of the Government; but even there, however advantageous in other respects, the sand-banks prevent the entry of large vessels. These ports would require to be artificially corrected; but it becomes necessary, in the first place, to inquire if the localities are such as to warrant a belief that this expensive remedy would be durable in its effects. It is to be observed, however, that we still know too little of the coasts of New Santander and Texas, particularly that part to the north of the Lake of S. Bernard or Carbonera, to be able to assert that in the whole of this extent nature presents the same obstacles and the same bars.

While civilization is in its infancy, gigantic projects are much more attractive than simple ideas of easier execution. Thus, instead of establishing a system of small canals for the internal navigation of the valley, the minds of the inhabitants have been bewildered, since the time of the viceroy Count Revillagigedo, with vague speculations on the possibility of a communication by water between the capital and the port of Tampico. Seeing the water of the lakes descend by the mountains of Nochistongo into the Rio de Tula (called also Rio de Moctezuma), and by the Rio de Panuco into the Gulf of Mexico, they entertain the hope of opening the same route to the commerce of Vera Cruz. Goods to the value of more than 4,000,000*l.* are annually transported on mules from the Atlantic coast over the interior table-land, while flour, hides, and metals descend from the central table-land to Vera Cruz. The capital is the emporium of this immense commerce. The road, which, if no canal is attempted, is to be carried from the coast to Perote, will cost nearly a million sterling. Hitherto the air of the port of Tampico has appeared not so prejudicial to the health of Europeans, and the inhabitants of the cold regions of Mexico, as the climate of Vera Cruz. Although the bar of Tampico prevents the entry into the port of vessels drawing more than from 14 to 20 feet water, it would still be preferable to the dangerous anchorage among the shallows of Vera Cruz. From these circumstances a navigation from the capital to Tampico would be desirable, whatever expense might be requisite for the execution of so bold an undertaking.

Expense, however, is not to be feared in a country where a private individual, the Count de la Valenciana, dug, in a single mine, three shafts at an expense of above 350,000*l.* Nor can we deny the possibility of carrying a canal into execution from the valley of Tenochtitlan to Tampico. In the present state of hydraulic architecture, boats may be made to pass over elevated chains of mountains, wherever nature offers points of separation which communicate with two principal recipients.

It remains for us to speak at the end of this chapter of the epidemical disease which prevails on the eastern coast of New Spain, and which during a great part of the year is an obstacle not only to European commerce, but also to the interior communications between the shore and the table-land of Anahuac. The port of Vera Cruz is considered as the principal seat of the yellow fever (*vomito prieto* or *negro*), to which Europeans landing in Mexico at the period of the great heats frequently fall victims. Some vessels prefer landing at Vera Cruz in the beginning of winter, when the tempests *de los nortes* begin to rage, to exposing themselves in summer to the effects of the *vomito*, and to undergoing a long quarantine on their return to Europe. These circumstances have frequently a very sensible influence on the supply of Mexico and the price of commodities. This destructive scourge produces still more serious effects on the internal commerce. The mines are in want of iron, steel, and mercury, whenever the communication is interrupted between Xalapa and Vera Cruz. We have already seen that the commerce between province and province is carried on by caravans of mules ; and the muleteers, as well as the merchants who inhabit the cold and temperate regions of the interior of New Spain, are afraid of descending towards the coast, so long as the *vomito* prevails at Vera Cruz.

The farm of *l'Encero*, near Vera Cruz, which I

found to be 3043 feet above the level of the ocean, is the highest limit of the *vomito*. We have already observed that the Mexican oaks descend no further than that place, being unable to vegetate in a heat sufficient to develop the germ of the yellow fever. Individuals born and brought up at Vera Cruz are not subject to this disease.

The Whites and the Mestizos who inhabit the interior table-land of Mexico, of which the mean temperature is 60° and 62° Fahr., and where the thermometer sometimes falls below the freezing point, are more liable to contract the *vomito*, when they descend from l'Encero to the Plan del Rio, and from thence to la Antigua and the port of Vera Cruz, than the Europeans or inhabitants of the United States, who come by sea. The latter, passing by degrees into the southern latitudes, are gradually prepared for the great heats which they experience on landing ; but the Spanish Mexicans, on the other hand, suddenly change their climate, when, in the space of a few hours, they are transported from the temperate region to the torrid zone. The environs of Vera Cruz are frightfully arid. On arriving by the Xalapa road, we find near *la Antigua*, a few cocoa trees which ornament the gardens of that village ; and they are the last great trees to be discovered in the desert. The excessive heat which prevails in the town is increased by the hillocks of moving sands (*meganos*) formed by the impetuosity of the north winds, and sur-

P

rounding it on the south and south-west side.
The suffocating heat which prevails in this
parched and naked plain, has a powerful effect
on individuals whose nervous system has never
been accustomed to so violent an irritation. The
heat, added to the fatigues of the journey, dis-
poses the organs more easily to receive the delete-
rious miasmata of the yellow fever : the ravages of
that pestilential malady will be greatly diminished,
therefore, by shortening that part of the road which
crosses the arid plains of the sea coast.

Persons born at Vera Cruz are not liable to
contract the *vomito* in their native country ; and
in this respect they possess a great advantage over
the inhabitants of the United States, who suffer
from the insalubrity of their own climate. Another advantage of the torrid zone is, that the Europeans, and in general all individuals born in temperate climates, are never twice attacked with the
yellow fever.

It is however certain that the *vomito*, which is
endemical at Vera Cruz, Carthagena, and the Havannah, is the same disease with the yellow fever,
which since the year 1793 has never ceased to af-
flict the inhabitants of the United States.

It is incontestable that the *vomito* is not contagious at Vera Cruz. In most countries, the common people consider many diseases as contagious
which are of a very different character ; but no po-
pular opinion in Mexico has ever interdicted the

stranger not seasoned to the climate from approaching the beds of those attacked by the *vomito*. No
fact can be cited to render it probable that the im-
mediate contact or breath of the dying person is
dangerous to those not seasoned to the climate, who
may attend on the patient. On the continent of
equinoctial America, the yellow fever is not more
contagious than the intermittent fevers of Europe.

Pringle, Lind, and other distinguished physicians, consider our summer and autumnal bilious
affections as the first degree of yellow fever. A fee-
ble analogy is also discoverable in the pernicious intermittent fevers which prevail in Italy In the low
regions of Mexico, as well as in Europe, the sudden suppression of perspiration is one of the principal occasional causes of the gastric or bilious fevers.

The strangers who frequent Vera Cruz have
greatly exaggerated the dirtiness of the inhabitants.
For some time the police has taken measures for
the preservation of the salubrity of the air; and
Vera Cruz is at present not so dirty as many of
the towns of the south of Europe ; but these pre-
cautions must be continued for some years before
their good effects will be sensibly felt.

An intimate connexion is observed on the coast
of Mexico between the progress of diseases, and the
variations of the temperature of the atmosphere.
Two seasons only are known at Vera Cruz, that of
the tempest of the north (*los Nortes*) from the

autumnal to the spring equinox, and that of the breezes or south winds (*brizas*), which blow with considerable regularity between March and September. The month of January is the coldest in the year, because it is furthest from the two periods in which the sun passes through the zenith of Vera Cruz. The *vomito* generally begins first to rage in that town when the mean temperature of the month reaches 75° Fahr. In December, January, and February, the heat remains below this limit; and accordingly it seldom happens that the yellow fever does not entirely disappear in that season when a very sensible cold is frequently felt. The strong heats begin in the month of March, and the epidemical scourge begins at the same time. Although May is warmer than September and October, it is however in the two last months that the *vomito* commits the greatest ravages; for in every epidemic it requires a certain time before the germ of the disease is developed in all its energy; and the rains, which last from the month of June to the month of September, have an undoubted influence on the production of the miasmata which are formed in the environs of Vera Cruz.

The beginning and the close of the rainy season are dreaded the most under the tropics, because an excessive humidity arrests, almost as much as a great drought, the progress of putrefaction of the vegetable and animal substances which are accumu-

lated in marshy situations.   More than 90 inches
of rain-water fall annually at Vera Cruz; and in
the month of July 1803 alone, an accurate ob-
server, M. Costanzo, colonel of the corps of
engineers, collected more than 25 inches, which
is only one-third less than the quantity which falls
at London during the whole year.

It is a very remarkable fact, that during the
eight years which preceded 1794, there was not a
single example of *vomito*, although the concourse
of Europeans and Mexicans from the interior was
extremely great.

# CHAPTER VII.

*Mineral productions—quantity of gold and silver—copper,*
*tin, iron, lead, mercury, coal, salt.*

HAVING given a brief general view of the soil,
climate and population of the kingdom of Mexico,
it remains for us to exhibit a view of the mineral
productions which for two centuries and a half have
been the object of working the mines of New
Spain. The mountains of the New Continent,
like the mountains of the Old, contain iron, copper,
lead, and a great number of other mineral substances, indispensable to agriculture and the arts.
If the labour of man has, in America, been almost
exclusively directed to the extraction of gold and
silver, it is because the members of a society act
from very different considerations to those which
ought to influence the whole society. Wherever
the soil can produce both indigo and maize, the
former prevails over the latter, although the general
interest requires a preference to be given to those
vegetables which supply nourishment to man, over
those which are merely objects of exchange with
strangers. In the same manner, the mines of iron

or lead on the ridge of the Cordilleras, notwithstanding their richness, continue to be neglected,
because nearly the whole attention of the colonists
is directed to the veins of gold and silver, even when
they exhibit on trial but small indications of abundance. Such is the attraction of those precious
metals, which, by a general convention, have become
the representatives of labour and subsistence.

No doubt the people of Mexico can procure, by
means of foreign commerce, all the articles which
are supplied to them by their own country; but in
the midst of great wealth in gold and silver, want
is severely felt whenever the commerce with the
mother country, or with other parts of Europe or
Asia, has suffered any interruption, or whenever
a war throws obstacles in the way of maritime
communication. From five to six hundred thousand pounds in piastres are sometimes heaped up
in Mexico, while the manufacturers and miners are
suffering from the want of steel, iron, and mercury.
A few years before my arrival in New Spain, the price
of iron rose from about 16s. the 100lbs. to 10l.,
and steel from 24s. to 54l. In those times when
there is a total stagnation of foreign commerce,
the industry of the Mexicans is awakened for a
time, and they then begin to manufacture steel,
and to make use of the iron and mercury of the
mountains of America. The nation is then alive
to its true interest, and feels that wealth consists

in the abundance of objects of consumption, in that of *things*, and not in the accumulation of the *sign* by which they are represented. During the last war but one between Spain and America, they began to work the iron mines of Tecalitan, near Colima, in the intendancy of Guadalaxara. The *Tribunal de Mineria* expended more than 6000*l*. in extracting mercury from the veins of San Juan de la Chica; but the effects of so praiseworthy a zeal were only of short duration; and the peace of Amiens put an end to undertakings which promised to give to the labours of miners a direction more useful to the public prosperity. The maritime communication was scarcely well opened, when they again preferred to purchase steel, iron, and mercury in the markets of Europe.

In proportion as the Mexican population shall increase, and the inhabitants, from being less dependent on Europe, shall begin to turn their attention to the great variety of useful productions contained in the bowels of the earth, the system of mining will undergo a change. An enlightened administration will give encouragement to those labours which are directed to the extraction of mineral substances of an *intrinsic value;* individuals will no longer sacrifice their own interests and those of the public to inveterate prejudices; and they will feel that the working of a mine of coal, iron, or lead, may become as profitable as

that of a vein of silver.    In the present state of
Mexico, the precious metals occupy almost exclusively the industry of the colonists ; and
whenever we employ the word mine *(real, real
de minas)*, unless the contrary is expressly stated,
a gold or silver mine is to be uniformly understood.

Having been engaged from my earliest youth in
the study of mining, and having myself had the
direction for several years of subterraneous operations in a part of Germany which contains a great
variety of minerals, I was doubly interested in
examining with care the state of the mines and
their management in New Spain.    I had occasion
to visit the celebrated mines of Tasco, Pachuca,
and Guanaxuato, in which last place, where the
veins exceed in richness all that has hitherto been
discovered in other parts of the world, I resided
for more than a month ; and I had it in my power
to compare the different methods of mining practised in Mexico, with those which I had observed
in the former year in Peru.    Without, however,
entering into discussions of a minute and purely
technical nature, I shall confine myself in this
work to the examination of what is conducive to
general results.

What is the geographical position of the mines
which supply this enormous mass of silver, which
flows annually from the commerce of Vera Cruz
into Europe ?    Is this enormous mass of silver the

produce of a great number of scattered undertakings,
or is it to be considered as almost exclusively furnished by three or four metallic veins of extraordinary wealth and extent ?  What is the quantity of
precious metals annually extracted from the mines
of Mexico ?  And what proportion does this quantity
bear to the produce of the mines of the whole of
Spanish America ?  At how many ounces per 100lb
may we estimate the mean richness of the silver
ore of Mexico ?  What proportion is there between
the quantity of ore which undergoes melting,  and
that from which gold and silver are extracted by the
process of amalgamation ?  What influence has the
price of mercury on the progress of mining, and
what quantity of mercury is lost in the process of
Mexican amalgamation ?  Can we know with precision the quantity of precious metals which have
passed, since the conquest of Tenochtitlan, from
New Spain into Europe and Asia ? Is it probable,
considering the present method of working, and the
geological constitution of the country, that the annual produce of the mines of Mexico will admit of an
augmentation ?  Or shall we conclude, with several
celebrated writers, that the exportation of silver from
America has already attained its *maximum* ? These
are the general questions which we now propose
to discuss.   They are connected with the most important problems of political economy.

Long before the arrival of the Spaniards, the natives of Mexico, as well as those of Peru, were ac-

quainted with the use of several metals. They did not content themselves with those which were found in their native state on the surface of the earth, and particularly in the beds of rivers and the ravines formed by the torrrents; they applied themselves to subterraneous operations in the working of veins; they cut galleries and dug pits of communication and ventilation; and they had instruments adapted for cutting the rock. Cortez informs us in the historical account of his expedition, that gold, silver, copper, lead, and tin, were publicly sold in the great market of Tenochtitlan.

We must however refrain from going into the historical part of this subject; since, however entertaining it may be, it would lead us into details wholly unimportant for our present purpose.

We shall proceed to lay before our readers all the information concerning the produce of the mines which a residence in the country and access to the registers of the mints of Mexico, Lima, Santa Fé, and Popayan, have enabled us to collect. We believe it will be found more full and exact than any hitherto published.

The quantity of silver annually extracted from the mines of New Spain, does not depend so much on the abundance and intrinsic riches of the ores, as on the facility with which the miners procure the mercury necessary for amalgamation. We are not therefore to be surprised that the number of ounces of silver converted into piastres, at the mint of

Mexico, varies very irregularly. When, from the effect of a maritime war or from any other accident, the mercury fails for a year, and the following year it arrives in abundance, a very considerable produce of silver succeeds to a very limited fabrication of money.

In Saxony, where the small quantity of mercury which is wanted for the process of amalgamation, is procured with sufficient facility, the produce of the mines of Freiberg is so admirably equal, that from 1793 to 1799 it was never below 29,800lbs. troy, and never above 31,300lbs. troy of silver. In that country, the great droughts, which stop the working of the hydraulic wheels, and prevent the water from being drawn off, have the same influence on the quantity of silver delivered into the mint, as the scarcity of mercury in America.

From 1777 to 1803, the quantity of silver annually extracted from the Mexican ores has almost constantly been above 1,231,000lbs. troy of silver, and from 1796 to 1799 it was 1,662,000lbs. troy; while from 1800 to 1802 it remained below 1,294,900lbs. troy. But we cannot by any means infer from these data, that the mining operations in Mexico have not been so flourishing latterly. In 1801 the gold and silver obtained amounted only to 3,480,000l. ; while in 1803 the coinage again amounted, on account of the abundance of mercury, to 4,865,000l.

Abstracting the influence of accidental causes, we find that the mines and stream works of New

Spain actually produce on an average 4,322lbs. troy of gold, and 1,543,837lbs. troy of silver, of which the mean value amounts altogether to 4,620,000*l.*

About twenty years ago, this produce was only from 2,170,000*l.* to 3,467,000*l.*, and thirty years ago from 2,380,000*l.* to 2,400,000*l.* In the beginning of the eighteenth century, the quantity of gold and silver coined at Mexico was only from 1,085,000*l.* to 1,200,000*l* The enormous increase in the produce of the mines observable in latter years is to be attributed to a great number of causes, all acting at the same time; among which the first place must be assigned to the increase of population on the table-land of Mexico, the progress of knowledge and national industry, the freedom of trade conceded to America in 1778, the facility of procuring at a cheaper rate the iron and steel necessary for the mines, the fall in the price of mercury, the discovery of the mines of Catorce and Valenciana, and the establishment of the *Tribunal de Mineria.*

The two years in which the produce of gold and silver attained its *maximum*, were 1796 and 1797. In the former there were coined at the mint of Mexico, 25,644,000 piastres; and in the latter, 23,080,000 piastres. To judge of the effect produced by the freedom of trade, or rather from the cessation of the monopoly of the galleons, we have merely to remember that the value of the gold and silver coined at Mexico was, from 1766 to 1778,

191,589,179 piastres; and from 1779 to 1791, 252,525,412 piastres; so that from 1778, the increase has been more than a fourth part of the total produce.

The mines of New Spain have produced from 1690 to 1800, the enormous sum of 92,229,256 lbs. troy; and from 1690 to 1803, gold and silver to the value of 284,224,924*l.* sterling.

For a hundred and thirteen years, the produce of the mines has been constantly on the increase, if we except the single period frm 1760 to 1767. This increase becomes manifest, when we compare, every ten years, the quantity of the precious metals given in to the mint of Mexico, as is done in the following tables, of which the one indicates the value of the gold and silver in pounds sterling, and the other, the quantity of silver in pounds troy.

Progress of the mining operations of Mexico.

### Table I. *Gold and Silver.*

| Period. | | Value in pounds sterling |
|---|---|---|
| | | £.    *s.*    *d.* |
| From 1690 to 1699 | | 9,505,455   18   4 |
| 1700 | 1709 | 11,208,390   14   0 |
| 1710 | 1719 | 14,245,189   3   8 |
| 1720 | 1729 | 18,233,198   1   4 |
| 1730 | 1739 | 16,614,774   16   8 |
| 1740 | 1749 | 24,235,258   13   4 |
| 1750 | 1759 | 27,245,853   14   0 |
| 1760 | 1769 | 24,446,253   0   0 |
| 1770 | 1779 | 35,789,374   12   4 |
| 1780 | 1789 | 41,925,986   14   0 |
| 1790 | 1799 | 50,067,379   14   0 |
| Total from 1690 to 1799--£276,517,115   6   8 | | |

### Table II. *Silver alone.*

| Period. | | Silver. | |
|---|---|---|---|
| | | Troy lbs. | Oz. |
| From 1690 to 1699 | | 3,194,568 | 3 |
| 1700 | 1709 | 3,773,001 | 10 |
| 1710 | 1719 | 4,782,511 | 6 |
| 1720 | 1729 | 6,166,375 | 5 |
| 1730 | 1739 | 6,577,081 | 2 |
| 1740 | 1749 | 7,450,180 | 2 |
| 1750 | 1759 | 9,135,760 | 0 |
| 1760 | 1769 | 8,200,776 | 3 |
| 1770 | 1779 | 12,017,963 | 0 |
| 1780 | 1789 | 13,616,912 | 2 |
| 1790 | 1799 | 16,065,557 | 6 |
| Total from 1690 to 1799 | | 60,980,685 | 3 |

When we distinguish those periods in which the progress of mining has been most rapid, we find the following results :

| Periods. | Value of Gold and Silver, for an average year, in pounds sterling. | | | Progressive increase. | | |
|---|---|---|---|---|---|---|
| | £. | s. | a | £. | s. | d. |
| 1690 to 1720 | 1,182,746 | 10 | 0 | In 27 years 801,666 | 13 | 4 |
| 1721    1743 | 1,988,516 | 8 | 0 | | | |
| 1744    1770 | 2,568,545 | 8 | 4 | 25    433,333 | 6 | 8 |
| 1771    1782 | 3,731,848 | 9 | 4 | 19    1,148,333 | 6 | 8 |
| 1783    1790 | 4,228,700 | 17 | 8 | 12    498,333 | 6 | 8 |
| 1791    1803 | 4,837,261 | 17 | 4 | 10    311,666 | 13 | 4 |

This table, along with the preceding, proves that the periods during which the wealth of the mines have most increased, are from 1736 to 1745, from 1777 to 1783, and from 1788 to 1798; but the increase in general has been so little in proportion to the space of time, that the total produce of the mines was:

| £. | s. | d. | | |
|---|---|---|---|---|
| 866,666 | 13 | 4 | in | 1695 |
| 1,733,333 | 6 | 8 | - | 1726 |
| 2,600,000 | 0 | 0 | - | 1747 |
| 3,466,666 | 13 | 4 | - | 1776 |
| 4,333,333 | 6 | 8 | - | 1788 |
| 5,200,000 | 0 | 0 | - | 1795 |

from whence it follows that the produce has been

tripled in fifty-two years, and sextupled in a hundred years.

After gold and silver, it remains for us to speak of the other metals, called common metals, the working of which, as we have already stated in the beginning of this chapter, has been very much neglected. *Copper* is found in a native state, and under the forms of vitreous and oxidulated copper, in the mines of Ingaran, a little to the south of the Volcano of Jorullo, at San Juan Guetamo, in the intendancy of Valladolid, and in the province of New Mexico. The Mexican *tin* is obtained by means of washing, from the alluvial soil of the intendancy of Guanaxuato, near Gigante, San Felipe, Robledal and San Miguel el Grande, as well as in the intendancy of Zacatecas between the towns of Xeres and Villa Nueva. One of the ores of tin most common in Mexico is the *wood tin* of the English mineralogists. It appears that this mineral is originally found in veins which traverse trap-porphyries; but the natives, instead of working these veins, prefer the extracting of tin from the earth brought down the ravines. The intendancy of Guanaxuato in 1802 produced nearly 110 tons of copper, and 5 tons of tin.

The iron mines are more abundant than is generally believed, in the intendancies of Valladolid, Zacatecas, and Guadalaxara, and especially in the *provincias internas.*

R

These mines are only wrought with any degree of spirit during a period of maritime war, when a stop is put to the importation of steel and iron from Europe. The veins of Tecalitan, near Colima, were successfully wrought ten years ago, and afterwards abandoned. Ores of compact red iron-stone have been observed in the intendancy of San Luis Potosi near Catorce. I saw crystallized micaceous iron, near the village of Santa Cruz, east from Celaya, on the fertile table-land extending from Queretaro to Guanaxuato.

*Lead*, which is very rare in the north of Asia, abounds in the mountains of calcareous formation, contained in the north-east part of New Spain. The lead mines are not wrought with so much spirit as might be desired in a country where the fourth part of all the silver minerals are smelted.

Among the metals of which the use is the most limited, we have to name *zinc*, which is found, under the form of brown and black blende, in the veins of Ramos, Sombrerete, Zacatecas, and Tasco; *antimony*, which is common to Catorce and Los Pozuelos, near Cuencame; *arsenic*, which is found among the minerals of Zimapan, combined with sulphur, as orpiment. *Cobalt*, as far as I know, has never yet been discovered among the minerals of New Spain; and *manganese*, which M. Ramirez recently discovered in the island of Cuba, appears to me in general much less abundant in Equinoctial America, than it is in the temperate climates of the Old Continent.

*Mercury*, which is very remote from *tin*, with respect to its relative antiquity, or the period of its formation, is almost as uncommon as it is in every part of the globe. The inhabitants of New Spain have for centuries procured the mercury necessary in the process of amalgamation, partly from Peru and partly from Europe; and hence they are accustomed to consider their country as destitute of this metal. When however we consider the examinations carried on under the reign of Charles the Fourth, we must admit that few countries have so many indications of cinnabar, as the table-land of the Cordilleras from the 19th to the 22d degree of north latitude. In the intendancies of Guanaxuato and Mexico, we find it in many places. Sulphuret of mercury has been also discovered in the intendancy of Valladolid; at Los Pregones near Tasco, in the district of mines of the Doctor; and in the valley of Tenochtitlan to the south of Gassavé in the road from Mexico to Pachuca. The works carried on for the discovery of these different mineral repositories have been so frequently interrupted, and they have been conducted with so little zeal, and generally with so little intelligence, that it would be very imprudent to assert, as has been often done, that the mercury mines of New Spain are not worth working. It appears, on the contrary, from the interesting information which we owe to the labours of

M Chovel, that the veins of San Juan de la Chica, as well as those of the Rincon del Centeno, and the Gigante, are very deserving of the attention of the Mexican miners. Was it to be expected that super-ficial works which were merely begun, should in the very first years yield a net profit to the share-holders?

America in its present state is the tributary of Europe with respect to mercury; but it is probable that this dependence will not be of long duration, if the ties which unite the Colonies with the mother country remain long loosened, and if civilization is progressive in America. The spirit of enterprise and research will increase with the population; the more numerous are the inhabitants of the coun-try, the more will they learn to appreciate the na-tural wealth which is contained in the bowels of their mountains. If they discover no single mine equal in wealth to the celebrated one of Huancave-lica, they will work several at once, the united pro-duce of which will render the importation of mer-cury from Spain and Carniola unnecessary. These changes will be so much the more rapidly effected, as the Peruvian and Mexican miners shall feel them-selves impeded by the want of the metal necessary for amalgamation. The mineral depositaries of New Spain, if examined with care, and worked with constancy, may one day produce a very considerable quantity of mercury. The period approaches when the Spanish Colonies, being more united together, will be more attentive to their common interests : it becomes, therefore, of consequence to observe the indications of mercury in South America. Mexico and Peru, instead of receiving this metal from Europe, will one day, perhaps, be able to supply the Old world with it.

We may also hope that, in proportion as the inhabitants of the New world shall learn to profit by the natural wealth of the soil, the improvement of chemical knowledge will discover processes of amalgamation by which less mercury is consumed. By diminishing the consumption of this metal, and increasing the produce of the indigenous mines, the American miners will gradually learn to dispense with the mercury of Europe and China.

To complete the view of the mineral substances of New Spain, it remains for us to name coal, salt, and soda. The *coal*, of which I saw in the valley of Bogota beds at 7,500 feet of elevation above the level of the sea, in general appears to be very rare in the Cordilleras. In the kingdom of New Spain it has only yet been discovered in New Mexico ; it is however probable that it may be found in the secondary formations which extend to the north and north-west of the Rio Colorado, as well as in the plains of San Luis Potosi and Texas. There is already a coal mine near the sources of the Rio Sabina. In general, coal and rock salt abound to the west of the Sierra Verde near the lake of Timpanogos, in Upper Louisiana, and in those vast northern regions situated between the *stony mountains* of Mackenzie and Hudson's Bay.

Deposits of coal abound beyond the tropics in New Mexico, in the middle of the salt plains of Moqui and Nabajoa, and to the east of the Rocky Mountains, as also towards the sources of the Rio Sabina, in that immense basin covered with secondary formations, in which flow the Missouri and the Arkansas.

An able engineer, M. Lafond, whose map throws much light on these countries, observes, that eight leagues north from the post of Chichi there are hills abounding in coal, from which a subterraneous noise is heard at a distance like the discharge of artillery. Does this curious phenomenon announce a disengagement of hydrogen produced by a bed of coal in a state of inflammation?

In the whole inhabited part of New Spain, there is no rock salt like that of Zipaquira in the kingdom of Santa Fe, or of Wieliczka in Poland. The muriate of soda is no where found collected in banks or masses of considerable volume; it is merely disseminated in the argillaceous soil which covers the ridge of the Cordilleras.

The most abundant salt mine of Mexico is the lake of the *Peñon Blanco*, in the intendancy of San Luis Potosi, of which the bottom is a bed of clay which contains from 12 to 13 per cent. of muriate of soda. We ought also to observe, that were it not for the amalgamation of silver ores, the consumption of salt would be very inconsiderable in Mexico, because the Indians, who constitute a great part of the population, have never abandoned the old custom of seasoning their food with *chile* or pimento instead of salt.

### Note A.

In speaking of the common metals which may be found in Mexico, I think the probability of their value, as an object of research, is overrated. Not that I doubt that they may be found, and perhaps in some instances abundantly; but unless fuel could be supplied in much larger quantity than at present, it cannot pay to work them.—For instance, iron and copper require such a great weight of coal that they cannot be worked to advantage without it; and when we take into account the expense of transporting and erecting machinery, the fuel required for merely draining the mines, the rate of wages of the miners of Mexico, and the charge of carrying the produce to the coast, we shall see at once, that though all these expenses may be borne by silver and gold mines, nothing but a great falling off in the supply from other countries, and a proportionable advance in price, can warrant the application of them to mines of the inferior metals.

An exception may be made in respect to mercury and lead.— The former may indeed be reckoned as a precious metal, and one of which the supply is limited, being only now found in Spain and Germany : it is also, according to the present practice, essential in Mexico for the extraction of gold and silver from the ores : and though I am of opinion that, if fuel can be obtained, it would be better to discontinue the use of mercury, yet I would strongly recommend M. de Humboldt's remarks to the attention of persons working mines in Mexico, and that every inquiry and research should be made as to veins likely to produce quicksilver.

If smelting should ever be extensively practised in Mexico instead of amalgamation, lead would be the substitute for quicksilver, and a great consumption of it would take place, as in the process much would be dissipated or destroyed. This demand for it on the spot would render it valuable, and it would be applied in the state of ore. There is also every reason to think that the lead ores of Mexico may frequently contain silver in sufficient proportion to make it worth while to work them.

J. T.

## Note B.

*Coal.*—M. de Humboldt mentions this substance in the preceding chapter as having hitherto been found only in New Mexico, which is far too distant north for the supply of any of the mines now likely to be worked. It has however been also found in Peru and Chili, and some late accounts warrant the belief that it may be yet discovered within reach of the silver mines.

In a letter which I had the honour to receive, containing some information from M. de Humboldt himself, dated at Paris, on the 12th Jan. last, (1824,) he tells me, that " he thinks that he " has insisted too much in his works upon the difficulties of " supplying fuel for steam engines : That this difficulty is not " so great in general in Mexico as in Peru, as far as relates to " wood ; because, in the latter, nature has deposited the mineral " treasures at such great elevations, that they are found almost " at the highest limits of all vegetation ; whereas, upon the ta-" ble-land of Mexico, though wood is not plentiful, yet a good " deal is to be found, as at Guanaxuato, from its proximity to " the Sierra de Santa Rosa: That there are also good woods " near Real del Monte, at l' Oyamel, and at Cerro del Sacal."

He also says, " that some coal has been found, but that he " does not know of any in the domains of Count Regla," which had been reported to be the case ; and he goes on to observe, " that the formations of basalt and amygdaloid, which are com-" mon there, might indicate the presence of Lignite or Bovey " coal, which would be very useful."

This observation of M. de Humboldt has, in some degree, been confirmed, as there have lately arrived in England some specimens of a kind of coal from the district he speaks of, which, though not exactly the same as the one he mentions, is nearly allied to it, and appears to be what Professor Jameson has called *pitch coal.* It has the appearance of jet, is found in several coal-fields in Scotland, in some in England, and in Hungary, where the minerals generally remarkably resemble those of Mexico.

The letter above mentioned goes on to say, " that he had " seen secondary formations resting upon the metalliferous por- " phyries about Actopan and Totonilcos; so that, geognostically " speaking, it is possible that true coal might be discovered " there." Some further remarks on this subject will be found in the next chapter.—J. T.

S

# CHAPTER VIII.

*Geological description of the mining districts of Mexico.*

WHEN we examine the solid mass of our globe, we soon perceive that some of the substances, which descriptive mineralogy has made known to us separately, are found in *constant associations*, and that those associations, which are called compound rocks, do not vary, like organized beings, according to the difference of latitude, or of the temperature under which they are placed. Geognosts, who have travelled through the most distant countries, have not only found, for the most part, in the two hemispheres, the same simple substances, quartz, feldspar, mica, garnet, and hornblende; but they have also observed that mountainmasses display every where the same rocks; that is, the same assemblages of mica, quartz, and feldspar, in granite; of mica, quartz, and garnets, in micaslate; and of feldspar and hornblende, in syenite. If it has sometimes been considered, that a rock belongs exclusively to a single portion of the globe, subsequent researches have shown, that it also occurs in regions the most distant from its first locality. Thus we are almost led to admit, that the formation of rocks has been independent of the diversity of climates, and perhaps anterior to its existence.* There is an identity even in those rocks where organized bodies are the most variously modified.

Transition clay-slate† forms far greater masses in the globe than primitive clay-slate. The latter is generally subordinate to mica-slate; as an independent formation, it is as rare in the Pyrenees and the Alps, as in the Cordilleras. In South America, between the parallels of 10° north and 7° south, I saw transition clay-slate only on the southern declivity of the littoral chain of Venezuela, at the entrance of the Llanos of Calaboza. The basin of the Llanos, the bottom of an ancient lake covered with secondary formations (red sandstone, zechstein, and clay-gypsum), is bounded by a band of intermediary formation of clay-slate, black limestone, and euphotide, connected with transition greenstone. Gneiss and mica-slate, between the valleys of Avague and the Villa de Ceura, constitute only one formation on which clay-slate reposes in conformable position, in the ravines of Malpasso and Piedras azules (direction N. 52° E.; inclin. 70° towards the N.W.), of which the lower

* Humboldt, Geography of Plants, 1807, p. 115. Idem, Views of the Cordilleras, vol. i. p. 122.

† The *transition clay-slate* in Cornwall is called *killas,* and indeed the same general term includes *primitive clay-slate.* This remark will enable the miners of that county to understand the description of rocks in the text.—J  T.

beds are green, steatitic, and mixed with hornblende, and the upper are of a greyish-green and
darkish-blue colour. This clay-slate contains (like
that of Steben, in Franconia, the duchy of Nas-
sau, and of Peschels-Mühle in Saxony) beds of
greenstone, sometimes massive, at other times of
a globular structure.

The famous vein of Guanaxuato in New Spain,
which, from 1786 to 1803, has produced yearly,
on an average, 343,000 lbs. troy of silver, also traverses transition clay-slate. This rock, in its lower
strata, passes, in the mine of Valenciana, (at the
height of 932 fathoms above the level of the sea,)
to a talcose slate; and I described it in my *Political
Essay* as placed on the limit of the primitive and
intermediary formations. A more particular examination of the relations of position which I noted
on the spot, and the comparison of the beds of
syenite and serpentine which have been pierced in
digging the great shaft, with the beds that are
interposed in the transition formations of Saxony,
of the Bochetta of Genoa, and of the Cotentin,
convinced me that the clay-slate of Guanaxuato
belongs to the most ancient intermediary formations. We do not know whether its stratification
be *parallel* and *conformable* with that of the granite-
gneiss of Zacatecas, and of Peñon blanco, which
probably supports it, the contact of these formations
not having been observed; but almost all the
porphyry-rocks on the great table-land of Mexico

follow the general direction of the chain of mountains (N. 40°, 50° W.). This *perfect concordance*
(gleichförmigkeit der lagerung) has been observed
between the primitive gneiss and the transition
clay-slate of Saxony (Friedricks-walde; valleys of
Müglitz, Seidewitz, and Lockwitz); it proves that
the formation of the intermediary series immediately succeeded that of the last beds of the primitive
series.    In the Pyrenees, as M. de Charpentier has
observed, the former of these series is found in a
different position (not parallel), sometimes in
*transgressive position* (übergreifende lagerung)
with the latter.    I shall observe, on this occasion,
that the parallelism between the stratification of
two *consecutive formations*, or the absence of this
parallelism, does not alone decide the question
whether the two formations are united or not in the
same primitive or secondary series; it is rather the
sum of these geognostic relations that solves that
problem.    The clay-slate of Guanaxuato is very
regularly stratified (direct. N. 46° W.; inclin. 45°
S.W.), and the form of the valleys has no influence
on the direction or inclination of the strata.    We
distinguish there three varieties, which may be
considered as three epochas of formation; a clay-
slate of a silvery lustre, and steatitic, passing to a
talc-slate (talk-schiefer); a greenish clay-slate, with
a silky lustre, resembling chlorite slate; finally, a
black clay-slate, in very thin laminæ, surcharged
with carbon, staining the figures like ampelite and
the marly slate of zechstein, but not effervescing

with acids. I have named these varieties in the
order in which I observed them from below upwards, in the mine of Valenciana, which is 263
fathoms in perpendicular depth; but in the mines of
Mellado, Animas, and Rayas, the supercarburetted
clay-slate *(hoja de libro)* occurs beneath the green
and steatitic variety; and it is probable, that the
strata which pass to talc-slate, chlorite, and ampelite, alternate several times with each other.

The thickness of this formation of transition
clay-slate, which I found at the mountain of Santa-
Rosa near Los Joares, where the Indians collect
ice in small artificial basins, is more than 3000
feet. It contains in subordinate beds, not only
syenite (like the transition clay-slate of the Cotentin), but also, which is very remarkable, serpentine,
and a hornblende-slate that is not greenstone. In
digging in the massive rock, the great shaft of
Valenciana, which has cost nearly 292,000*l.*, the
following strata were found, reckoning downwards
for ninety-four fathoms of depth : an ancient conglomerate, representing the red sandstone; black
transition clay-slate, strongly carburetted, in very
thin laminæ; clay-slate, blueish-grey, and containing
magnesia; hornblende-slate, greenish-black, a little
mixed with quartz and pyrites, destitute of feldspar,
not passing to greenstone, and altogether similar
to the hornblende-slate (hornblend-schiefer) which
forms beds in primitive gneiss and mica-slate;
green serpentine of uneven fracture and fine grain,
dull, but translucent on the edges, containing much

pyrites, destitute of garnets, and diallage metalloid (schillerspath) mixed with talc and steatite; hornblende-slate; syenite, or a granular mixture of much darkish-green hornblende, yellowish quartz, and a little lamellar and white feldspar. This syenite splits into very thin layers; the quartz and feldspar are so irregularly spread, that they sometimes form small veins in a paste of hornblende. The syenite is the largest of these eight interposed beds, of which the direction and inclination are exactly parallel to that of the whole rock; it is more than 180 feet thick; and as I saw in the deepest working of the mine (*planes* of San Bernardo), at 172 fathoms below the bed of syenite, carburetted clay-slate occurring again, identical with that in which new shafts are beginning to be sunk, no doubt can remain that hornblende-slate alternating twice with serpentine, and serpentine alternating probably with syenite, form beds subordinate to the great mass of clay-slate of Guanaxuato. The connexion which we have just remarked between hornblende-rocks and serpentine, is found in other parts of the globe, in formations of euphotide of different ages; for instance, at Heidelberg near Zell in Franconia; at Keilwig in the northern extremity of Norway; at Portsoy in Scotland; and at the island of Cuba, between Regla and Guanavacoa*.

* The *syenite* here spoken of will best be understood in Cornwall, as a species of *elvan*; which term, however, more properly belongs to what is now called *porphyry*.—J. T.

I saw no remains of organized bodies, nor beds of porphyry, grauwacke, nor lydian stone, in the transition clay-slate of Guanaxuato, which is the rock richest in silver that has hitherto been found; but this clay-slate is covered in conformable position in some places by transition porphyries very regularly stratified (los Alamos de la Sierra); in some by greenstone and syenites alternating thousands of times together (between Esperanca and Comangillas); and in others, either by a calcareous conglomerate or by transition limestone of a blueish-grey colour, mixed with clay, and fine-grained (ravine of Acabuca), or by red sandstone (Marfil). These relations of the clay-slate of Guanaxuato, with the rocks which it supports, and some of which (the syenites) appear first as subordinate beds, suffice to place it among the transition formations; above all, they justify this result in the opinion of those geognosts who are acquainted with the observations which have been recently published on the intermediary formations of Europe. With respect to lydian stone, there can be no doubt that it is contained on some points not yet explored in the clay-slate of Guanaxuato; for I found the former substance frequently imbedded in large fragments in the ancient conglomerate (red sandstone) which covers the clay-slate between Valenciana, Marfil, and Cuevas. Thirty miles to the south of Cuevas, between Queretaro and la Cuesta de la Noria, in the middle of a Mexican table-land, a transition clay-slate appears beneath the porphyry, darkish-gray, and passing both to siliceous slate *(schistoïd jasper kiesel-schiefer)* and lydian stone. Many fragments of this latter substance are found near the Noria scattered in the fields. The rocks with argentiferous veins of Zacatecas, and a small part of the veins of Catorce, according to the report of two well-informed mineralogists, MM. Sonneschmidt and Valencia, also traverse transition clay-slate, which contains true beds of lydian stone, and which appears to rest on syenites. This super-position would prove, according to what has been observed of the great shaft of Valenciana, that the clay-slates of Mexico constitute (as at Caucasus and in the Cotentin) the same formation with the transition syenites and euphotides, and that perhaps they alternate with the latter rocks.

It is in porphyries and porphyritic greenstones, that at the north of the equator, in Mexico and in Hungary, the immensely rich gold and silver mines have been discovered; for although the metalliferous rock of Schemnitz (*saxum metalliferum* of Born) may perhaps be posterior to the transition lime-stones, containing some indistinct organic remains, this position, in the opinion of a celebrated geognost, M. Beudant, is too uncertain to separate formations so closely allied as those of New Spain and Hungary. The syenites with zircons, the transition granites and porphyries of Norway, which MM. de Buch and Hausmann have made us acquainted

T

with, are not only posterior, (Stromsoë, Krogsko-
ven) to grauwacke and a clay-slate that alternates
with orthoceratite-limestone, but these rocks also
cover (Skeen) immediately a quartzite *(quartzfels)*
that represents grauwacke, and reposes on a black
limestone destitute of alternating beds of clay-slate.

The property which certain porphyries and porphyritic syenites possess of being eminently metalliferous, ought not, I think, to oppose the union of
the rocks of Mexico, Hungary, Saxony and Norway.
The ores of gold and silver do not form contempo-
rary beds, but are veins of extraordinary size. Some
transition porphyries, several of which we should be
tempted to place among trachytes because they contain true beds of phonolite with glassy feldspar, participate in these mineral riches, which, among the
rocks posterior to primitive formations, were long
thought to be found exclusively in carburetted and
micaceous clay-slate, grauwacke, and transition
limestone. There exist in the same regions groups
of porphyries and syenites, very analogous, in their
mineralogical composition and their position, to the
rocks containing the rich mines of Schemnitz or
New Spain, and which, nevertheless, are found entirely destitute of metals. This is the case with
almost all the transition porphyries of South America. The great workings of Peru, those of Hual-
gayoc or Chota, and Llauricocha or Pasco, are not
in porphyry, but mountain limestone. The famous
Cerro del Potosi, in the republic of Buenos-Ayres,

is composed of clay-slate (transition ?) covered by porphyries that contain disseminated garnets.

If the great argentiferous and auriferous deposits which have formed for ages the wealth of Hungary and Transylvania, are found solely amidst syenites and porphyritic greenstones, we must not thence conclude that the case is the same in New Spain. The Mexican porphyries no doubt offer insulated examples of immense riches. At Pachuca, the pit of del Encino alone furnished annually, during a long time, more than 18,500lbs. troy of silver; in 1726 and 1727, the two workings of La Biscaina and Xacal gave together 333,000lbs. troy; that is, almost twice as much as all Europe and Asiatic Russia produced in the same interval. These same porphyries * of Real del Monte, which are connected by their upper beds with porphyritic trachytes and pearl-stone, with obsidian of Cerro de las Navajas, furnished, by the working of the mine of La Biscaina, to the Count of Regla, from 1762 to 1781, more than 3,384,000*l*. These riches, however, are still inferior to those which are drawn in the same country from transition formations which are not porphyritic. The *veta negra* of Sombrerete, which traverses a compact limestone containing nodules of lydian stone, has furnished the example of the greatest abundance of silver which has been observed

* Porphyry is what is called *Elvan* in Cornwall, where it is usually found to run in channels or courses in the killas or clay-slate; in Mexico it forms larger masses.—J. T.

in the two hemispheres; the family of Fagoaga, or of
the Marquis del Apartado, drew from thence in a
few months a neat profit of 870,000*l.* The produce
of the mine of Valenciana, worked in transition
slate, has been so constant, that to the end of the last
century it never ceased to furnish anually, during
forty years successively, above 222,000lbs. troy of
silver. In general, in the central part of New Spain,
where porphyries are frequent, it is not that rock
which affords the precious metals in the three great
workings of Guanaxuato, Zacatecas, and Catorce.
These three mining districts, which yield the half
of all the Mexican gold and silver, are situated between the 18th and 23d degrees of north latitude.
The miners there work on metalliferous mineral deposits, almost entirely in intermediary formations
of clay-slate, grauwacke, and alpine limestone; I
say almost entirely, for the famous *Veta madre* de
Guanaxuato, richer than Potosi, and furnishing till
1804, on an average, a sixth of the silver which
America pours into the circulation of the whole
world, traverses both clay-slate and porphyry. The
mines of Belgrado, San Bruno, and Marisanshez,
opened in the porphyritic part at the south-east of
Valenciana, are but of small importance. Other
workings carried on in the porphyries of Real del
Monte, Moran, Pachuca, and Bolaños, do not now
furnish above 62,000lbs. troy, or a twenty-fifth part
of the silver exported (1803) from the port of Vera
Cruz. I thought it proper here to state these

facts, because the denomination of *metalliferous porphyries* which I have often used in my works, might lead to the error of considering the metallic riches of the New World as procured in great part from transition porphyries. The more we advance in the study of the constitution of the globe in different climates, the more we are convinced that there scarcely exists one rock anterior to mountain limestone which has not been found in some countries extremely argentiferous. The phenomenon of these ancient veins in which our metallic riches are deposited, (perhaps as the specular iron and muriate of copper are deposited in modern times in the fissures of lava,) is a phenomenon that appears in some degree independent of the specific nature of rocks.

In advancing to the north towards Sopilote, Mescala, and Tasco, we again lose sight of porphyry. Primitive granite re-appears, but is soon hid by a porphyry, the mineralogical composition of which presents very remarkable characters ; it is blueish-gray, a little argillaceous by decomposition, and contains large crystals of whitish-yellow feldspar (rather lamellar than glassy), pyroxene of nearly a leek-green, and a little uncrystallized quartz. This stratified porphyry is covered, towards the south, with the same conglomerate limestone that abounds on the table-land of Chilpansingo ; towards the north (Sopilote, Estola, Mescala) with a grayish compact limestone traversed by veins of carburetted lime. The limestone of Estola is not always spongy or vesicular in its whole mass, like the formation of Masatlan, but contains large insulated caverns like the limestone of Peregrino. Whilst travelling in those mountains, I had no doubt remaining, that the rocks of Cañada de Sopilote and of Alto del Peregrino are identical with our alpine limestone *(zechstein)* of Europe, which succeeds, according to the age of its formation, to the red sandstone, or, when that is wanting, to the transition rocks. Near Mescala, a little north of Sopilote, rich silver veins, analogous to the veins of Tasco and Tehuilotepec, traverse the alpine limestone. The rock in the valley of Sopilote, that covers the porphyry of the group of Zumpango, exhibits the same sinuous and contorted beds that are seen at Achsenberg, on the bank of the lake of Lucerne, and in other mountains of alpine limestone in Switzerland. I observed that the upper beds of the formation of Sopilote and Mescala passed progressively to whitish-gray, were destitute of veins of calcareous spar, and presented a dull, compact, or conchoidal fracture. They divide, nearly like the limestone of Pappenheim, into very thin layers. It seems to be the passage from the alpine to the Jura limestone, two formations which immediately cover each other in Switzerland, the Apennines, and several parts of equinoctial America, but which in the south of Germany are separated from each other

by several interposed formations (by the sandstone
of Nebra, or *bunte sandstein,* by *muschelkalk,* and
the white sandstone or *quadersandstein).*

Near the village of Sochipala, the mountain limestone is covered by gypsum, and between Estola and
Tepecuacuilco, there appears beneath the mountain
limestone (directed sometimes N. 48° E., with inclination of 40° at the east; sometimes N. 48° E. ;
with inclination 50° to south-east) a porphyry, as-
paragus-green, with a base of compact feldspar, divided into very thin strata like that of Achichintla,
and almost destitute of disseminated crystals. This
rock resembles phonolitic porphyry *(porphyr-schie-
fer)* of the trachyte formation. In advancing towards the mines of Tehuilotepec and Tasco, we find
the same rock covered with a quartzose sandstone
having a cement of argillaceous limestone, and analogous to the *weiss liegende* (lower arenaceous bed
of zechstein) of Thuringia. This quartzose sandstone again announces the proximity of mountain
limestone; and in fact, on this sandstone and perhaps immediately on porphyry (as at Zumpango,
and the Alto de los Caxones), near the salt lake of
Tuspa, an immense mass of mountain limestone
reposes, often cavernous, and containing some pe-
trifactions of trochi and other univalve shells.
This limestone of Tuspa, indubitably posterior to
all the porphyries which I have just described, contains beds of specular gypsum, and beds of slaty and
carburetted clay, which we must not confound with

grauwacke-slate. It is generally blueish gray, compact and crossed by veins of carbonate of lime.   In
many places, instead of being cavernous, it passes
to a very compact white formation, analogous to the
limestone of Pappenheim.  I was struck with these
variations of texture, which M. de Buch and myself
had also observed in the Apennines (between Fo-
sombrono, Furli, and Fuligno), and which seem to
prove that, where the intermediary members of the
series were not developed, the formations of alpine
and Jura limestone are more closely connected than
is generally admitted.  The rich silver veins of
Tasco, which formerly yielded 99,000lbs. troy of
silver annually, traverse both limestone and a clay-
slate that passes to mica-slate ; for, notwithstanding the identity of the limestone formations of Tasco
and Mescala, which are both argentiferous, the former of those, wherever it has been pierced in mining
(Cerro de S. Ignacio), has not been found superposed to porphyry like the limestone of Mescala,
but covering a more ancient rock than porphyry, a
mica-slate (dir. N. 50° E.; incl. 40°—60°, most
frequently at N. W. sometimes at S. E.) destitute
of garnets, and passing to primitive clay-slate.   It
was proper to enter into these details on the formations that succeed porphyries, because it is only in
making known the nature of *superposed* rocks, that
geognosts can be enabled to decide on the place
which Mexican porphyries ought to occupy in the
order of formations.   A sketch of a geognostic ta-

ble has its value only inasmuch as we connect the rock we wish to make known, to those by which it is immediately succeeded above and below. Mineralogical facts alone may be presented singly ; positive geognosy is a science occupied with the relation and connexion of facts ; and in describing any one portion of the globe, we ought not to limit our view, and stop at the study of a particular bed.

*Central table-land, valley of Mexico ; tract between Pachuca, Moran, and La Puebla.* An enormous mass of transition porphyry rises to the *mean* height of 1200 to 1400 fathoms above the level of the sea. It is covered in the valley of Mexico, and at the south towards Cuernavaca and Guchilaque, with basaltic and cellular amygdaloid (*tetzontli* in Mexican); and towards the east and north-east (between Tlascala and Totonilco) with secondary formations. The porphyry, probably hid at first beneath the mountain limestone of Mescala and then in the Llanos of San Gabriel (near the bridge of Istla) beneath trachytic conglomerates and a porous amygdaloid, is identical with that which reappears, 45 miles further north, and 800 fathoms higher, on the banks of the lake of Tezcuco. In the fine valley of Mexico the porphyritic rock pierces the cellular amygdaloid in the hills of Chapoltepec, of Notre Dame de la Guadeloupe, and of Peñol de los Baños. It exhibits several very remarkable varieties : 1. reddish-gray, a little argillaceous, with-

out distinct stratification, containing crystals of
hornblende, and common feldspar in equal parts
(level dug in the rock of Chapoltepec); 2. black
or darkish-gray (sometimes fissile and spongy) stratified by beds from 3 to 4 inches thick, with a basis
of compact feldspar, fracture dull, smooth, or im-
perfectly conchoidal, resembling more the fracture
of lydian stone than that of pitchstone, containing
small crystals of glassy feldspar and olive-green
pyroxene, almost destitute of hornblende, and often
covered at their surface by superb masses of reni-
form hyalite, or Muller's glass (Peñol de los Baños;
dir. N. 60° W.; incl. 60° N. E.) ; 3. red, earthy,
with a quantity of large crystals of common decomposed feldspar (salt-works of the lake of Tezcuco,
where the Peñol is covered by ancient Aztic sculp-
tures). The porphyry of the valley of Mexico furnishes not only springs of pure water, which is conveyed to the town by long and magnificent aqueducts,
but also acidulated thermal waters, some warm, and
others cold. Here are also found (and this is a very
remarkable fact) naphtha and petroleum (promontory
of the sanctuary of Guadeloupe), as in the primitive
mica-slate of the vicinity of Araya and Cumana.
Although this porphyry appears below the porous
amygdaloid, and is seen (Cerro de las Cruces and
Tiangillo, Cuesta de Varientos and Capulalpan,
Cerro Ventoso, and Rio Frio) in all the circular
outline of the basin of Tenochtitlan, (the bottom
of an ancient lake partly dried,) it is only towards

the north-east (Pachuca, Real del Monte, and Moran) that it has been found to be argentiferous.

Several rich veins traverse a mass of porphyry above 700 feet in thickness, from the mine of San Pedro, at the summit of Cerro Ventoso (1461 fathoms), as far as the bottom of the ancient wells of Encino (1170 fathoms), in the Real de Pachuca. This rock, which would have formerly been called petrosilex, or hornstone-porphyry, is generally greenish-gray, sometimes prase-green, with a scaly fracture, and giving fragments with sharp edges. The paste is probably a compact feldspar, having a large proportion of silica; and contains, not quartz and mica, but crystals of common feldspar and hornblende. In general, the latter substance is not very abundant, and when the porphyry is argillaceous, or merely earthy, we recognise the hornblende only by spots with striated surfaces, and of a very dark green. The beds which are argillaceous and softer (clay porphyry of Moran) appear to be below the harder and more tenacious beds. Strata of phonolite (*klingstein*) are found subordinate to both; it is smoke-gray, or leek-green, divided into tables or plates that are very sonorous. It is not, however, altogether a porphyry slate of the trachyte formation; for the phonolitic mass does not contain thin crystals of glassy feldspar, but crystals of grayish-white common feldspar, constantly accompanied with a little hornblende. All these argentiferous porphyries of Moran and Real del Monte are very re-

gularly stratified (general direction as in the valley
of Mexico, N. 60° W., incl. 50°—60° at N. E.):
they are irregularly columnar only in the Organos of
Actopan (Cerro de Mamanchota, summit 1527 fathoms) and the Monjas of Totonilco el Chico; if indeed the rock of Organos, the mass of which is 3000
feet thick, reckoning only the porphyries visible above
the neighbouring plains, is identical with the rock
of Moran. The latter contains fewer crystals of
hornblende ; neither of these rocks is fissile or porous, and it is at the foot of the grotesque peaks
of Monjas that the rich veins of Tononilco el Chico
are found. The argentiferous porphyries of Pachuca
and Moran which I have just described, present no
character that should separate them from the transition formation: they are even covered, between
the baths of Totonilco el Grande and the cavern of
Madre de Dios, or the pierced rock, by enormous calcareous masses, and by sandstone and gypsum.

  *Group of porphyries of Guanaxuato.* It is this
group that determines most clearly the relative
age, or, to express myself with more precision, the
*maximum* of the antiquity of the Mexican porphyries; if indeed those of which we have just indicated the positions are of the same formation as
the porphyries of Guanaxuato. The superposition
of those porphyries on rocks belonging to intermediary formation is evident. Near the farm of
Noria, and in the Cañada de Queretaro, a slaty
olive-green porphyry, containing glassy feldspar in

microscopic crystals, is superposed on a transition
clay-slate with lydian stone.   This superposition is
equally certain near Guanaxuato, and particularly
near Santa Rosa de la Sierra.   The porphyries of
this district have in general a concordant position
(a parallel direction and inclination) with the strata
of clay-slate.   They are eminently metalliferous;
and the famous vein of Guanaxuato *(Veta Madre)*,
making the same angle with the meridian as the
veins of Zacatecas, Tasco and Moran (N. 50° W.),
has been worked successively on a length of 12,000
fathoms, and a thickness of 20 to 25 fathoms.   It
has furnished, in 230 years, more than 39,000,000*l.*,
and traverses both porphyry and transition-slate.
The first of these rocks forms, at the east of Guanaxuato, gigantic masses, that have at a distance
the most singular aspect, resembling walls and
bastions.   These perpendicular ridges, rising more
than 200 fathoms above the surrounding plains,
bear the name of *buffas;* they are destitute of
metals, appear to have been heaved up by elastic
fluids; and are regarded by the Mexican miners,
who see them placed also at Zacatecas on a very
metalliferous transition clay-slate, as a natural
indication of the riches of those countries.   When
we consider the porphyries of La Buffa de Guanaxuato, and those of the formerly celebrated
mines of Belgrado de San Bruno, la Sierra de
Santa Rosa, and Villalpando, in the same point
of view, we think we perceive in their latest strata,

passages to rocks which in Europe are generally placed among trachytes.

In the vicinity of Guanaxuato, porphyries predominate, which have a paste of compact feldspar, are gray and olive-green, and contain imbedded lamellar feldspar (not glassy), either in crystals almost microscopic (Buffa) or in very large crystals (mines of San Bruno and Tesoro). Decomposed hornblende, which probably tinges with green the whole mass of these rocks, is only distinguished by irregular spots. In ascending towards the Sierra (Puerto de Santa Rosa, Puerto de Varientos), the porphyry is often composed of balls with concentric layers; its paste becomes darkish-gray, semi-vitreous (pitchstone-porphyry), and contains a little crystallized mica and grains of quartz. The auriferous veins near Villalpando traverse a green porphyry with a base of phonolite, in which we perceive only some small and thin crystals of glassy feldspar. It is difficult to distinguish this rock from trachytic porphyry-slate; I have seen it covered with an earthy yellowish-white porphyry (mine of Santa Cruz), and with an ancient conglomerate (mouth of the mine of Villalpando), which evidently represents the red sandstone, and the lower beds of which pass to grauwacke.

The porphyries of the equinoctial region of Mexico contain, although rarely, besides some disseminated garnets (Izmiquilpan and Xaschi), sulphuret of mercury (San Juan de la Chica; Cerro del Fraile, near the Villa of San Felipe; Gasave, at the northern extremity of the valley of Mexico), tin (El Robedal, and la Mesa de los Hernandez), and alumstone (Real del Monte, according to M. Sonneschmidt). This latter substance seems to give to the porphyritic rocks a nearer affinity to real trachytes; although in South America (peninsula of Araya, Cerro del Distiladero and Chupariparu) I saw a clay-slate which belonged rather to the primitive than to the intermediary formation, traversed by veins, I will not say, of alumstone (*alumstein*), but of native alum, of which the Indians sell pieces of the size of an inch at the market of Cumana. The cinnabar of the porphyries of San Juan de la Chica, the argillaceous beds of Durasno containing both coal and cinnabar and placed on a porphyry with much hornblende, are phenomena well worthy of attention. The geognosts who, like myself, attach more importance to the position than to the mineralogical composition of rocks, will, no doubt, connect the porphyries and clays of Davasno with the deposites of mercury which the formation of the red sandstone and porphyry exhibits in both hemispheres (duchy de Deuxponts and Cuenca, between Quito and Loxa). The last beds of the transition formation are found every where in close connexion with the most ancient beds of the secondary formation.

The celebrated silver vein of Bolaños contains its greatest riches in an amygdaloid interposed in porphyry. In Hungary, England, Scotland, and even in Germany, rocks of amygdaloid and porphyry belong to grauwacke, to clay-slate, to transition limestone, to red sandstone, and to coal sandstone. The metalliferous porphyry of Guanaxuato simply covers clay-slate, without forming in it subordinate beds ; but a syenite analogous to that which occurs in the mine of Valenciana, in the midst of intermediary clay-slate, alternates thousands of times, on a surface of more than twenty square leagues, with transition greenstone, between the mine of the Esperanza and the village of Comangillas. In that region the syenitic rock is destitute of metals, but at Comanja it is argentiferous, as it is also in Saxony and in Hungary.

I had the opportunity of observing the formation of red sandstone in the equinoctial region of the New Continent, north and south of the equator, in six different places ; in New Spain (from 1100 to 1300 fathoms high), in the steppes or Llanos of Venezuela (30—50 fathoms), in New Granada (50—1800 fathoms), on the southern table-land of the province of Quito (1350—1600 fathoms), and in the western valley of the Amazon (200 fathoms).

The schists and transition porphyries of Guanaxuato (table-land of Anahuac), of which we have given a detailed description above, are covered with a formation of red sandstone. This formation fills the plains of Celaya, Salamanca, and Burras (900 fathoms) ; it there supports limestone very analogous to that of Jura, and lamellar gypsum. It extends by Cañada de Marfil to the mountains that surround the town of Guanaxuato, and appears in insulated spots in the Sierra de Santa Rosa, near Villalpando (1330 fathoms). This Mexican sandstone has the most striking resemblance with the *rothe todte liegende* of Mansfeld in Saxony. It contains angular fragments of lydian stone, syenite, porphyry, quartz, and flint *(splittriger hornstein)*. The cement that unites these fragments is argillo-ferruginous, very tenacious, yellowish-brown, and often (near the river of Serena) of a brick-red colour. Beds of coarse conglomerate, containing fragments two or three inches in diameter, alternate with a fine-grained conglomerate, sometimes even (Cuevas) with a sandstone consisting uniformly of grains of quartz. Coarse conglomerates abound more in plains and ravines than on the heights. I thought I perceived in the most ancient beds (mine of Rayas) a passage from the red sandstone to grauwacke; the pieces of imbedded syenite and porphyry become very small; their outlines are indistinct and appear as if softened into the mass. This conglomerate *(frijolillo de Rayas)* must not be confounded with that of the mine of Animas, which is whitish-gray, and contains fragments of compact limestone. In the red sandstone of Guanaxuato, as well as in that of Eisleben in Saxony, the cement is often so abundant (road from Guanaxuato to

Rayas and Salgado) that the imbedded fragments are no longer distinguished. Argillaceous beds, from three to four inches thick, then alternate with the coarse conglomerate. The great formation of red sandstone, superposed on metalliferous clay-slate, appears in general only when supported by transition porphyry (Belgrade, Buffa de Guanaxuato); but we see it distinctly placed on the latter rock at Villalpando. I found no petrified shells, nor any trace of coal or fossil wood in the red sandstone of Guanaxuato. These combustible substances occur frequently in other parts of New Spain, especially in those which are least elevated above the level of the sea. In the interior of New Mexico, coal is known not far from the banks of the Rio del Norte; other deposites of it probably are hid in the plains of Nuevo Sant-Ander and the Texas. At the north of Natchitoches, near the coal-mine of Chica, subterraneous detonations are heard from time to time, from an insulated hill, occasioned perhaps by the inflammation of hydrogen gas mixed with atmospheric air. Fossil wood is common in the red sandstone that extends towards the north-east of the town of Mexico. It is also found in the immense plains of the intendance of San Luis Potosi, and near the town of Altamira. The coal of Durasno (between Tierra-Nueva and San Luis de la Paz) is placed below a bed of clay containing fossil wood, and over a bed of sulphuret of mercury which covers the porphyry.

GEOLOGY OF MINING DISTRICTS. 155

Does it belong to very recent lignites? or, ought we not rather to admit that these combustible substances of Durasno, these clays and semi-vitreous porphyries *(pechstein porphyre)*, globular and covered with mammillated hyalite, porphyries which in other parts of Mexico (San Juan de la Chica, Cerro del Fraile near the Villa of San Felipe) contain deposites of sulphuret of mercury, are connected with the great formation of red sandstone? There is no doubt that this formation is as rich in mercury in the new continent as in the west of Germany; it is found there when the porphyries are wanting (Cuenca, table-land of Quito); and if the union of veins of tin with veins of cinnabar, in the porphyries of San Felipe, appear at first to remove porphyritic rocks which abound in mercury from those of the red sandstone, we must recollect that transition clay-slate and porphyries (Hollgrund near Steben, Hartenstein) are also sometimes stanniferous in Europe.

I place in the suite of coal-sandstones of Guanaxuato, a formation that is somewhat doubtful, which I have already described, in my *Political Essay on New Spain*, by the name of *lozero*, or feldspathic conglomerate; it is an arenaceous rock, reddish-white, and sometimes apple-green, which divides, like sandstone *(leuben* or *waldplatten-stein* of Suhl), in very thin plates *(lozas)*; it contains grains of quartz, small fragments of clay-slate, and a quantity of crystals of feldspar partly

x 2

broken and partly entire. These various substances
are connected together in the *lozero* of Mexico, as
in the rock of porphyritic aspect of Suhl, by an
argillo-ferruginous cement (Cañada de Serena, and
almost the whole mountain of that name). It is
probable that the destruction of the porphyry has
had great influence on the formation of the feldspathic sandstone of Guanaxuato. The most experienced mineralogist might at first be led to take
it for a porphyry with an argillaceous base, or
for a porphyritic breccia. Around Valenciana
the *lozero* forms masses of 200 fathoms in thickness, and which exceed in elevation the mountains
formed by the intermediary porphyry. Near to
Villalpando a feldspathic conglomerate, with very
small grains, alternates by beds one or two feet
thick, twenty-eight times with slate-clay of a
darkish brown. I saw every where this conglomerate or *lozero* reposing on the red sandstone,
and at the south-west declivity of Cerro de Serena,
in descending towards the mine of Rayas, it appeared to me sufficiently evident that the *lozero*
forms a bed in the coarse conglomerate of Marfil.
I doubt, consequently, if this remarkable formation
can belong to trachytic pumice-conglomerates,
as M. Beudant seems to think from its analogy
with some rocks in Hungary. The argillaceous
cement becomes often so abundant that the imbedded parts are scarcely visible, and the mass
passes to compact clay-stone *(thonstein)*. In this

state the *lozero* furnishes the fine building-stone of
Queretaro, (quarries of Caretas and Guimilpa,)
which is so much esteemed for architecture.   I
have seen columns fourteen feet high, and two feet
and a half in diameter, flesh-red, brick-red, or
peach colour.   When in contact with the atmosphere those fine colours change to gray, probably
by the action of the air on the dendritic manganese
contained in the fissures of the rock.   The columns
of Queretaro have a smooth fracture, like that of
the lithographic Jura limestone.   With difficulty
we discover in these clay-stones *(argilolites)* some
very small fragments of clay-slate, quartz, feldspar, and mica.   I will not decide, if the unbroken
crystals of *lozero* or feldspathic sandstone are developed in the mass itself, or are found there acci-
dentally.   I shall here confine myself to the observation, that in Europe this red sandstone and
these porphyries are also sometimes characterized
by a *local suppression* of crystals and imbedded
fragments.   The *lozero* appears to me to be a
formation of superposed sandstone, perhaps even
subordinate to the red sandstone ; and if no rock
entirely similar is found in  the ancient continent,
we see, at least, the first germ of this kind of
pseudo-porphyritic structure in the layers of sandstone with feldspar crystals, broken or entire,
which are sometimes imbedded in the great formation of red sandstone of Mansfeld and Thuringer-
wald.

### Note 1.

An attentive perusal of the preceding observations on the geology of those parts of Mexico which contain the richest mines, will present striking resemblances, in some points, to what is observed in England. It is only within a few years, that the coincidence between the position of the most productive mines of Cornwall, with the junctions of different rocks has been much noticed. My own attention was first called to it by the communication of observations made in different parts of Europe by my friend Mr. Greenough, and I believe I was afterwards instrumental in calling the attention of our practical miners to the circumstance. The truth of the remark is now universally admitted in that district, where it will appear that our great mines are either near the junction of the killas (clay-slate) with the granite, or they are in killas which is intersected by channels of elvan (inclined beds of porphyry). So prevalent is the opinion now become, that some of the most intelligent miners would hesitate to recommend trials which involve much expense, on lodes or veins discovered where the different rocks are not thus associated, or in what has in Cornwall been significantly called a *clean country*.

Our lead mining districts in England are also to be found near junctions, either where the coal measures rest on the limestone, as in North Wales, or where rocks are interstratified, as in Derbyshire, Yorkshire, or Cumberland and Durham.

We see this theory confirmed in Mexico : in the succeeding chapter we shall find that at Guanaxuato the richest veins in the world are in killas, containing beds of syenite, and in porphyries, which we should call elvan; and that the best mines on this extraordinary lode are near the junction of the rocks.

At Sombrerete the lode is in limestone containing lydian stone, a kind of flinty slate nearly allied to chert, which in England is found with the limestone near some of our best lead mines, and is esteemed a favourable circumstance, as it is also at Ecton mine for copper.

In Zacatecas and Catorce, where the mines have been extremely rich, we find them in intermediary formations of clay-slate, grauwacke and limestone. The veins of Tasco traverse both limestone and clay-slate.

Real del Monte, Moran and Pachuca, which are nearly together, and Bolaños which is very distant from them, exhibit porphyry as the prevalent rock: we observe, however, that it is stratified with beds which are of the argillaceous kind, and that strata of phonolite, which is a kind of basalt or whin stone, occur in them; and that amygdaloid, another rock of the same nature, forms junctions at no great distance.

We cannot too much value the industry and accuracy of the learned author, which have enabled us to compare facts so important, at such a distance from our usual means of information.                                                                                   J. T.

## Note 2.

The *lozero* of Guanaxuato, which M. Humboldt places in the suite of coal sandstones, will deserve particular attention on the part of those who may undertake the mines of that important district. It does not indeed appear that any coal has been discovered there; but as this rock seems to resemble some of the sandstones which occur among coal formations, and as fuel for steam-engines and smelting will be an article of the utmost importance, no effort should be spared for its discovery, and no exertion should be abandoned while any chance exists.                                                                            J. T.

## CHAPTER IX.

*Geological constitution of mines—position and extent of
mineral veins—elevation of mines—comparative wealth
of mines—distance between principal mines—nature of
ores—mean riches of ores.*

As the subject of the disposition of the mineral
treasures of Mexico in the bosom of the earth—
the direction, inclination, and character of the
veins, is of primary importance, we shall communicate the result of some further observations
on those interesting phenomena, together with
some details as to the comparative wealth of the
most celebrated veins.

Those who have studied the geological constitution of a mining country of great extent, know
the difficulty of reducing to general ideas the observations made on a great variety of beds and
metalliferous veins. These difficulties are increased
when it happens, as in the mountains of Mexico,
that the *veins*, the *beds*, and the *masses (stock-
werke)*, are scattered in an infinity of mixed rocks
of very different *formations*. If we possessed an
accurate description of the four or five thousand
veins actually wrought in Mexico, or which have
been wrought within the two last centuries, we

should undoubtedly perceive, in the materials and structure of these veins, analogies indicative of a simultaneous origin; we should find that the matters comprising the veins are partly the same with those which are exhibited in the veins of Saxony and Hungary, and on which M. Werner, the first mineralogist of the age, has thrown so much light. But we are yet very far from being acquainted with the metalliferous mountains of Mexico; and notwithstanding the great number of observations collected by myself in travelling through the country in different directions, for a length of more than 1200 miles, I shall not venture to sketch a general view of the Mexican mines, considered under their geological relations; I shall content myself with merely indicating the rocks which yield the greatest part of the wealth of New Spain.

In the present state of the country, the veins or lodes are the object of the most considerable operations; and the ores disposed in *beds* or in *masses* are not frequent. The Mexican lodes are for the most part found in *primitive* and *transition* rocks, and rarely in the rocks of *secondary* formation.

On taking a general view of the metalliferous repositories, we find that the Cordilleras of Mexico contain veins in a great variety of rocks, and that those rocks, which at present furnish almost the whole silver annually exported from Vera Cruz, are, *primitive slate* or killas, *grauwacke,* and *alpine limestone,* intersected by the *principal veins* of Guanaxuato, Zacatecas, and Catorce.

The *porphyries* of Mexico may be considered for the most part as rocks eminently rich in ores of gold and silver. The more we study the geological constitution of the globe on a large scale, the more we perceive that there is scarcely a rock which has not in certain countries been found eminently metalliferous. The wealth of the veins is for the most part totally independent of the nature of the beds which they intersect.

In proportion as the north of Mexico shall be examined by intelligent geologists, it will be perceived that the metallic wealth of Mexico does not exclusively belong to primitive formations and transition rocks, but extends also to those of *secondary formation.* I know not whether the lead which is procured in the eastern parts of the intendancy of San Luis Potosi is found in veins or beds; but it appears certain, that the veins of silver of the Real de Catorce, as well as those of the Doctor and Xaschi near Zimapan, traverse *alpine limestone;* and this rock rests on pudding-stone, with siliceous cement, which may be considered as the most ancient of secondary formations. The alpine limestone, and the jura limestone, contain the celebrated silver mines of Tasco and Tehuilotepec, in the intendancy of Mexico; and it is in these calcareous rocks that the numerous veins which in this country have been very early wrought, display the greatest wealth. Mines in Europe are usually worked either on a great number of small veins, or on fewer depositories of minerals of great size, as at Clausthal, the Harz, and near Schemnitz in Hungary. The Cordilleras of Mexico offer frequent examples of these two methods of operation; but the districts of mines of the most constant and considerable wealth, Guanaxuato, Zacatecas, and the Real del Monte, contain only one principal vein each *(veta madre)*. The vein called *halsbruckner spath,* of which the extent is $6\frac{1}{2}$ feet, and which has been traced for a length of 339 fathoms, is spoken of as a remarkable phenomenon at Freiberg. The *veta madre* of Guanaxuato, from which there have been extracted, during the course of the last ten years, nearly 4,000,000lbs. troy of silver, is of the extent of from 130 to 150 feet, and it is wrought from Santa Isabella and San Bruno to Buena-Vista, a length of more than 6944 fathoms.

In the New Continent the metallic wealth is deposited by nature on the very ridge of the Cordilleras, and sometimes in situations within a very small distance from the limit of perpetual snow. The most celebrated mines in Mexico are at absolute heights of from 5900 to 9840 feet.

We have mentioned in another place the advantage which, in working the Mexican mines, is derived from the most important veins being in a middle region, where the climate is not unfavourable to agriculture and vegetation. The large town of Guanaxuato is placed in a ravine, the bottom of which is somewhat lower than the level of the lakes of the valley of Tenochtitlan. We are ignorant of the absolute heights of Zacatecas and the Real de Catorce; but these two places are situated on table-lands seemingly more elevated than the level of Guanaxuato. However, the temperate climate of these Mexican towns, which are surrounded with the richest mines in the world, is a contrast to the cold and exceedingly disagreeable climate of Micuipampa, Pasco, Huancavelica, and other Peruvian towns.

The 1,544,000lbs. of silver which are annually sent to Europe and Asia, from the ports of Vera Cruz and Acapulco, are the produce of a very small number of mines. The three districts which we have frequently had occasion to name, Guanaxuato, Zacatecas, and Catorce, supply more than the half of that sum. The vein of Guanaxuato alone yields more than a fourth part of the whole silver o Mexico, and a sixth part of the produce of all America.

The following is the order in which the richest mines of New Spain follow one another, arranging them according to the quantity of money actually drawn from them:

Guanaxuato, in the Intendancy of the same name.

Catorce, in the Intendancy of San Luis Potosi.
Zacatecas, in the Intendancy of the same name.
Real del Monte, in the Intendancy of Mexico.
Bolaños, in the Intendancy of Guadalaxara.
Guarisamey, in the Intendancy of Durango.
Sombrerete, in the Intendancy of Zacatecas.
Tasco, in the Intendancy of Mexico.
Batopilas, in the Intendancy of Durango.
Zimapan, in the Intendancy of Mexico.
Fresnillo, in the Intendancy of Zacatecas.
Ramos, in the Intendancy of San Luis Potosi.
Parral, in the Intendancy of Durango.

The veins of Tasco, Tlapujahua, Sultepeque, Moran, Pachuca, and Real del Monte, and those of Sombrerete, Bolaños, Batopilas, and Rosario, have afforded from time to time immense wealth; but their produce has been less uniform than that of the mines of Guanaxuato, Zacatecas, and Catorce.

The silver extracted in the 37 mining districts into which the kingdom of Mexico or New Spain is divided, is deposited in the *Provincial Treasuries,* established in the chief places of the Intendancies; and it is from the receipts of these *caxas reales* that we are to judge of the quantity of silver furnished by the different parts of the country. The following is an account of the receipts of 11 Provincial Treasuries:

From 1785 to 1789, there were received in the *Caxas Reales* of

|  | Silver—lbs. troy. |
|---|---|
| *Guanaxuato*  -  -  -  -  -  - | 1,500,000 |
| *San Luis Potosi* (Catorce, Charcas, San Luis Potosi)  -  -  -  -  - | 910,000 |
| *Zacatecas* (Zacatecas, Fresnillo, Sierra de Pinos) | 730,000 |
| *Mexico* (Tasco, Zacualpa, Zultepeque)  - | 640,000 |
| *Durango* (Chihuahua, Parral, Guarisamey, Cosiguiriachi)  -  -  -  - | 545,000 |
| *Rosario* (Rosario, Cosala, Copala, Alamos)  - | 410,000 |
| *Guadalaxara* (Hostotipaquillo, Asientos de Ybarra)  -  -  -  -  - | 306,000 |
| *Pachuca* (Real del Monte, Moran)  - | 274,000 |
| *Bolaños*  -  -  -  -  -  -  - | 219,000 |
| *Sombrerete*  -  -  -  -  - | 195,000 |
| *Zimapan* (Zimapan, Doctor)  -  -  - | 150,000 |
| Sum for five years, | 5,879,000 |

That part of the Mexican mountains which at present contains the greatest quantity of silver, is situated between the parallels of 21 and $24\frac{1}{2}$ degrees. The celebrated mines of Guanaxuato are distant, in a straight line, from those of San Luis Potosi, 90 miles only : from San Luis Potosi to Zacatecas the distance is 102 miles ; from Zacatecas to Catorce 93, and from Catorce to Durango 222 miles. It is remarkable enough that this metallic wealth of Mexico and Peru should be placed at an almost equal distance in the two hemispheres from the equator.

The silver supplied by the veins of Mexico is

extracted from a great variety of ores, which from the nature of their mixture bear an analogy to those of Saxony, the Harz, and Hungary. The greatest quantity of silver annually brought into circulation, is derived from those ores which the Saxon miner calls by the name of *durre erze*, especially from *sulphuret of silver* (or vitreous silver), from *arsenical (fahlerz)* and *antimonial gray copper*, from *muriate of silver*, from *prismatic black silver*, and from red silver ore. We do not name native silver among these ores, because it is not found in sufficient abundance to admit of any very considerable part of the total produce of the mines of Mexico being attributed to it.

*Sulphuret of silver* and *black prismatic silver* are very common in the veins of Guanaxuato and Zacatecas, as well as in the *veta Biscaina* of Real del Monte. The silver extracted from the ore of Zacatecas exhibits the remarkable peculiarity of not containing gold. The richest gray copper *(fahlerz)* is that of Sierra de Pinos, and the mines of Ramos. In the latter, the *fahlerz* is accompanied with *glaserz*, with variegated copper ore, sulphuret of zinc, and vitreous copper, which is only wrought for the extraction of the silver, without applying the copper to any use. The antimoniated gray copper described by Mr. Karsten is found at Tasco, and in the mine of Rayas, south-east from Valenciana. The muriate of silver, which is so seldom found in the veins of Europe, is very

abundant in the mines of Catorce, Fresnillo, and
the Cerro San Pedro, near the town of San Luis
Potosi. That of Fresnillo is frequently of an olive
green, which passes into leek-green. Superb
specimens of this colour have been found in the
mines of Vallcrecas, which belong to the district
de los Alamos in the intendancy of Sonora. In the
veins of Catorce, the muriate of silver is accompanied with molybdate of lead and phosphate of
lead. From the last analysis of Mr. Klaproth, it
appears that the muriate of silver of America is a
pure mixture of silver and muriatic acid, while
that of Europe contains oxide of iron, alumine,
and especially a little sulphuric acid. The red
silver ore constitutes a principal part of the wealth
of Sombrerete, Cosala, and Zolaga, near Villalta,
in the province of Oaxaca. From this ore more
than 425,000lbs. troy of silver have been extracted
in the famous mine of *la Veta Negra* near Sombrerete, in the space of from five to six months.
It is affirmed that the mine which produced this
enormous quantity of metal, the greatest which
was ever yielded by any vein on the same point of
its *mass*, was not 16 fathoms in length. The true
*white silver ore* is very rare in Mexico. Its
*grayish white* variety, very rich in lead, is found,
however, in the intendancy of Sonora, in the veins
of Cosala, where it is accompanied with argentiferous galena, red silver, brown blende, quartz,
and sulphate of barytes. This last substance,

which is very uncommon among the lodes of
Mexico, is to be also found at the Real del Doctor,
near Baranca de las Tinajas, and at Sombrerete,
particularly in the mine called Campechana.
Fluor-spar has been only found hitherto in the
veins of Lomo del Toro, near Zimapan, at Bolaños
and Guadalcazar, near Catorce. It is constantly
of a grass green or violet blue colour.

In some parts of New Spain, the operations of
the miner are directed to a mixture of brown oxide
of iron and native silver, disseminated in particles
imperceptible to the naked eye. This ochreous
mixture is the object of considerable operations
at the mines of Angangueo, in the intendancy of
Valladolid, as well as at Yxtepexi, in the province
of Oaxaca. The ores of Angangueo, known by
the name of *colorados*, have a clayey appearance.
Near the surface, the brown oxide of iron is mixed
with native silver, with sulphuret of silver, and
black prismatic silver *(sprodglaserz)*, all three in
a state of decomposition. At great depths, the
vein of Angangueo contains only galena and iron
pyrites, yielding but a small quantity of silver.
Hence the blackish *pacos*, of the mine of Aurora
d'Yxtepexi, which must not be confounded with
the *negrillos* of Peru, owe their richness rather to
the *glaserz*, than to the imperceptible filaments
of native dendritic silver. The vein is very unequal
in its produce, sometimes sterile, and sometimes
abundant. The *colorados* of Catorce, particularly

z

those of the mine of Conception, are of a tile-red colour, and mixed with muriate of silver. In general it is observed both in Mexico and Peru, that those oxidated masses of iron which contain silver, are peculiar to that part of the veins nearest to the surface of the earth. The *pacos* of Peru present to the eye of the geologist a very striking analogy with the earthy masses called by the miners in Germany the *iron hat (eiserne huth)* of the veins*.

*Native silver*, which is much less abundant in America than is generally supposed, has been found in considerable masses, sometimes weighing more than 440lbs. avoird., in the mines of Bato-pilas in New Biscay. Native silver is constantly accompanied by *glaserz* in the veins of Mexico, as well as in those of the mountains of Europe. These very minerals are frequently found united in the rich mines of Sombrerete, Madroño, Ramos, Zacatecas, Hapujaha and Sierra de Penos. From time to time small branches or cylindrical fila-ments of native silver are also discovered in the celebrated vein of Guanaxuato ; but these masses have never been so considerable as those which

---

* The ochreous mixtures here described as common in Mexico, Peru and Germany, answer so exactly to the *gossans* of Cornwall that there is no doubt of their being the same ; and we have at the mines of Wheal Duchy and Wheal St. Vincent in Calstock in that county, instances of gossan rich in silver, and similar in most respects to the *pacos* and *colorados* above mentioned.—J. T.

were formerly drawn from the mine *del Encino* near Pachuca and Tasco, where native silver is sometimes contained in foliated gypsum. At Sierra de Penos near Zacatecas, this metal is constantly accompanied with blue radiated copper crystallized in small four-sided prisms.

A great part of the silver annually produced in Europe, is derived from the *argentiferous sulphuret of lead*. In Mexico, the greatest part of the veins contain likewise some argentiferous galena ; but there are very few mines in which the lead ore is a particular object of their operations. Among the latter, we can only include the mines of the districts of Zimapan, Parral, and San Nicholas de Croix. I observed that at Guanaxuato, as well as several other mines in Mexico*, and every where in Saxony, the varieties of galena contain the more silver, the finer they are in the grain.

A very considerable quantity of silver is produced from the smelting of iron pyrites (*mundic*), of which New Spain sometimes exhibits several varieties richer than the *glaserz* itself. It has been found in the Real del Monte, on the vein of Biscaina, near the pit of San Pedro, the ton of which contained

---

* Among the varieties of galena, particularly rich in silver, and of very fine grain, may be specified those of the new mine of Talpan, in the Cerro de las Vegas, belonging to the district of Hostotipaquillo. This galena, which sometimes passes into *compact antimonial sulphuret of lead,* is accompanied with much copper pyrites and carbonate of lime.

even so much as 450oz. troy of silver.   At Sombrerete,   the abundance of  pyrites disseminated
in the red silver ore, is a great obstacle to the process of amalgamation.

We have described the ores which produce the
Mexican silver, and it remains for us to examine into
the *mean riches* of these minerals, considering them
as all mixed together.   It is a very common prejudice in Europe, that great masses of native silver
are extremely common in Mexico and Peru, and that
in general the mineralized silver ores destined to
amalgamation or smelting, contain more ounces
of silver to the ton, than the *poor* ores of Saxony
and Hungary.   Full of this prejudice, I was doubly
surprised, on my arrival in the Cordilleras, to find
that the number of *poor mines* greatly surpasses
those of the mines to which in Europe we give the
name of *rich*.   A traveller who visits the famous
mine of Valenciana in Mexico, after having examined the *metalliferous* repositories of Clausthal,
Freiberg, and Schemnitz, can scarcely conceive how
a vein, which for a great part of its extent contains
the sulphuret of silver disseminated in the lode in
almost imperceptible particles, can regularly supply 230,000oz. per month, a quantity of silver
equal to the half of what is annually furnished by all
the mines of Saxony.   It is no doubt true that *blocks*
of *native silver* (*papas de plata*) of an enormous
weight, have been extracted from the mines of Batopilas in Mexico and Guantahajo in Peru ; but

when we study attentively the history of the principal mines of Europe, we find that the *veins* of
Kongsberg in Norway, Schneeberg in Saxony, and
the famous metallic repository of Schlangenberg in
Siberia, have produced masses of much more considerable bulk.   We are not in general to judge
from the size of the blocks, of the wealth of the
mines of different countries.   France does not altogether produce more than 5000lbs. troy of silver
annually ; and yet there are veins in that country
(those of *Sainte-Marie-aux-Mines*) from which
amorphous masses of native silver have been extracted, of the weight of 66lbs. avoird.

It appears that at the period of the formation of
veins in every climate, the distribution of silver
has been very unequal ; sometimes concentrated in
one point, and at other times disseminated in the
lode, and allied with other metals.   Sometimes in
the midst of the poorest ores we find very considerable masses of native silver ; a phenomenon
which appears to depend on a particular operation
of chemical affinities, of whose mode of action
and laws we are completely ignorant.   The
silver, instead of being concealed in galena, or in
pyrites in a small degree argentiferous, or of being
distributed throughout all the *mass of the vein* over
a great extent, is collected into a single mass.   In
that case the riches of a point may be considered
as the principal cause of the poverty of the neighbouring ores ; and hence we may conceive why the

richest parts of a vein are found separated from
one another by portions of the lode almost altogether destitute of metals.

Although the New Continent, however, has not
hitherto exhibited native silver in such considerable
blocks as the Old, this metal is found more abundantly
in a state of perfect purity in Peru and Mexico, than
in any other quarter of the globe.   In laying down
this opinion, I am not considering the native silver
which appears in the form of lamellæ, branches, or
cylindrical filaments, in the mines of Guantahajo,
Potosi, and Gualgayoc, or in Batopilas, Zacatecas,
and Ramos.  I found my opinion rather on the
enormous abundance of the ores called *pacos* and
*colorados*, in which silver is not *mineralized*, but
dissemimated in such small particles, that they can
only be perceived by means of a microscope*.

The result of the investigations made by Don
Fausto d'Elhuyar, the director general of the mines
of Mexico, and by several members of the superior
council of mines, is, that in uniting together all the
silver minerals annually extracted, it would be found

* The most considerable copper mines of England have
always owed their importance more to the quantity than the
quality of their ores, and experienced men know that it is but
delusive to depend upon rich specimens.

Where profit is, however, to be derived by working mines
which yield their produce in a disseminated state, the value of
good management, and of the application of machinery, becomes the more important, and the results have often proved
the most beneficial.—J. T.

from the mixture, that their mean produce is from 0.0018 to 0.0025 of silver, that is to say, in the common language of miners, that one hundred pounds of ore, or 1200 ounces troy, *contain from three to four ounces of silver.* This important result is confirmed by the testimony of an inhabitant of Zacatecas, who had the direction of considerable metallic operations in several districts of mines of New Spain, and who has lately published a very interesting work on the American amalgamation. M. Garces expressly says, " that the " great mass of Mexican ores is so poor, that the " 1,878,400lbs. troy of silver annually produced by " the kingdom in good years, are extracted from " 500,000 tons of mineral, partly smelted, and " partly amalgamated." According to these numbers, the mean riches would only amount to 48 ounces per ton, a result which differs very much from the assertion of a traveller, very estimable in other respects, who relates that the veins of New Spain are of such extraordinary wealth, tnat the natives never think of working them when the minerals contain less than a third of their weight in silver, or 43lbs. troy per cwt. * As the most erroneous ideas have

* These accounts of the produce of metal from the ores, seem to imply throughout that the calculation is made on the whole mass of stuff drawn out of the mines, and not upon what we should call in England the clean ores. The processes of dressing or washing in Mexico seem to be so imperfect, that by the improvements that would naturally be introduced, the ores would probably be reduced to a very different state ; more rich in

been spread through Europe respecting the *contents* of the ores of America, I shall proceed to give a more minute description of the districts of mines of Guanaxuato, Tasco and Pachuca, which I had occasion to visit.

At Guanaxuato, the mine of the Count de la Valenciana produced between the 1st January 1787 and the 11th June 1791, the sum of 1,034,500lbs. troy of silver, which were extracted from 84,368 *montones* of ores. In the table * containing the general state of the mine, a *monton* is estimated at 32 cwt. ; from whence it follows that the mean riches of the minerals was twenty years ago 102 ounces of silver per ton. Applying the same calculation to the produce of the single year 1791, we shall find 186 ounces per ton. At this period, when the mine was in the most flourishing condition, in the total mass of ores there were :

produce, though smaller in quantity. Much advantage may be expected from attention to this circumstance.—J. T.

* *Estado de la mina Valenciana, remitido por mano del Excellentiss. Señor virey de Nueva España al Secretario de Estado Don Antonio Valdes.* (Manuscript.) I have followed the numbers contained in the table drawn up by Don Joseph Quixano, the administrator of the Valenciana. A *monton* (a heap of ores reduced to powder) is reckoned at 35 cwt. at Guanaxuato ; at 30 at the Real del Monte, Pachuca, Zultepeque, and Tasco ; at Zacatecas and Sombrerete, at 20 ; at Fresnillo at 18 ; and at 15 at Bolaños. As the wealth of the ore is determined from the *contents of the monton,* the exact knowledge of the measure is of great importance in metallurgical calculations.

Oz.

$\frac{5}{1000}$ of rich ores *(polvillos* and *xabones)*, containing
   per ton - - - - - - - - 3360
$\frac{28}{1000}$ of rich ores *(apolvillado)* - - - - 1400
$\frac{152}{1000}$ of rich ores *(blanco bueno)* - - - - 460
$\frac{815}{1000}$ of poor ores *(granzas, tierras ordinarias, &c.)* - 60

The quantity of rich ores was consequently, to that of the poor ores, nearly in the proportion of 3 to 14. The ores which only contained 60 ounces per ton, supplied in 1791 (we are always speaking of the Valenciana mine alone) more than 123,508lbs. troy of silver; while there was a sufficient quantity of rich ores (from 60 to 3,360 ounces per ton) to yield a produce of more than 247,000lbs troy. At present, the *mean* richness of the whole vein of Guanaxuato may be estimated at 80 ounces of silver per ton of ores. The South West part of the vein, which intersects the mine of Rayas, yields, however, minerals, of which the *contents* generally amount to more than 450 ounces per ton.

In the district of the mines of Pachuca, they divide the produce of the vein of Biscaina into three classes, of which the richness varied in 1803 from 32 to 160 ounces per *monton* of 30 *quintals.* The minerals of the first class, which are the richest, contain from 144 to 160; and those of the second class, from 56 to 80 ounces troy. The poorest ores which form the third class are only computed at 32 ounces of silver per *monton.* The result is, that the *good* contains 100 ounces; the *middling* 80 ounces; and the *worst* about 50 ounces of silver per ton.

2 A

In the district of mines of Tasco, the minerals
of Tehuilotepec contain in a *tarea* of four *montones*
or 5 tons, 15lbs. troy of silver ; those of Guautla
yield 45 ; their mean wealth is consequently about
50 ounces of silver per ton of minerals.

It is not then, as has been too long believed,
from the intrinsic richness of the ores, but rather
from the great abundance in which they are found
in the bowels of the earth, and the facility with
which they can be wrought, that the mines of America are to be distinguished from those of Europe *.
The three districts of mines which we have just alluded to, furnish alone about 500,000lbs. of silver,
and from the whole of these data we cannot entertain a doubt that the *mean contents* of the Mexican
ores do not amount, as we have already stated, to
more than from 60 to 80 ounces of silver per ton.
Hence these ores, though somewhat richer than
those of Freiberg, contain much less silver than
the ores of Annaberg, Johann-Georgenstadt, Ma-
rienberg, and other districts of the *Obergebirge* in
Saxony.   From 1789 to 1799, there have been
extracted *communibus annis* from the mines of the
district of Freiberg, 7,838 tons, which have yielded
30,230lbs. troy of silver ;  so that the mean contents

---

* The silver ores of Peru do not in general appear to be
richer than those of Mexico : the *contents* are estimated not by
the *monton*, but by the *caxon* (chest), which contains 24 cargas,
reckoning each carga at ten *arrobas* or 250lbs.   At *Potosi*, the
*mean* richness of the minerals is $\frac{53}{100}$ ; in the mines of Pasco,
$1\frac{3}{50}$ ounces per 100lbs.

were 25 ounces per ton of minerals. But in the mines of the *Obergebirge* the mean riches have amounted to 200, and at very fortunate periods even to 300 ounces per ton.

We have thus taken a general view of the rocks in which the principal mines of New Spain are found; we have examined on what points, in what latitudes, and at what elevations above the level of the sea, nature has collected the greatest quantity of metallic wealth; and we have indicated the ores which furnish the immense quantity of silver which annually flows from the one continent to the other. It remains for us to afford some details relative to the most considerable mining operations. We shall confine ourselves to three of these *groups of mines* which we have already described, to the central group, and those of Tasco and Biscaina. Those who know the state of mining in Europe will be struck with the contrast between the great mines of Mexico, for example, those of the Valenciana, Rayas, and Tereros, and the mines which are considered as very rich in Saxony, the Harz, and Hungary. Could the latter be transported to the midst of the great works of Guanaxuato, Catorce, or the Real del Monte, their wealth, and the quantity of their produce, would appear as insignificant to the inhabitants of America, as the height of the Pyrenees compared with the Cordilleras.

2 A 2

# CHAPTER X.

*Number of mines—laws respecting mines—quantity of silver raised—state of mining operations—condition of mines—smelting—amalgamation.*

THE kingdom of Mexico in its present state contains nearly 500 places (*reales y realitos*) celebrated for the mines in their environs. It is probable that these 500 *reales* comprehend nearly three thousand mines (*minas*), designating by that name the whole of the subterraneous works which communicate with one another, by which one or more metallic depositories are worked. These mines are divided into 37 districts, over which are placed the same number of Councils of Mines, called *Diputaciones de Mineria*.

In taking a general view of the mineral wealth of New Spain, far from being struck with the value of the actual produce, we are astonished that it is not much more considerable. It is easy to foresee that this branch of public industry will continue augmenting as the country shall become better inhabited, as the smaller proprietors shall obtain greater security for good government and for the enjoyment of property, and as geological and chemical knowledge shall become more generally diffused. Several obstacles have already been re-

moved since the year 1777, or since the establishment of the supreme council of mines, which has
the title of *Real Tribunal general del importante
cuerpo de Mineria de Nueva España*, and holds
its sittings in the palace of the Viceroy at Mexico. Till that period the proprietors of mines were
not united into a corporation, or the Court of Madrid, at least, would not recognise them as an established body by a constitutional act.

The legislation of the mines was formerly in infinite confusion, because, at the beginning of the
conquest, under the reign of Charles the Fifth, a
mixture of Spanish, Belgic, and German laws was
introduced into Mexico ; which laws, from the
difference of local circumstances, were inapplicable
to those distant regions. The erection of the supreme council of mines, the head of which bears a
name celebrated in the annals of chemical science,
was followed by the establishment of the school of
mines, and the compilation of a new code of laws,
published under the title of *Ordonanzas de la Mineria de Nueva España.* The council or *Tribunal
general* is composed of a director, two deputies
from the body of miners, an assessor, two consul-
tors, and a judge, who is head of the *juzgado de
alzadas de mineria.* On the *Tribunal general*
depend the thirty-seven *councils of provincial mines*
or *diputaciones de mineria*, of which the names
have been already mentioned. The proprietors of
mines (*mineros*) send their representatives to the

provincial councils, and the two general deputies who reside at Mexico, are chosen from among the deputies of the districts. The body of miners of New Spain has, besides, *apoderados*, or representative proprietors at Madrid, whose business it is to treat immediately with the ministry, as to the interest of the colonies, in whatever respects the mines. The students of the *colegio de mineria*, instructed at the expense of the state, are distributed by the *Tribunal* among the head towns of the different *diputaciones*. It cannot be denied that the representative system followed in the new organization of the body of Mexican miners, possesses great advantages. It preserves public spirit in a country where the citizens, scattered over an immense surface, do not sufficiently feel the community of their interests ; and it gives the supreme council a facility of collecting considerable sums, whenever any great or useful undertaking is proposed. It is to be desired, however, that the director of the *tribunal* should possess more influence on the progress of the operations in the provinces, and that the proprietors of mines, less jealous of what they call their liberty, were more enlightened as to their true interests.

The *Supreme Council* possesses an income of more than 40,000*l*. sterling. The king granted it on its establishment two thirds of the royal right of signiorage, which amounts to a *real de plata*, or about sixpence per troy ounce of silver delivered in to the mint. This revenue is destined for the salaries of the members of the *tribunal*, the support of the school of mines, and to raise a fund for assistance or advances (*avios*) to the proprietors of the mines. These advances, as we have already observed, have been given with more liberality than discernment. A miner of Pachuca at one time obtained 36,000*l.*; and the share-holders of the *mina de agua* of Temascaltepec, received 46,400*l.*; but this assistance never produced any results. The tribunal during the last years of the war of Spain with France and England, was compelled to make a gratuitous present to the court of Madrid, of 104,200*l.*, and to lend it 625,000*l.* besides, 250,000*l.* of which have never been repaid. To support these extraordinary expenses, they were compelled to have recourse to borrowing; and at present the half of the revenues of the supreme council of mines is employed in paying the interest of that capital. They have increased by one half the *signorial impost*, till the period of the liquidation of the debts contracted by the tribunal; and in place of thirteen grains, the miners are obliged to pay twenty per ounce of silver. In this state of things the tribunal can no longer make advances to the miners, who for want of funds are frequently unable to carry on useful undertakings. Great capitals formerly employed in mining, are now destined to agriculture, and the proprietors of mines would again require those establishments (*bancos de plata, compañias refac-*

*cionarias\** ò *de habilitacion y avios*) which advanced to the miners considerable sums of money
at a large interest.

All the metallic wealth of the Spanish colonies
is in the hands of individuals.  The Government
possesses no other mine than that of Huancavelica
in Peru, which has been long abandoned ; it is not
even proprietor of the great levels, as several sovereigns of Germany are.

From the information given by us in this chapter, it is almost unnecessary to agitate the question,
whether the produce of the silver mines of Mexico
has attained its *maximum*, or whether there is any
probability that it will still augment in the time to
come.  We have seen that three mining districts,
those of Guanaxuato, Catorce, and Zacatecas, alone
furnish more than the half of the whole silver of
New Spain, and that nearly one fourth of it is furnished by the mine of Guanaxuato.  One mine
which has only been known for forty years, that of
Valenciana, has sometimes alone furnished in one
year as much silver as the whole kingdom of Peru.
It is but thirty years since the veins of the Real de
Catorce began to be worked, and yet by the discovery of these new mines the metallic produce of
Mexico was increased nearly one sixth.  If we consider the vast extent of ground occupied by the

* *Real cedula sobre la compañia refaccionaria propuesta por
el Genoves Domingo Reborato, del* 12 *Marzo* 1744.—*Don Josef
Bustamente, Informe sobre la habilitacion de los Mineros,* 1748.

Cordilleras, and the immense number of mineral
depositories which have never yet been attempted *,
it is very possible that New Spain, under a better
administration, and inhabited by an industrious
people, may alone one day yield, in gold and silver,
the 15,600,000*l.*, at present furnished by the whole
of America. In the space of a hundred years, the
annual produce of the Mexican mines rose from
one to four millions sterling. If Peru does not
exhibit an equal augmentation of wealth, it is because this unfortunate country has not increased
its population, and because, being worse governed
than Mexico, industry found more difficulties to
overcome. Besides, nature has deposited the precious metals in that country at enormous elevations,
in situations where, on account of the very high price
of provisions, the working becomes extremely expensive. The abundance of silver is in general
such in the chain of the Andes, that when we reflect on the number of mineral depositories which
remain untouched, or which have been very super-
ficially wrought, we are tempted to believe, that the
Europeans have as yet scarcely begun to enjoy the
inexhaustible fund of wealth contained in the New
World. When we cast our eyes over the mining
district of Guanaxuato, which, on the small space
of a few thousand square yards, supplies annually
the seventh or eighth part of all the American sil-

* Especially from Bolaños to the Presidio de Fronteras.

ver, we shall see that the 340,000lbs. troy, which are annually extracted from the famous *veta madre*, are the produce of only two mines, the Valenciana and that of the Marquis de Rayas, and that more than four-fifths of this vein have never yet been attempted. It is very probable, however, that in uniting the two mines of Fraustros and Mellado, and clearing them out, a mine would be found of equal wealth with that of Valenciana. The opinion that New Spain produces only perhaps the third part of the precious metals which it could supply under happier political circumstances, has been long entertained by all the intelligent persons who inhabit the principal districts of mines of that country, and is formally announced in a Memoir presented by the deputies of the body of miners to the King in 1774, a production drawn up with great wisdom and knowledge of local circumstances. Europe would be inundated with precious metals, if they were to work at the same time, and with all the means afforded by the improvements in the art of mining, the mineral depositories of Bolaños, Batopilas, Sombrerete, Rosario, Pachuca, Moran, Zultepec, Chihuahua, and so many others which have been long and justly celebrated. I am aware, that in thus expressing myself, I am in direct contradiction with the authors of a great number of works of Political Economy, in which it is affirmed that the mines of America are partly exhausted, and partly too deep to be worked any longer with advantage. It is true,

no doubt, that the expenses of the mine of Valenciana have doubled in the space of ten years, but
the profits of the proprietors have still remained
the same ; and this increase of expense is much
more to be attributed to the injudicious direction
of the operations than to the depth of the shafts.

When we take a general view of the mining operations of New Spain, and compare them with those
of the mines of Europe, we are surprised at still
finding in its infancy an art which has been practised in America for three centuries, and on which,
according to the vulgar prejudice, the prosperity
of these ultramarine establishments depends.

Since the brilliant period of the reign of Charles
the Fifth, Spanish America has been separated from
Europe, with respect to the communication of dis-
coveries useful to society. The imperfect knowledge which was possessed in the 16th century relative to mining and smelting, in Germany, Biscay, and the Belgic provinces, rapidly passed into
Mexico and Peru, on the first colonizaion of these
countries ; but since that period, to the reign of
Charles the Third, the American miners have learned hardly any thing from the Europeans, but the
blasting with powder * those rocks which resist the
effect of tools.

German miners have since been sent, at the expense of the Court, to Mexico, Peru, and the king-

* This art was only introduced into the mines of Europe
towards the year 1613. (*Daubuisson*, t. i. p. 95.)

2 B 2

dom of New Granada ; but their knowledge has
been of no utility, because the mines of Mexico
are considered as the property of the individuals,
who direct the operations, without the Government
being allowed to exercise the smallest influence.

We shall not here undertake to detail the defects which we believe we have observed in the administration of the mines of New Spain, but shall
confine ourselves to general considerations, remark-
ing whatever appears to us worthy of fixing the attention of the European traveller.    In the greatest
number of the Mexican mines the operations with
the *pointrole,* a sort of wedge somewhat resembling that called by Cornish miners the *gad,* which
requires the greatest address on the part of the
workman, are very well executed.  The *mallet* might
indeed be somewhat less heavy ; it is the same
tool which the German miners used in the time of
Charles the Fifth.  Small moveable forges are placed
in the interior of the mines, to re-forge the point
of the pointroles when they are unfit for working.
I reckoned 16 of these forges in the mine of Valenciana ; and in the district of Guanaxuato the
smallest mines have at least one or two.   This arrangement is very useful, particularly in mines which
employ as many as 1500 workmen, and in which
there is consequently an immense consumption of
steel.  I cannot say much in praise of the method
of blasting with powder.  The holes for the reception of cartridges are generally too deep, and the

miners are not sufficiently careful in diminishing the mass of rock intended to yield to the explosion. A great waste of powder is consequently occasioned by these defects. The mine of Valenciana consumed *, from 1794 to 1802, powder to the amount of 150,000l., and the mines of New Spain annually require from 12 to 14,000 cwt. It is probable that two-thirds of this quantity is uselessly employed.

The timber-work is very carelessly performed, though it ought the more to engage the consideration of the proprietors, as wood is every year becoming more scarce on the table-land of Mexico. The masonry employed in the shafts and levels †, and especially the walling with lime, deserves great praise. The arches are formed with great care, and in this respect the mines of Guanaxuato may stand a comparison with whatever is most perfect at Freiberg and Schemnitz. The shafts, and still more the galleries or levels, have generally the defect of being dug of too great dimensions, and of occasioning, by that means, exorbitant expenses. We find levels at

* In 1799, 13,731l. sterling ; in 1800, 14,840l. sterling ; in 1801, 16,953l. sterling ; in 1802, 17,312l. sterling. The miner is paid at Guanaxuato, for a hole of 4 feet 11 inches in depth, ten shillings ; for a hole of 6 feet 3 inches in depth, 7s. 6d. ; without including powder and tools, which are furnished to him. In the mine of Valenciana, nearly 600 holes *by two men each* are made every 24 hours.

† Especially in the mines of Valenciana, Guanaxuato, and the Real del Monte.

Valenciana\*, executed with the viewof making trial on a poor vein, of a height of 26 or 29 feet. It is an erroneous opinion, that this great height facilitates the renovation of the air; the ventilation depends on the equilibrium and difference of temperature between two neighbouring columns of air. They believe also, equally without foundation, that, in order to discover the nature of a powerful vein, very large drifts are requisite, as if, in mineral veins of from six to eight fathoms in width, it were not better to cut from time to time small cross drifts, for the purpose of discovering whether the mass of the vein begins to grow richer. The absurd custom of cutting every level of such enormous dimensions, prevents the proprietors from multiplying the means of trial, so indispensable for the preservation of a mine and the duration of the works. At Guanaxuato, the breadth of the oblique shafts dug stairwise is from five to six fathoms; and the perpendicular shafts are generally three, four, or five fathoms in diameter. The enormous quantity of ores extracted from the mines, and the necessity of working in them the ropes attached to six or eight whims, necessarily occasion the shafts of Mexico to be made of greater dimensions than those of Germany; but the attempt which has been made at Bolaños to separate by beams the ropes of the whims, has sufficiently proved that the breadth of the shafts may be

* Canon de la Soledad.

diminished without any danger of the ropes en-
tangling in their oscillatory motion.   It would in
general be very useful to make use of kibbles instead
of leathern bags suspended by ropes for the extraction of the ores.

The greatest fault observable in the mines of New
Spain, and which renders the working of them extremely expensive, is the want of communication
between the different works.   They resemble ill-
constructed buildings, where, to pass from one adjoining room to another, we must go round the
whole house.   The mine of Valenciana is justly
admired on account of its wealth, the magnificence
of its walling, and the facility with which it is entered
by spacious and commodious stairs ; yet it exhibits
only a union of small works irregularly conducted ;
they are as it were *cul de sacs*, and without any lateral
communication.  I mention this mine, not because
it is more faulty than the others in the distribution
of its labours, but because we might naturally suppose it to be better organized.   As subterraneous
geometry had been entirely neglected in Mexico, till
the establishment of the School of Mines, there
is no plan in existence of the works already executed.
Two works in that labyrinth of cross levels and interior winzes, may happen to be very near each other,
without its being possible to perceive it.  Hence the
impossibility of introducing, in the actual state of
most of the mines of Mexico, the wheeling by means
of barrows, and an economical disposition of the

ore plats. A miner brought up in the mines of
Freiberg, and accustomed to see so many ingenious
means of conveyance practised, can hardly conceive
that in the Spanish colonies, where the ores are poor
though very abundant, all the metal which is taken
from the vein is carried on the backs of men. The
Indian *tenateros*, who may be considered as the
beasts of burden of the mines of Mexico, remain
loaded with a weight of from 250 to 380 pounds
for a space of six hours. In the levels of Valenciana and Rayas, they are exposed, as we have already observed in speaking of the health of the miners, to a temperature of from 71° to 77° Fahr.;
and during this time they ascend and descend several
thousands of steps in shafts of an inclination of 45°.
These *tenateros* carry the minerals in bags *(costales)*
made of the thread of the *pité*. To prevent their
shoulders from being hurt, (for the miners are generally naked to the middle) they place a woollen covering *(frisida)* under this bag. We met in the mines
files of fifty or sixty of these porters, among whom
there are men above sixty, and boys of ten or twelve
years of age. In ascending the stairs they throw
the body forwards, and rest on a staff, which is generally not more than a foot in length. They walk
in a zigzag direction, because they have found from
long exerience, as they affirm, that their respiration
is less impeded when they traverse obliquely the
current of air which enters the pit from without.
We cannot sufficiently admire the muscular

strength of the Indian and Mestizo *tenateros* of
Guanaxuato, especially when we ourselves are oppressed with fatigue in ascending from the bottom
of the mine of Valenciana, without carrying the
smallest weight. The *tenateros* cost the proprietors
of Valenciana more than 620*l.* weekly; and they
reckon that there are three men destined to carry
the ores to the depositaries to one workman
*(barenador)* who blows up the vein by means of
powder. These enormous expenses of transportation would perhaps be diminished exceedingly, if
the works communicated with each other by winzes,
or by levels adapted for conveyance by wheel-bar-
rows or rail-roads, Well contrived operations would
facilitate the extraction of minerals and the circulation of air, and would render unnecessary this great
number of *tenateros*, whose strength might be employed in a manner more advantageous to society,
and less hurtful to the health of the individual.
Winzes communicating from one gallery to another,
and serving for the extraction of ores, might be provided with windlasses to be wrought by men, or
whims to be moved by cattle. For a long time (and
this arrangement undoubtedly deserves the attention
of the European miner) mules have been employed
in the interior of the mines of Mexico. At Rayas
these animals descend every morning without guides
and in the dark, the steps of a shaft of an inclination of from 42° to 46°. The mules distribute themselves of their own accord in the different places

2 c

where the machines for drawing water are fixed, and their step is so sure, that a lame miner was accustomed several years ago, to enter and leave the mine on one of their backs. In the district of the mines of Peregrino, at the *Rosa de Castilla*, the mules sleep in subterraneous stables, like the horses which I saw in the famous rock salt mines of Wieliczka in Gallicia.

The smelting and amalgamation works of Guanaxuato and Real del Monte are so placed, that two navigable levels, with their openings near Marfil and Omitlan, might serve for the carriage of ores, and render every sort of draught above this level superfluous. Besides, the descents from Valenciana to Guanaxuato, and from Real del Monte to Regla, are so rapid, that they would admit of the construction of rail-ways, on which waggons loaded with the ores destined for amalgamation might be easily rolled along.

We have already spoken of the truly barbarous custom of drawing off the water from the deepest mines, not by means of pump apparatus, but by means of bags attached to ropes which roll on the cage of a whim. The same bags are used in drawing up the water and the ores: they rub against the walls of the shafts, and it is very expensive to keep them in repair. At the Real del Monte, for example, these bags only last seven or eight days; and they commonly cost five, and sometimes seven and eight shillings a piece. A bag full of water, suspended to the cage of a whim with eight horses, *(malacate doble)* weighs 1250 pounds : it is made of two hides sewed together. The bags used for the whims called *simple,* those with four horses *(malacates sencillos)* are only half the size, and are made of one hide. In general the construction of the whims is extremely imperfect; the bad custom also prevails of forcing the horses, by which they are made to go at far too great a speed. I found this speed at the shafts of San Ramon at Real del Monte no less than ten feet and a half per second ; at Guanaxuato in the mine of Valenciana from thirteen to fourteen feet ; and every where else I found it more than eight feet. Don Salvado Sein, Professor of Natural Philosophy at Mexico, has proved in a very excellent paper on the rotatory motion of machines, that, notwithstanding the extreme lightness of the Mexican horses, they produce only the *maximum* of effect on the whims, when exerting a force of 175 pounds they walk at a pace of from five to six feet in the second.

It is to be hoped that pumps, moved either by horse-engines of a better construction, or by water wheels, or by pressure engines, will at last be introduced in the mines of New Spain If wood and coal, which has only yet been discovered in New Mexico, should be found sufficiently abundant for employing the steam-engine, the use of it would be of great advantage in the inundated mines of Bolaños, as well as in those of Rayas and Mellado.

2 c 2

It is in the draining the mines of water that we particularly feel the indispensable necessity of having plans drawn up by subterraneous surveyors *(geome-tres)*. Instead of stopping the course of the water, and bringing it by the shortest road to the shaft where the machines are placed, they frequently direct it to the bottom of the mine, to be afterwards drawn off at a great expense. In the district of mines of Guanaxuato nearly two hundred and fifty workmen perished in the space of a few minutes on the 14th of June 1780; because, not having measured the distance between the works of San Ramon and the old works of *Santo Christo de Burgos,* they had imprudently approached this last mine while carrying on a drift in that direction. The water of which the works of Santo Christo were full, flowed with impetuosity through this new gallery of San Ramon into the mine of Valenciana. Many of the workmen perished from the sudden compression of the air, which, in taking vent, threw to great distances pieces of timber, and large masses of rock. This accident would not have happened, if, in regulating the operations, they could have consulted a plan of the mines.

After the picture which we have just drawn of the actual state of the mining operations, and of the bad management which prevails in the mines of New Spain, we cannot be astonished at seeing works which for a long time have been most productive, abandoned whenever they reach a considerable depth, or whenever the veins appear less abundant in metals. We have already observed, that in the famous mine of Valenciana, the annual expenses rose in the space of fifteen years from 90,000*l.* to 180,000*l.* sterling. Indeed, if there be much water in this mine, and if it require a number of whims to draw it off, the profit must, to the proprietors, be little or nothing. The greater part of the defects in the management which I have pointed out, have been long known to a respectable and enlightened body, the *Tribunal de Mineria* of Mexico, to the professors of the School of Mines, and even to several of the native miners, who, without having quitted their country, know the imperfection of the old methods: but we must repeat here, that changes can only take place very slowly among a people who are not fond of innovations. It is a prejudice to imagine, that the wealth of the mines of New Spain renders unnecessary the intelligence and the economy which are requisite in other mines. We must not confound the abundance of ores with their intrinsic value. The most part of the ores of Mexico being low in produce, as all those who do not allow themselves to be dazzled by false calculations well know, an enormous quantity of stuff impregnated with metals must be extracted, in order to produce 1,540,000lbs. troy of silver. Now it is easy to conceive that in mines of which the different works are badly disposed, and without any communication with one another, the expense of extraction must be increased in an alarming manner, in proportion as the shafts *(pozos)* increase in depth, and the levels *(cañones)* become more extended.

The working of the mines has long been regarded as one of the principal causes of the depopulation of America. It would be difficult to deny, that at the first epoch of the conquest, and even in the seventeenth century, many Indians perished from the excessive labour to which they were compelled in the mines. They perished without posterity, as thousands of African slaves annually perish in the West Indian plantations from fatigue, want of nourishment and of sleep. In Peru, at least in the most southern part, the country is depopulated by the mines, because the barbarous law of the *mita* is yet in existence, which compels the Indians to remove from their homes into distant provinces, where hands are wanted for extracting the subterraneous wealth.

In the kingdom of New Spain, at least within the last thirty or forty years, the labour of the mines is free; and there remains no trace of the *mita*, though a justly celebrated author* has advanced the contrary. No where do the people enjoy in greater security the fruit of their labours

* Robertson, History of America, vol. ii. p. 373.

than in the mines of Mexico; no law forces the
Indian to choose this species of labour, or to prefer
one mine to another; and when he is displeased
with the proprietor of the mine, he may offer his
services to another master who may pay perhaps
more regularly. These unquestionable facts are
very little known in Europe. The number of persons employed in subterraneous operations, who
are divided into several classes *(Barenadores,
Faeneros, Tenateros, Bureteros)*, does not exceed
in the whole kingdom of New Spain 28 or 30,000.
Hence there is not more than $\frac{1}{200}$ of the whole population immediately employed in the mines.

The mortality among the miners of Mexico is
not greater than what is observed among the other
classes. We may easily be convinced of this by
examining the bills of mortality in the different
parishes of Guanaxuato and Zacatecas. This is a
phenomenon, so much the more remarkable, as
the miner in several of these mines is exposed to a
temperature 11° above the mean temperatures of
Jamaica and Pondicherry. I found Fahrenheit's
thermometer at 93° at the bottom of the mine of
Valenciana *(en los planes)*, a perpendicular depth
of 1681 feet, while at the mouth of the pit in the
open air, the same thermometer sinks in winter to
39° or 40°. The Mexican miner is, consequently,
exposed to a change of temperature of more than
54°. This enormous heat of the Valenciana mine
is not the effect of a great number of men and

lights collected into a small space; it is much more owing to local and geological causes.

It is curious to observe how the Mestizoes and Indians called *tenateros*, employed in carrying minerals on their backs, remain for six hours at a time loaded with a weight of from 225 to 350 pounds, and constantly exposed to a very high temperature, ascending without intermission eight or ten times successively, stairs of 1800 steps. The appearance of these robust and laborious men would have wrought a change in the opinions of the Raynals, Pauws, and many other authors, who have declaimed against the degeneracy of our species in the torrid zone. In the Mexican mines, lads of seventeen years of age are able to carry masses of stone of a hundred pounds weight. This occupation of *tenateros* is accounted unhealthy, if they enter more than three times a week into the mines. But the labour which rapidly ruins the most robust constitutions is that of the *barenadores*, who blow up the rock with powder. These men rarely pass the age of 35, if from a thirst of gain they continue their severe labour for the whole week. They generally pass no more than five or six years at this occupation, and then betake themselves to other employments less injurious to health.

The art of mining is daily improving, and the pupils of the School of Mines at Mexico gradually diffuse correct notions respecting the circulation of air in pits and galleries. Machines are beginning to be introduced, in place of the old method of carrying minerals and water on men's backs up stairs of a rapid ascent. In proportion as the mines of New Spain resemble more and more those of Europe, the miner's health will be less injured by the influence of the foul air, and the excessively prolonged efforts of muscular motion.

From five to six thousand persons are employed in the amalgamation of the minerals, or the preparatory labour. A great number of these individuals pass their lives in walking barefoot over heaps of brayed metal, moistened and mixed with muriate of soda, sulphate of iron, and oxide of mercury, by the contact of the atmospheric air and the solar rays. It is a remarkable phenomenon to see these men enjoy the most perfect health. The physicians who practise in places where there are mines unanimously assert, that the nervous affections, which might be attributed to the effect of an absorption of oxide of mercury, very rarely occur. At Guanaxuato part of the inhabitants drink the very water in which the amalgamation has been purified *(aqua de lavaderos)* without feeling any injury from it. This fact has often struck Europeans not intimately acquainted with the principles of chemistry. The water is at first of a grayish-blue colour, and contains in suspension black oxide of mercury, and small globules of native mercury and amalgamation of silver. This metallic mixture

2 D

gradually precipitates, and the water becomes limpid. It can neither dissolve the oxide of mercury nor the muriate of mercury, which is one of the most insoluble salts we know. The mules are very fond of this water, because it contains a little muriate of soda in solution.

We have already said, that the labour of a miner is entirely free throughout the kingdom of New Spain. No Indian or Mestizo can be compelled to devote himself to the working of mines. It is absolutely false, though the assertion has been re-peated in works of the greatest estimation, that the Court of Madrid sends out galley slaves to work in the gold and silver mines. The mines of Siberia have been peopled by Russian malefactors, but in the Spanish colonies this species of punish-ment has been fortunately unknown for centuries. The Mexican miner is the best paid of all miners; he earns at the least from 1*l.* to 1*l.* 4*s.* per week of six days, while the wages of labourers who work in the open air, husbandmen for example, are 6*s.* 3*d.* on the central table-land, and 7*s.* 6*d.* near the coast. The miners, *tenateros* and *faeneros*, occu-pied in transporting the minerals to the plats (*despachos*), frequently gain more than 4*s.* 10*d.* per day of six hours. Honesty is by no means so common among the Mexican as among the German or Swedish miners; they make use of a thousand tricks to steal rich specimens of ores. As they are almost naked, and are searched on leaving the mine in the most indecent manner, they conceal small morsels of native silver, or red sulphuret and muriate of silver, in their hair, under their arm-pits, and in their mouths. It is a most shocking spectacle to see in the large mines of Mexico, hundreds of workmen, among whom there are a great number of very respectable men, all compelled to allow themselves to be searched on leaving the shaft or level. A register is kept of the minerals found in the hair, in the mouth, or other parts of the miners' bodies. In the mine of Valenciana at Guanaxuato, the value of these stolen minerals amounted between 1774 and 1787 to the sum of 63,000*l.* sterling.

In the interior of the mines much care is employed in controuling the *tenateros*, by whom the ores are carried towards the shaft from the place of operation. At Valenciana, for example, they know to within a few pounds the quantity of work containing ore which daily goes out of the mine. I say, the work, for the rock is never there an object of extraction, and is employed to fill up the vacancies formed by the extraction of the minerals. At the plats of the great shafts, two chambers are dug in the wall, in each of which two persons (*despachadores*) are seated at a table, with a book before them containing the names of all the miners employed in the carriage. Two balances are suspended before them, near the counter. Each *tenatero* loaded with ores presents himself at the

2 D 2

counter; and two persons stationed near the balances judge of the weight of this load by raising it lightly up. If the *tenatero*, who on the road has had time to estimate his load, believes it lighter than the *despachador*, he says nothing, because the error is advantageous to him; but on the other hand, if he believes the weight of the ore he carries in his bag to be greater than it is estimated, he demands that it should be weighed, and the weight which is thus determined is entered in the book of the *despachador*. From whatever part of the mine the *tenatero* comes, he is paid at the rate of one *real de plata** for a load of $2\frac{1}{4}$ cwt., and one *real* and a half for a load of $3\frac{1}{4}$ cwt. per journey. There are some *tenateros* who perform in one day from eight to ten journeys, and their pay is regulated from the book of the *despachador*. This mode of reckoning is no doubt highly deserving of praise; and we cannot sufficiently admire the celerity, the order, and the silence with which they thus determine the weight of so many thousand quintals of ores, which are furnished by veins of 6 or 8 fathoms in breadth, in a single day.

These ores, which are separated from the sterile rocks in the mine itself by the master miners (*quebradores*), undergo three sorts of preparation, viz. at the places for jigging or washing the ores, where women work; under the stamping mills; and under the *tahonas* or *arastras*. These tahonas

* Sixpence-halfpenny.

are machines in which the work is ground under very hard stones, which have a rotatory motion, and weigh upwards of seven or eight cwt. They are not yet acquainted with washing with the tub (*setz wäsche*), nor washing on sleeping tables *(tables dormantes) (liegende-heerde)*, or percussion *(stossheerde)*. The preparation under the stumps *(mazos)* or in the *tahonas*, to which I shall give the name of *edge mills*, on account of their resemblance to some oil and snuff mills, differs according as the ore is destined to be smelted or amalgamated. The mills properly belong only to this last process; however, very rich metallic grains called *polvillos*, which have passed through the trituration of the tahona, are also smelted.

The quantity of silver extracted from the ores by means of mercury, is in the proportion of $3\frac{1}{2}$ to 1 of that produced by smelting. This proportion is taken from the general table formed by the provincial treasuries, from the different districts of mines of New Spain. There are, however, some of those districts, for example those of Sombrerete and Zimapan, in which the produce from smelting exceeds that of amalgamation.

Silver *(plata quintada)* extracted from the Mines
of New Spain, from the 1st January 1785 to
the 31st December 1789.

| Provincial treasuries receiving the fifth. | Silver extracted by amalgamation. | Silver extracted by smelting. |
|---|---|---|
| Mexico . . . . . . . . | 950,185 | 104,835 |
| Zacatecas . . . . . . . | 1,031,360 | 173,631 |
| Guanaxuato . . . . . . | 1,937,895 | 531,138 |
| San Luis Potosi . . . . . | 1,491,058 | 24,465 |
| Durango . . . . . . . . | 536,272 | 386,081 |
| Guadalaxara . . . . . . | 405,357 | 103,615 |
| Bolaños . . . . . . . . | 336,355 | 27,614 |
| Sombrerete . . . . . . . | 136,395 | 184,205 |
| Zimapan . . . . . . . . | 1,215 | 247,002 |
| Pachuca . . . . . . . . | 269,536 | 185,500 |
| Rosario . . . . . . . . | 477,134 | 191,368 |
| Total in lbs. troy | 7,572,762 | 2,159,454 |

In times of peace, amalgamation gains a gradual ascendancy over smelting, which is generally
badly managed. As wood is becoming yearly more
scarce on the ridge of the Cordilleras, which is the
most populous part, the diminution of the produce
of smelting is very advantageous to the manufactories which require a great consumption of combustibles. In time of war the want of mercury
arrests the progress of amalgamation, and compels
the miner to endeavour to improve the process of
smelting. M. Velasquez, the director general of
the mines, supposed even in 1797, before the dis-

covery of the rich mines of Catorce, where there is scarcely any smelting, that of all the ores of New Spain two-fifths were smelted, and the other three-fifths amalgamated.

The limits prescribed by us in the execution of this work, do not permit us to enter into any detail of the processes of amalgamation used in Mexico. It is sufficient to give a general idea of them, to examine the chemical phenomena which are exhibited in the greatest part of these processes, and to show the difficulties which in the New Continent oppose the introduction of the method invented in Germany in 1786, by Born, Ruprecht, and Gellert.

The ancients knew the property which mercury possesses of combining with gold; and they made use of amalgamation in gilding copper, and collecting the gold contained in their worn out dresses, by reducing them to ashes in clay vessels. It appears certain, that before the discovery of America the German miners used mercury, not only in washing auriferous earths, but also in extracting the gold disseminated in veins, both in its native state, and mixed with iron pyrites, and with the gray copper ore. But the amalgamation of silver ores, and the ingenious process now used in the New World, to which we owe the greater part of the valuable metals existing in Europe, or which have flowed from Europe to Asia, go no further back than the year 1557. It was invented in

Mexico by a miner of Pachuca of the name of Bartholome de Medina.

Cold amalgamation was found so profitable in Mexico, that in 1562, five years after the first discovery of the process of Medina, there were already 35 works at Zacatecas in which minerals were treated with mercury, notwithstanding Zacatecas is three times further from Pachuca than the old mines of Tasco, Zultipeque, and Tlapujahua.

The Mexican miners do not appear to follow any very fixed principle, in the selection of the ores submitted to smelting or amalgamation; for we see them smelt in one district of mines, the same mineral substances which in another they believe can only be managed with mercury. The ores which contain muriate of silver, for example, are sometimes smelted with carbonate of soda *(tequesquite)*, and sometimes destined to the processes of hot and cold amalgamation; and it is frequently only the abundance of mercury, and the facility in procuring it, which determine the miner in the choice of his method. In general they find it necessary to smelt the very rich *meagre ores*, those which contain from 6lbs. to $7\frac{1}{2}$lbs. troy of silver per cwt., argentiferous sulphuret of lead, and the ores mixed of blende and vitreous copper. On the other hand, they find it profitable to amalgamate the *pacos* or *colorados*, destitute of metallic lustre; native, vitreous, red, black, and horn-silver; *fah lore* rich in silver; and all the meagre ores which are disseminated in very small particles in the gangue.

The ores destined for amalgamation must be triturated, or reduced to a very fine powder, to present the greatest possible contact with the mercury. This trituration under the *arastras* or mills, of which we have already spoken, is of all the metallurgical operations that which is executed in the greatest perfection in most of the Mexican works. In no part of Europe have I ever seen pulverized ores or powdered *schlich* so fine, and of so equal a grain, as in the great *haciendas de plata* of Guanaxuato, belonging to Count de la Valenciana, Colonel Rul, and Count Perez Galvez. When the ores are very pyritous, they are burnt *(quemar)* in the open air in heaps, on beds of wood, as at Sombrerete, or in *schlich* in reverberating furnaces *(comalillos)*. The latter I found at Tehuilotepec: they are 38 feet in length, without chimneys, but managed by two fires, the flames of which traverse the laboratory. This chemical preparation of the ores is however very rare in general; the size of the fragments of substances to be amalgamated, and the want of combustibles on the table-land of New Spain, render the process equally difficult and expensive.

The dry braying is done by *mazos*, eight of which work together, kept in motion by hydraulic wheels or by mules. The brayed ore *(granza)* passes through a hide pierced with holes; and it is reduced to a very fine powder under the *arastras* or *tahonas*, which are called *sencillas* or *de marco*, according as they are furnished with two or four blocks of porphyry or basalt (*piedras voladoras*), which revolve in a circle from 29 to 38 feet in circumference. From 12 to 15 of these *arastras*, or mills, are generally ranged in a row under one shed; and they are moved by water, or by mules which are relieved every eight hours. One of these machines brays in the space of 24 hours, from 660 to 880lbs. avoirdupois of ores. The moist *schlich* (*lama*) which leaves the *arastras*, is sometimes washed again in cisterns (*estanques de deslamar*), the construction of which, in the district of mines of Zacatecas, has been recently carried to perfection by M. Garcès. When the ores are very rich, as in the mine of Rayas at Guanaxuato, they are only reduced under the stones of the mills to the size of coarse sand (*xalsonte*), and they separate by washing the richest metallic grains (*polvillos*), which are destined for smelting. This very economical operation is called *apartar polvillos*.

I have been assured, that when they are about to amalgamate silver ores which are very poor in gold, they pour mercury into the vessel or trough, on the bottom of which the stones of the *arastras* turn: the auriferous amalgamation then goes on in proportion as the ore is reduced to powder, the rotatory motion of the *piedras voladeras* being favourable to the combination of the metals. I had

no opportunity of seeing this operation, which is
not practised at Guanaxuato. In some great amalgamation works of New Spain, the *arastras* are
still unknown; they are contented with the braying
of the *mazos;* and the *schlich* which comes from
under them is passed through sieves (*cedazos* and
*tolvas*). This comminution is very imperfect; a
powder of an unequal and coarse grain amalga-
mates very ill; and the health of the workmen suffers greatly, in a place where a cloud of metallic
dust is perpetually flying about.

The moistened *schlich* is carried from the mills
or *arastras*, into the court of amalgamation (*patio*
or *galera*), which is generally paved with flags.
The flour is ranged in piles (*montones*) which contain from 15 to 35 cwt. Forty or fifty of these *montones* form a *torta,* by which name they call a heap of
moistened *schlich*, which they leave exposed to the
open air, and which is frequently from 60 to 100 feet
in breadth, by 20 to 24 inches in thickness. The
materials used in amalgamation, which process is
generally carried on in a paved court (*en patio*),
are muriate of soda (*sal blanca*), sulphate of iron
and copper (*magistral),* lime, and vegetable ashes.

It is by the contact of these different substances,
namely, moistened ore in powder, mercury, muriate of soda, sulphates of iron and copper, and
lime, that the amalgamation of silver, in the process of cold amalgamation (*de patio y por cruto*),
takes place. They begin at first by mixing salt

2 E 2

with the metallic powder, and they stir (*repassar*) the paste (*torta*). According to the purity of the salt used, they give each cwt. of *schlich*, a quantity which varies from two and a half to twenty-four pounds. They leave the mineral mixed with salt (*metal ensalmorado*) for several days, in order that the latter may dissolve and be equally distributed. If the *azoguero* judges the metals to be *warm* (*calientes*), that is to say in a state of oxidation, and naturally charged either with sulphates of iron and copper which rapidly decompose in the air, or with muriate of silver, he adds lime to *cool* the mass; and this operation is called *curtir los metales con cal*. But they use *magistral*, if the *schlich* appears too cold (*frios*); for example, if it proceeds from ores which display great metallic lustre; if it contains sulphate of lead (*negrillos agalenados*), or pyrites difficult to decompose in the humid air; and this operation is called *curtir con magistral*. They attribute to the sulphate of iron and copper, the property of heating the mass; and they only consider it as well prepared, when, moistened and held in the hand, it causes a sensation of heat. In this case the sulphuric acid, which is concentrated in the acid sulphate, attracts the water, and, combining with it, gives out caloric.

We have described two processes of chemical preparation of minerals, *salting* (*el ensalmorar*), and *tanning* (*curtir*) with lime or magistral. After the interval of some days they begin to incorporate (*incorporar*) the mercury with the metallic powder. The quantity of mercury is determined by the quantity of silver which they think will be drawn from the minerals; and they generally employ in the incorporation (*en el incorporo*) six times the quantity of mercury which the paste contains of silver. They allow from three to four pounds of mercury for half a pound of silver; and with the mercury, or shortly afterwards, they add to the mass, magistral, according to the nature, or (to use the barbarous language of the *azogueros*) according to the temperature of the minerals (*segun los grados de frialdad*). They allow from one to seven pounds of magistral to each pound of mercury; and if the mercury assumes a lead colour (*color aplomado,*) it is a mark that the paste is working, or that the chemical action has begun. To favour this action, and to augment the contact of the substances, they stir the mass (*se da repasso*) either by causing about twenty horses or mules to run round for several hours, or by setting workmen to tread the *schlich*, who for whole days go about barefooted in this metallic mud. Every day the *azoguero* examines the state of the powder; and he makes the trial (*la tentadura*) in a small wooden trough (*xicara*), that is to say, he washes a portion of *schlich* with water, and judges from the appearance of the mercury and the amalgam, if the mass is too cold or too warm. When the mercury takes an ash colour (*en lis ce-*

*nicienta*), when a very fine gray powder is separated from it which sticks to the fingers, they say the paste is too hot ; and they cool it by the addition of lime. But if, on the other hand, the mercury preserves a metallic lustre, if it remains white, and covered with a reddish or gilt pellicle (*telilla roxiza o de tornasol morado* or *en lis dorada*) ; if it does not appear to act upon the mass, the amalgamation is then considered to be too cold, and they endeavour to heat it (*calentar*) by a mixture of magistral.

In this manner during the space of two, three, and even five months, the paste is balanced between the *magistral* and the lime, for the effects are very different according to the temperature of the atmosphere, the nature of the ores, and the motion given to the *schlich*. If they imagine that the action is too strong, and that the mass is working too much, they allow it to repose : or if they wish to accelerate the amalgamation, and increase the heat, they repeat the stirring more frequently, sometimes employing men, and sometimes mules. If the amalgamation is formed too quickly, and appears in the form of small globules, called *pasillas* or *copos*, they feed the *paste* (*si ceba la torta*) by again adding mercury with a little magistral, and sometimes with salt. When from the exterior characters the *azoguero* judges that the mercury has united with the whole silver contained in the ores, and that the paste has yielded (*ha rendido*), the metallic muds are thrown into vats of wood or stone. Small mills provided with sails placed perpendicularly, turn round in these vats. These machines (*tinas de cal y canto*), which are particularly well executed at Guanaxuato, have a resemblance to those established at Freiberg for washing the remains of the amalgamation. The earthy and oxidated parts are carried away by the water, while the amalgam and the mercury remain in the bottom of the vat. As the force of the current carries away at the same time some globules of mercury, in the great works, Indian women are employed in gathering this metal from the water used in washing. They separate the amalgam collected at the bottom of the *tinas del lavadero* from the mercury, by pressing it through sacks ; and they mould it into pyramids, which they cover with a reversed crucible in the shape of a bell. The silver is separated from the mercury by means of distillation. In the process which I have been describing, they lose in general from $1\frac{1}{2}$ to $1\frac{3}{4}$lb. of mercury for each pound of silver. In the process of amalgamation introduced into Saxony by MM. Gellert and Charpentier, the consumption of mercury is $\frac{2}{16}$ per pound of silver, or eight times less than the proportion used in Mexico.

We have described the cold amalgamation (*por crudo y de patio*), without roasting the ores, and by exposing them in a court to the open air. Medina was only acquainted with the use of salt, and sulphates of iron and copper ; but in 1586, fifteen years after his process was introduced into Peru, Carlos Corso de Leca, a Peruvian miner, discovered the *beneficio de hierro*. He advised the mixture of small plates of iron with the metallic powder, affirming that by this mixture more then nine-tenths of the mercury would be saved. This process, as we shall afterwards see, is founded on the decomposition of the muriate of silver by the iron, and on the attraction of this metal for the sulphur. It is now but very little followed by the Mexican *azogueros*. In 1590, Alonzo Barba proposed the hot amalgamation in copper vats. This process is called the *beneficio de cazo y cocimiento*, which was proposed by M. Born, 1786. The loss of mercury is much less by it than in the *beneficio por patio*, because the copper of the vessels serves to decompose the muriate of silver, while at the same time the heat favours the operation, either in rendering the action of the affinities more powerful, or in giving motion to the liquid mass which enters into ebullition. This hot amalgamation is used in several of the mines of Mexico, which abound in *horn-silver* and *colorados*. Juan de Ordoñez, whose work has been already quoted, even advised amalgamation by means of stoves. In 1676, Juan de Corrosegarra discovered a process which is very much in use at present, called the *beneficio de la pella de plata* ; and in which silver already formed is added to the mercury of the amalgam. It is said, that this amalgam (*pella*) favours the extraction of the silver, and that the loss of mercury is so much less, as the amalgam disseminates itself with greater difficulty into the mass. A fifth method is the *beneficio de la colpa*, in which, instead of an artificial *magistral*, which contains much more of the sulphate of copper than of the sulphate of iron, they use *colpa*, which is a natural mixture of acid sulphate of iron and iron oxidated to the *maximum*. This *beneficio de la colpa*, extolled by Don Lorenzo de la Torre, offers part of the advantages which we have just pointed out in speaking of the amalgamation by iron.

Since the practice of amalgamation of silver ores was introduced into Europe, and since the learned of every nation met at the metallurgic congress of Schemnitz*, the confused theory of Barba, and the Mexican *azogueros*, has been succeeded by sounder ideas, better adapted to the present state of chemistry. It is supposed that the practice of Freiberg, where a mass of roasted ores is amalgamated in a very few hours, will be gradually introduced into the amalgamation of Mexico, where the ores are generally not roasted, and where they remain exposed in the open air to the sun and the rain for several months.

The enormous waste of mercury which we observe in the American process of amalgamation

---

* Properly Szkleno or Glashutte, near Schemnitz.

proceeds from several causes which act simulta-
neously.  If in the process *por patio* all the silver
extracted were owing to a decomposition of muriate of silver by mercury, there would be lost a
quantity of mercury which would be to that of the
silver in the muriate, nearly as 4 : 7. 6 ; for this
ratio is that of the respective oxidations of the two
metals.  Another and perhaps the most considerable part of the mercury is lost, because it remains
disseminated in an immense mass of the moistened powder (*schlich*) ; and this division of the metal is so great, that the most careful washing is not
sufficient to unite the particles concealed in the
residue.  A third cause of the loss of the mercury
must be sought for in its contact with the salt water, in its exposure to the open air and the rays of
the sun for the space of three, four and even five
months.  These masses of mercury and *schlich*,
which contain a great number of heterogeneous
metallic substances, moistened by saline solutions,
are composed of an infinite number of small *galva-
nic piles*, of which the slow but prolonged action
is favourable to the oxidation of the mercury, and
the play of chemical affinities.

It results from these researches, that the use of
fire will sensibly improve the process of amalgamation.  If the minerals to be treated are only vitreous silver, iron filings alone would be perhaps
sufficient to lay the silver bare, and separate it from
the sulphur which retards its union with the mer-

cury. But as in all the other silver ores there are, besides sulphur, different metals combined with the silver, the simultaneous employment of muriate of soda, and sulphates of copper and iron, becomes necessary to favour the disengagement of the muriatic acid, which combines with the copper, iron, antimony, lead and silver. The muriates of iron, copper, zinc, and arsenic, and even that of lead, remain dissolved; and the muriate of silver, which is next to insoluble, is decomposed by contact with the mercury.

The amalgamation, such as we have described it, serves to extract all the silver from the ores which have been treated by mercury, provided the *azoguero* be experienced, and thoroughly know the aspect or external character of the mercury, by which to judge if the paste is in want of lime or sulphate of iron. At Guanaxuato, where this operation is best managed, ores are successfully amalgamated which contain only 15 ounces of silver per ton. M. Sonneschmidt found only $\frac{3}{4}$ of an ounce of silver in the residue of amalgamation proceeding from ores of which the ton contained from 700 to 900 ounces of silver. In the works of Regla, on the other hand, the *schlich* frequently undergoes washing before the mercury has extracted all the silver in the paste; and it is believed at Mexico, that the father of the present proprietor of the famous mine of Biscaina threw, with the refuse, an enormous mass of silver into the river.

2 f 2

After treating of the amalgamation in use in America, it remains for us to touch upon a very important problem, that of the quantity of mercury annually required by the mines of New Spain. Mexico and Peru depend very much upon the abundance and low price of the mercury for the quantity of silver which they produce. When the mercury fails them, which happens often in periods of maritime war, the mines are not so briskly worked; and the ores accumulate on their hands without their being able to extract the silver from them. Rich proprietors, who possess in their magazines ores to the amount of two or three millions of francs, are frequently in want of the necessary money to make head against the daily expenses of their mines. On the other hand, the more mercury is wanted in Spanish America, either on account of the flourishing state of the mines, or the process of amalgamation followed there, the more the price of this metal rises in Europe. The small number of countries which nature has supplied with it, Spain, the department of Mont-Tonnerre, Carniola, and Transylvania, gain by this rise; but the districts of silver mines in which the process of amalgamation is the more desirable, as they are in want of the necessary combustibles for smelting, feel very disadvantageously the necessity for great importations of mercury into America.

Mexico consumes annually upwards of 2,000,000 pounds troy of mercury. In 1803, a very useful project was formed in Spain of supplying Mexico for several years, in order that in the unforeseen case of a war, the amalgamation might not be impeded by the want of mercury ; but this project (*del requesto*) shared the fate of so many others which have never been executed. Before 1770, when the working of mines was far from being so considerable as at present, New Spain received no other mercury but that of Almaden and Huancavelica. The German mercury furnished by the Austrian Government, of which the greatest part is from Idria, was only introduced into Mexico after the falling in of the subterraneous works of Huancavelica, at a time when the mine of Almaden was inundated in the greatest part of its works, and yielded a very inconsiderable produce. But in 1800 and 1802, this last mine was again in such a flourishing state, that it could alone have furnished more than 20,000cwt. of mercury per annum, and there were sufficient grounds to conceive the hope of a termination of the necessity for recurring to German mercury, for the supply of Mexico and Peru. There have been years, when 10 or 12,000cwt. of this last mentioned mercury have been imported at Vera Cruz. Upon the whole, from 1762 to 1781, the amalgamation works of New Spain destroyed the enormous quantity of 25,124,200lbs. troy, of which the value in America amounted to more than 2,400,000*l*.

When the price of mercury has progressively lowered, the working of the mines has gone on increasing. In 1590, under the Viceroy Don Luis de Velasco II., a cwt. of mercury was sold in Mexico for 40*l*. 10*s*. But in the 18th century, the value of this metal had diminished to such a degree, that in 1750 the court distributed it to the miners at 17*l*. 15*s*. Between 1767 and 1776, its price was 13*l*. 9*s*. per cwt. In 1777, under the administration of the Minister Galvez, a royal decree fixed the price of the mercury of Almaden at 8*l*. 17*s*. 6*d*., and that of Germany at 13*l*. 13*s*. At Guanaxuato, these two sorts of mercury are increased by the expensive carriage on the backs of mules, from 8*s*. 8*d*. to 10*s*. 10*d*. per cwt.

The impartial distribution of mercury *(el re-partimiento del azogue)* is of the greatest consequence to the prosperity of the mines of New Spain. Unfortunately, however, the viceroys and those persons who were about them, under the old government, were jealous of the right of administering this branch of the royal revenue. They knew very well that to distribute mercury, and especially that of Almaden, which is one third cheaper than that of Idria, was to concede a favour; and in the colonies, as every where else, it is profitable to favour the richest and most powerful individuals. From this state of things, the poorest miners, those of Tasco, Temascaltepec, or Copala, could not procure mercury, when the great works of Guanaxuato and Real del Monte had it in abundance.

The following table* proves the influence of the price of mercury on its consumption. The diminution of this price, and the freedom of trade with all the ports of Spain, have jointly contributed to the progress of mining.

| Periods. | Price of a cwt. of mercury. | | | Total consumption of mercury. |
|---|---|---|---|---|
| | £. | s. | d. | |
| 1762—1766 | 17 | 15 | 0 | 35750 cwt. |
| 1767—1771 | 13 | 9 | 0 | 42000 |
| 1772—1777 | 13 | 9 | 0 | 53000 |
| 1778—1782 | 8 | 17 | 6 | 59000 |

It was known in Mexico in 1782, that China possesses mercury mines; and it was imagined that nearly 15,000 cwt. might be annually drawn from Canton. The Viceroy Galvez sent thither a cargo of otter skins by way of exchange for the mercury; but this project, wise in itself, was badly executed. The Chinese mercury obtained from Canton and Manilla was impure, and contained a great deal of lead; and its price amounted to 17*l*. 6*s*. 8*d*. the cwt. Even at this price, only a very small quantity could be procured. Since 1793, this

---

* Influxo del precio del azogue sobre su consumo, por Don Antonio del Campo Marin. (MS.)

important object has been totally lost sight of; yet it is deserving of the utmost attention, especially at a time when the Mexicans experience great difficulty in procuring mercury from the Continent of Europe.

From all the researches which I could make, the whole of Spanish America, namely, Mexico, Peru, Chili, and the kingdom of Buenos Ayres, (for elsewhere the process of amalgamation is unknown,) annually consume more than 25,000 cwt. of mercury, the price of which in the Colonies amounts to more than 250,000*l.* sterling. M. Heron de Villefosse, in an interesting table which contains the quantity of each metal extracted from the mines over the whole globe, estimates the mercury annually drawn from those of Europe at 36,000 cwt. From these data we find that mercury is, after cobalt, the rarest of all metals, and that it is even twice as rare as tin.

The following table indicates the quantity of mercury lost in the processes of amalgamation, used in different districts of mines, to extract the silver from the ore. A loss *(perdida y consumo)* of 100lbs. of mercury is computed

|  | lbs. troy of silver. |
|---|---|
| In the mines of Guanaxuato, for about - | 65 |
| In the mines of the intendancy of Guada-laxara - - - - - - | 58 |

In the mines of Pachuca, Zacatecas, Som-
brerete, Guadiana, Durango, Parral, Zichu,
Tonala, Comanja, Zerralbo, Temextla,
Alchichica, Tepeaca, Zimapan, Cairo and
Tlapa   -   -   -   -   -   -   52
In the mines of Chichiapa, Tetala, Tasco,
Santa Theresa de Leiba y Banos, Ituquaro,
Tehuistla, San Esteban de Albukquerque,
and Chiconasi   -   -   -   -   -   48
In the mines of Temascaltepec, Ayuteco,
and Chautla de la Sal   -   -   -   -   44
In the mines of Zacualpa, San Luis Potosi,
Guautla, Sultepec, and Tlapujahua   42

The Government regulates the distribution
(*repartimiento*) of silver, according to these data,
and the quantity of silver annually extracted from
the different districts of mines.

The amalgamation of a hundred weight of ores,
which contain from three and a half to four ounces
of silver, costs in Mexico, including the loss of
mercury, from four to five shillings. M. Sonneschmidt calculates the loss of mercury at ten, twelve,
or fourteen ounces for eight ounces of silver; and
he reckons 8 ounces of mercury consumed (*azogue
consumido*), and from 3 to 6 ounces lost (*azogue
perdido*).

From December 1801 till August 1804, Spain
received from its colonies 23,250,094*l.* in gold
and silver, and 13,725,961*l.* in agricultural pro-

duce. From 1788 to 1795 the total importation
was only at an average, from seven to ten millions
sterling per annum.

The produce of the mines of Spanish America
varies a seventh from year to year, or more than
310,000lbs. troy of silver. We have estimated
this produce for the Spanish and Portuguese colonies at 17,291 kilogrammes of gold, or 75,217
Castilian marcs, and at 795,581 kilogrammes or
4,460 Castilian marcs of silver, which together are
of the value of 9,400,000*l.* Europe, Siberia, and
America furnish per annum 57,368lbs. in gold,
and 2,175,000lbs. in silver, or to the value of
10,755,000*l.*

NOTE 1.

The Baron de Humboldt proves to us in these remarks that
he is well acquainted with practical mining, and that his information is likely to be most valuable on that account. I would
particularly direct the attention of English Miners to what is
said (page 189) respecting the great size of the shafts and
levels, particularly of the latter, and to the influence justly
drawn in the following page, that this has prevented the proprietors from making trials which are so indispensable for the
preservation of a mine.

If these works have not been properly carried on, it may be
so much the better for those who are about to commence a new
system of operations. Every miner from Cornwall knows that
the greater part of the profits on the Mines of that country
have of late arisen from a judicious system of exploring ground
which had formerly been neglected. It is hoped that experience
so valuable for the enterprize in question, will be actively and
successfully applied.

I have seen many Mines in England and Wales to which
M. de Humboldt's remark might have been justly applied, and
which were abandoned for want of the trials he recommends.
The working of these having been resumed of late years and

conducted on a better system, they have become very profitable.

The untried ground on the veins between different mines on the same lode, or the high ground standing, should be accurately inspected. There is evidence enough in this chapter that much is to be done, and that a great probability exists of beneficial results.

I need hardly say any thing on the mode of drawing the water or the ores, the improvements with respect to which, have been considerable in England in the last twenty years. Every one who is sent to manage mines in Mexico, should of course understand these improvements well.    J. T.

### Note 2.

On the mode of dressing the ores we have no very precise information ; the author praises the trituration or grinding to a fine powder : this is necessary where amalgamation is used, but would be less so for smelting. It appears, however, that their machines only grind from 660 to 880 lbs. in 24 hours. A good stamping mill with 3 heads would probably do 4 times as much; and as 24 heads would be worked by a small steam engine, such a machine would do the work of between 30 and 40 of their mills : consequently, ores that would not pay in the old method, would give large profits by the new. I have said elsewhere, that I conceive it to be a great object to dress the ores as clean as possible, and to reduce the bulk to the smallest possible quantity. This I think must be true, whether amalgamation be used, or smelting, with a scarcity of fuel.

It appears that the pyritous ore, or mundic containing silver, which is often very plentiful, is sometimes calcined in reverberatory furnaces or burning-houses. This operation appears to be ill performed, and must be attended to. I should think it an essential process for those ores which are very valuable.

In page 206, we are told that smelting is badly performed.

The improvement of this process, as well as of that of dressing, will of course demand great attention. Their importance may be estimated by their effect on the consumption of quicksilver, the cost of which, as stated in the latter part of the chapter, forms one of the most formidable deductions from the profits of the mines.    J. T.

# CHAPTER XI.

*Intendancy of Guanaxuato.—Situation—extent—cultiva-*
*tion—population—towns—mining districts—geological*
*constitution.*

WE shall now subjoin some more particular details
concerning the mining districts, and the intendancies
in which they are situate; taking them in the order
of their comparative wealth and importance.

I. *Intendancy of Guanaxuato.*

| Extent in North Latitude. | Extent in West Longitude. | Population in 1803. | Extent of Surface in square Leagues. | No. of Inhabitants to the square League. |
|---|---|---|---|---|
| From 20° 55' to 21° 30' | From 102° 30' to 103° 45' | 517,300 | 8199 | 695 |

This province, wholly situated on the ridge of the
Cordillera of Anahuac, is the most populous in New
Spain. The population is also more equally distributed here than in any of the other provinces.
Its length, from the lake of Chapala to the north-
east of San Felipe, is 156 miles, and its breadth,
from the Villa de Leon to Celaya, 93 miles. Its
territorial extent is nearly the same as that of the

kingdom of Murcia; and in relative population it exceeds the kingdom of the Asturias. Its relative population is even greater than that of the departments of the *Hautes-Alpes, Basses-Alpes, Pyrenées Orientales*, and the *Landes*. The most elevated point of this mountainous country seems to be the mountain de los Llanitos in the Sierra de Santa Rosa. I found its height above the level of the sea 9235 feet.

The cultivation of this fine province, part of the old kingdom of Mechoacan, is almost wholly to be ascribed to the Europeans, who arrived there in the 16th century, and introduced the first germ of civilization. It was in these northern regions, on the banks of the Rio de Lerma, formerly called Tololotlan, that the engagements took place between the tribes of hunters and shepherds, called in the historians by the vague denominations of Chichimecs, who belonged to the tribes of the Pames, Capuces, Samues, Mayolias, Guamanes, and Guachichiles Indians. In proportion as the country was abandoned by these wandering and warlike nations, the Spanish conquerors transplanted to it colonies of Mexican or Aztec Indians. For a long time agriculture made more considerable progress than mining. The mines, which were of small celebrity at the beginning of the conquest, were almost wholly abandoned during the seventeenth and eighteenth centuries; and it is not more than thirty or forty years since they

became richer than the mines of Pachuca, Zacatecas, and Bolaños.   Their metallic produce, as we
shall hereafter explain, is now greater than the produce of Potosi or any other mine in the two continents ever was.

There are in the intendancy of Guanaxuato
3 *ciudades* (viz. Guanaxuato, Celayo, and Salva-
tierra) ; 4 *villas* (viz. San Miguel el Grande, Leon,
San Felipe and Salamanca) ; 37 villages or *pueblos ;*
33 parishes *(paroquias) ;* 448 farms or *haciendas ;*
225 individuals of the secular clergy, 170 monks
and 30 nuns ; and in a population of more than
180,000 Indians, 52,000 subject to tribute.

The most remarkable towns of this intendancy
are the following :

Population.

*Guanaxuato,* or Santa Fe de Gonna-
joato.   The building of this city was
begun by the Spaniards in 1554.   It received the royal privilege of *villa* in 1619 ;
and that of *ciudad* the 8th December
1741.   Its present population is :

Within the city *(en el casco de la ciudad)*   .     .     .     .     .     .     41,000

In the mines surrounding the city, of
which the buildings are contiguous, at
Marfil Santa Ana, Santa Rosa, Valenciana, Rayas, and Mellado     .     .     29,600
                                    ―――――――
                                     70,600

Among whom there are 4500 Indians. Height
of the city at the Plaza Mayor near 6836 feet.
Height of Valenciana at the mouth of the new pit
*(tiro nuevo)* 7586 feet. Height of Rayas at the
mouth of the gallery 7075 feet.

*Salamanca,* a pretty little town, situated in a
plain which rises insensibly by Temascatio, Burras
and Cuevas, towards Guanaxuato. Height 5762
feet.

*Celaya.* Sumptuous edifices have recently been
constructed at Celaya, Queretaro, and Guanaxuato.
The church of the Carmelites at Celaya has a fine
appearance. It is adorned with Corinthian and
Ionic columns. Height 6018 feet.

*Villa de Leon,* in a plain eminently fertile in
grain. From this town to San Juan del Rio are
to be seen the finest fields of wheat, barley, and
maize.

*San Miguel el Grande,* celebrated for the industry of its inhabitants, who manufacture cotton
cloth.

The hot wells of San Jose de Comangillas are
in this province. They issue from a basaltic opening. The temperature of the water, according to
experiments made jointly by myself and Mr. Roxas,
is 205°·3 Fahr. thermometer.

*Disputaciones de Mineria,* or Districts.

### 1. Guanaxuato.

*Reales,* or places surrounded with Mines :

Guanaxuato : Villalpando; Monte de San Nico-
las; Santa Rosa; Santa Ana ; San Antonio de las
Minas ; Comanja ; Capulin ; Comanjilla ; Gigante ;
San Luis de la Paz ; San Rafael de los Lobos ;
Durasno ; San Juan de la Chica ; Rincon de Cen-
teno ; San Pedro de los Pozos ; Palmos de Vega ;
San Miguel el Grande ; San Felipe.

The district of Guanaxuato is as remarkable for
its natural wealth as for the gigantic labours of man
in the bowels of the mountains.

In the centre of the intendancy of Guanaxuato
on the ridge of the Cordillera of Anahuac, rises a
group of porphyritic summits known by the name
of the Sierra de Santa Rosa. This group of mountains, partly arid, and partly covered with straw-
berry trees and evergreen oaks, is surrounded with
fertile and well cultivated fields. To the north of
the *Sierra,* the *Llanos* of San Felipe extend as far
as the eye can reach ; and to the south, the plains
of Irapuato and Salamanca exhibit the delightful
spectacle of a rich and populous country. The
*Cierro de los Llanitos,* and the *Puerto de Santa
Rosa,* are the most elevated summits of this group

of mountains. Their absolute height is from 9000 to 9300; but as the neighbouring plains, which are part of the great central table-land of Mexico, are more than 6000 feet above the level of the sea, these porphyritic summits appear but as inconsiderable hills to the eye of a traveller accustomed to the striking appearance of the Cordilleras. The famous vein of Guanaxuato, which has alone, since the end of the sixteenth century, produced a mass of silver equal to nearly 58,000,000*l.*, crosses the southern slope of the Sierra Santa de Rosa.

In going from Salamanca to Burras and Temascatio, we perceive a chain of mountains which, bounding the plains, stretches from the south-east to the north-west. The crest of the vein follows this direction. At the foot of the Sierra, after passing the farm of Xalapita, we discover a narrow ravine, dangerous to pass at the period of the great swells, called the *Canada de Marfil*, which leads to the town of Guanaxuato. The population of that town, as we have already observed, is more than 70,000 souls. One is astonished to see in this wild spot, large and beautiful edifices in the midst of miserable Indian huts. The house of Colonel Don Diego Rul, who is one of the proprietors of the Valenciana mine, would be an ornament to the finest streets of Paris and Naples. It is fronted with columns of the Ionic order, and the architecture is simple, and remarkable for great purity of

2 H

style. The erection of this edifice, which is almost uninhabited, cost more than 33,000*l.*—a considerable sum in a country where the price of labour and materials is very moderate.

The name of Guanaxuato is scarcely known in Europe; yet the riches of the mines of this district are much greater than those of the metalliferous depositary of Potosi. The latter was discovered in 1545 by Diego Hualca an Indian, and has produced, (according to information never yet made public,) in the space of two hundred and thirty-three years, 57,068,488 lbs. troy of silver, worth 170,789,344*l.* sterling.

|  | Pounds Sterling. |  | lbs. Troy. |
|---|---|---|---|
| From 1556—1578.... | 10,619,112 | or | 3,548,328 |
| 1579—1736.... | 132,469,881 | — | 44,264,213 |
| 1737—1789.... | 27,700,351 | — | 9,255,947 |
|  | 170,789,344 |  | 57,068,488 |

The produce of the vein of Guanaxuato is almost double that of the Cerro de Potosi. There is actually drawn from this vein (for it alone furnishes all the silver of the mines of the district of Guanaxuato), in average years, about 300,000 lbs. troy *of silver, and* 1000 lbs. troy *of gold.*

It is found from official papers, that the district of mines of Guanaxuato has produced in 38 years gold and silver to the value of 35,750,000*l.* sterling, and that from 1786 to 1803, the annual average produce has been 342,231 lbs. troy of silver, equal to 1,059,655*l.* sterling. All the veins of Hungary and Transylvania together, yield only 55,686 lbs. troy of silver.

Taking four averages of years, of which three are of ten and one of eight years, we shall have the following results:

| Periods. | Value of the total produce of gold and silver extracted from the mines of Guanaxuato. | Silver for an average year. | Value of gold and silver for an average year. |
|---|---|---|---|
| | Pounds Sterling. | lbs.Troy. | Pounds Sterling. |
| 1766—1775 | 6,569,442 | 210,609 | 656,944 |
| 1776—1785 | 10,116,786 | 324,997 | 1,011,678 |
| 1786—1795 | 10,547,910 | 345,191 | 1,054,790 |
| 1796—1803 | 8,516,325 | 339,273 | 1,064,521 |

The rocks known in the district of Guanaxuato, are clay-slate and chlorite-slate *(killas)*, which are considered to be of primitive formation.

In sinking the great shaft at the Valenciana mine, they went through floors of syenite, hornblende-slate, and true serpentine.

There are resting on some parts of the clay-slate of this district, porphyry and old sandstone. The porphyry forms gigantic masses on the surface. The sandstone occurs at lower elevations, and is a breccia with an argillaceous cement.

2 H 2

This formation serves again as a basis to other secondary beds, such as limestone and gypsum.

Floors or courses of greenstone are also sometimes found in the primitive rocks.

Such is the geological constitution of the country at Guanaxuato. The vein *(veta madre)* traverses clay-slate as well as porphyry; and in both of these rocks it has proved very rich in ore. Its mean direction is h. $8\frac{4}{3}$ of the miner's compass*; and is nearly the same with that of the *veta grande* of Zacatecas, and of the veins of Tasco and Moran, which are all western veins *(spathgänge).* The inclination of the vein of Guanaxuato is 45 or 48 degrees to the south-west. We have already stated, that it has been wrought for a length of more than 39,000 feet; and yet the enormous mass of silver which it has supplied for the last hundred years,— sufficient of itself to produce a change in the price of commodities in Europe,—has been extracted from that part of the vein alone contained between the shafts of Esperanza and Santa Anita, an extent of less than 8500 feet. In this part we find the mines of Valenciana, Tepayac, Cata, San Lorenzo, Animas, Mellado, Fraustros, Rayas, and Santa Anita, which at different periods have enjoyed great celebrity.

The *veta madre* of Guanaxuato exhibits the extraordinary example of a fissure formed accord-

* Or N. 52°. W.

ing to the direction and inclination of the strata of the rock. Towards the south-east from the ravine of Serena, or from the mines of Belgrado and San Bruno, which are very fully wrought, to beyond the mines of Marisanchez, it runs through porphyritic mountains; and towards the north-east, from the shafts of Guanaxuato to the Cerro de Buena Vista and the Cañada de la Virgen, it traverses clay-slate *(thon schiefer)*. Its magnitude varies like that of all the veins of Europe. When not ramified, it is generally from 40 to 50 feet in breadth; sometimes it is even contracted to the width of 20 inches; and it is for the most part found divided into three masses *(cuerpos)*, separated either by rock *(caballos)*, or by parts of the gangue almost destitute of metals. In the mine of Valenciana the *veta madre* has been found without ramification, and of the breadth of 22 feet, from the surface of the ground to the depth of 93 fathoms. At this point it divides into three branches, and its extent, reckoning from wall to wall of the entire mass, is from 160 to 200 feet. Of these three branches of vein, there is in general but one which is rich in metals; and sometimes when all the three join, as at Valenciana near the pit of San Antonio, at a depth of 164 fathoms the vein contains immense riches to a width of more than 80 feet. In the *pertinencia de Santa Leocadia*, four branches are observable. A branch, of which the inclination is 65°, separates from the inferior branch *(cuerpo baxo)*, and cuts the rock of the wall.

The small ravines into which the valley of Marfil is divided, appear to have a decided influence on the richness of the *veta madre* of Guanaxuato, which has yielded the most metal where the direction of ravines and the slope of the mountains *(flaqueza del cerro)* have been parallel to the direction and inclination of the vein. When we stand on the elevation of Mellado, near the shaft which was sunk in 1558, we observe that the *veta madre* is in general most abundant in ores towards the north-west, towards the mines of Cata and Valenciana; and that to the south-east towards Rayas and Santa Anita, the produce has been at once richer, rarer, and more inconstant. Besides, in this celebrated vein there is a certain middle region which may be considered as a depositary of great riches; for above and below this region, the ores have yielded an inconsiderable share of silver. At Valenciana the rich ores have been in the greatest abundance, between 55 and 186 fathoms in depth below the mouth of the gallery. This abundance appeared at Rayas at the surface of the earth; but the level of Valenciana is pierced, according to my measurements, in a plain which is more than 511 feet above the level *(galerie d'ecoulement)* of Rayas; which might lead us to believe that the depositary of the great wealth of Guanaxuato is found in this part of the vein, between 6987 and 6199

feet of absolute height above the level of the ocean.
The deepest works of the mine of Rayas *(los
planes)* have never yet reached the lowest limit of
this middle region; while the bottom *(das tiefste)*
of the mine of Valenciana, the level of San
Bernardo, has unfortunately passed this limit more
than 230 feet. Hence the mine of Rayas continues
to furnish extremely rich ores, while at Valenciana
they have endeavoured for some years to supply by
the extraction of a greater quantity of ores the de-
ficiency in their intrinsic value.

The mineral substances which constitute the
mass of the vein of Guanaxuato, are common
quartz, amethyst, carbonate of lime, pearl spar,
splintery hornstone, sulphuret of silver, dendritic
native silver, prismatic black silver, deep red silver,
native gold, argentiferous galena, brown blende,
spar iron, and copper and iron pyrites. We observe besides, though much more rarely, crystallized
feldspar (the rhomboidal quartz of the Mexican
mineralogists), calcedony, small masses of spar-
fluor, capillary quartz *(haarformiger quartz)*, gray
copper ore *(fahlerz)*, and columnar carbonate of
lead. The absence of the sulphate of barytes and
muriate of silver distinguishes the formation of
the vein of Guanaxuato from that of Sombrerete,
Catorce, Fresnillo, and Zacatecas. Those mineralogists who are interested in the study of regular
forms, find a great variety of crystals in the mines
of Guanaxuato, and especially in the red and black

sulphuret of silver, and in the calcareous spar, and the brown spar.

The abundance of waters which filtrate through the crevices of the rock and the gangue, vary very much in the different points of the vein. The mines of Animas and Valenciana are entirely dry, though the works of the latter occupy a horizontal extent of 4920, and a perpendicular depth of 1640 feet. Between these two mines, in which the miner is incommoded by dust and heat*, lie the mines of Cata and Tepeyac, which remain inundated, because they do not possess sufficient mechanical force to draw off the water. At Rayas, it is drawn off in a very expensive manner by means of whims, worked by mules, placed under ground. One is astonished to see mines of such considerable wealth without any adit level, while the neighbouring ravines of Cata and Marfil, and the plains of Tenascatio, which are lower than the *bottom* of Valenciana, appear to invite the miners to undertake works which would both serve to draw off the water, and to transport the ores to the place where they are smelted and amalgamated.

The *Valenciana* is almost the sole example of a mine, which for forty years has never yielded less to its proprietors than from 80,000*l*. to 124,000*l*. per annum. It appears that the part of the vein extending from Tepeyac to the north-west, had

* From 71° to 80° Fahr.; the temperature of the exterior air being 62° Fahr.

not been much wrought towards the end of the 16th century. From that period the whole tract remained forsaken till 1760, when a Spaniard who went over very young to America, began to work this vein in one of the points which had till that time been believed destitute of metals *(emboras-cado)*. M. Obregon (the name of this Spaniard) was without fortune ; but as he had the reputation of being a worthy man, he found friends who from time to time advanced him small sums to carry on his operations. In 1766, the works were already 44 fathoms in depth, and yet the expenses greatly surpassed the value of the metallic produce. With a passion for mining equal to what some men display for gaming, M. Obregon preferred submitting to every sort of privation, to the abandoning his undertaking. In the year 1767 he entered into partnership with a petty merchant of Rayas, of the name of Otero. Could he then hope that in the space of a few years he and his friend would become the richest individuals in Mexico, perhaps in the whole world? In 1768 they began to extract a very considerable quantity of silver minerals from the mine of Va-lenciana. In proportion as the shafts grew deeper, they approached that region which we have already described as the depository of the great metallic wealth of Guanaxuato. In 1771 they drew from the *pertinencia de Dolores* enormous masses of sulphuret of silver, mixed with native and red silver. From that period till 1804, when I quitted

New Spain, the mine of Valenciana has continually yielded an annual produce of more than 583,380*l.* There have been years so productive, that the net profit of the two proprietors of the mine has amounted to about 250,000*l.* sterling.

M. Obregon, better known by the name of Count de la Valenciana, preserved in the midst of immense wealth the same simplicity of manners, and the same frankness of character, for which he was distinguished previous to his success. When he began to work the vein of Guanaxuato, above the ravine of San Xavier, goats were feeding on the very hill which ten years afterwards was covered with a town of seven or eight thousand inhabitants. Since the death of the old Count, and his friend Don Pedro Luciano Otero, the property of the mine has been divided among several families*. I knew at Guanaxuato two younger sons of M. Otero, each of whom possessed, in ready money, a capital of 271,835*l.* sterling, without including the actual revenue from the mine, which amounted to more than 16,600*l.* sterling.

The constancy and equality of the produce of the mine of Valenciana, is so much the more surprising, as the abundance of the rich mines has considerably diminished, and the expenses of the

---

* The property of Valenciana is divided into twenty-eight shares, called *barres,* of which ten belong to the descendants of the Count de la Valenciana, twelve to the family of Otero, and two to that of Santana.

works have increased in an alarming proportion, when they have reached a perpendicular depth of 273 fathoms. The piercing and walling of the three old whim shafts cost the Count de Valenciana nearly 260,000*l.* sterling, viz.

|  | £. |
|---|---|
| The square shaft of San Antonio or *tiro viejo*, 128 fathoms in perpendicular depth, and four whims - - | 86,000 |
| The square shaft of Santo Christo de Burgos, 82 fathoms in depth, and two whims - - - - | 22,000 |
| The hexagonal shaft of Nuestra Señora de Guadalupe (*tiro nuevo*) 186 fathoms in perpendicular depth, and six whims | 152,000 |
| Expense of the three shafts | 260,000 |

Within these twelve years they have begun to dig in the solid rock, in the roof of the vein, a new whim shaft (*tiro general*), which will have the enormous perpendicular depth of 281 fathoms, terminating at the actual bottom of the mine, or at the *planes of San Bernardo.* This shaft, which will be in the centre of the works, will considerably diminish the number of the 980 labourers (*tenateros*) employed as beasts of burden to carry the minerals to the upper places where ore is deposited. The whim shaft, which will cost more than 218,767*l.* sterling, is octagonal, and contains 87 feet of cir-

cumference. Its walling is most beautiful. It is
believed that they will reach the vein in 1815, although in the month of September 1803 the depth
did not exceed 100 fathoms. The piercing of
this shaft is one of the greatest and boldest undertakings to be found in the history of mines. It
may be questioned, however, whether for the sake
of diminishing the expenses of carriage and
draught, it was expedient to recur to a remedy
which is at once slow, expensive, and uncertain.

The expenses of working the mine of Valenciana have been on an average annually:

|                     |   |   |   | Pounds sterling. |
|---------------------|---|---|---|------------------|
| From 1787 to 1791   | - | - | - | 89,694           |
| From 1794 to 1802   | - | - | - | 194,708          |

Although the expenses are doubled, the profits
of the share-holders have remained nearly the same.

The following Table contains an exact state of
the mine for the last nine years.

| | PERIODS. | | | | | | | | | Total of the 9 years. |
|---|---|---|---|---|---|---|---|---|---|---|
| | 1794. | 1795. | 1796. | 1797. | 1798. | 1799. | 1800. | 1801. | 1802. | |
| Produce of the sale of the minerals of Valencia-na (pounds sterling) | 277,775 | 367,605 | 285,008 | 461,162 | 373,628 | 343,286 | 320,868 | 302,106 | 266,420 | 2,997,666 |
| Expenses of working (pounds st.) | 173,188 | 176,760 | 180,341 | 190,404 | 192,992 | 198,344 | 211,751 | 214,929 | 204,600 | 1,743,314 |
| Net profit divided among the shareholders (pounds sterling) | 104,587 | 190,845 | 104,667 | 270,758 | 180,636 | 144,942 | 109,117 | 87,177 | 61,820 | 1,254,352 |

The result of this table is, that the net profit of the shareholders has been latterly at an average of 139,372*l.*  In 1802 circumstances were extremely unfavourable.   The greater part of the ores were very poor, and their extraction attended with great expense ; and besides this, the produce was sold at very low prices, because the want of mercury impeded the amalgamation, and all the mines were incumbered with ores.   The year 1803 promised greater advantages to the proprietors, and they reckoned on a net profit of more than 109,383*l.*  I saw them sell weekly at Valenciana, silver ores to the amount of more than 5,850*l.*, the expenses of which amounted to 3,683*l.*  At Rayas the profit of the proprietor was greater, though the produce was less ; for this mine furnished more than 3,250*l.* worth of ores weekly, while the expense of working only amounted to 866*l.*  This was the effect of the richness of the ores, their concentration in the vein, the inconsiderable depth of the mine, and consequently a less expensive draught.

To form an idea of the enormous advances required in working the mine of Valenciana, it is sufficient here to mention, that in its present state there must be laid out annually,

£.
136,000 { in wages of miners, triers, masons, and other workmen employed in the mine.

44,000 { in powder, tallow, wood, leather, steel, and other materials necessary in mining.

Total expense £180,000

The consumption of powder alone has amounted to 16,668*l*., and that of steel to 6,250*l*. : the number of workmen who labour in the interior of the mine of Valenciana amounts to 1,800. Adding 1,300 individuals (men, women, and children) who labour at the whims, in the carriage of ores to the places where they are tried, we shall find 3,100 individuals are employed in the different operations of the mine. The direction of the mine is entrusted to an administrator with a salary of 2,500*l*., through whose hands upwards of 240,000*l*. annually pass. This administrator, who is under the controul of no one, has under his orders an overseer *(obersteiger, minero)*, the under overseers *(untersteiger, sottomineros)*, and nine master miners *(mandones)*. These head people daily visit the subterraneous operations, carried by men who have a sort of saddle fastened on their backs, and who go by the name of little horses *(cavallitos)*.

We shall conclude this account of the mine of Valenciana, with a comparative Table of the state of this Mexican work, and of that of the celebrated mine of Himmelsfürst in the district of Freiberg. I flatter myself that this Table will fix the attention of those who consider the study of the management of mines as an important object in political economy.

# Comparative Table of the Mines of America and Europe.

| | America. | Europe. |
|---|---|---|
| Average year at the end of the eighteenth century. | Mine of Valenciana, the richest of the Mexican mines. At the surface, 9280 feet above the level of the sea. | Mine of Himmelsfürst, the richest of the Saxon mines. At the surface, 1638 feet above the level of the sea. |
| Metallic produce - - | 221,538lbs. troy of silver | 6,154lbs. troy of silver. |
| Total expenses of the mine - - | 250,000l. sterling | 9,600l. sterling. |
| Net profit of the share-holders | 120,000l. sterling | 3,600l. sterling. |
| The ton of ores contains in silver - - - | 80 ounces | From 120 to 140 ounces silver. |
| Number of workmen - - | 3,100 Indians and Mestizoes, 1800 of whom are in the interior of the mine | 700 miners, of whom 550 are in the interior of the mine. |
| Wages of the miners - - - | From 3s. 6d. to 5s. | 1s. 6d. |
| Expense of powder | 16,000l. sterling (nearly 1,600 cwt.) | 1,080l. sterling (nearly 270 cwt.) |
| Quantity of ores smelted and amalgamated | 36,000 tons | 700 tons. |
| Veins - - - | A vein frequently divides into thin branches of from 150 to 200 feet of extent (in clay slate) | Five principal veins, from 60 to 90 feet extent (in gneiss). |
| Water - - - | No water | Eight cubic feet per minute. Two hydraulic wheels. |
| Depth of the mine | 278 fathoms | 178 fathoms. |

They reckoned in 1803, in the whole district of mines of Guanaxuato, 5000 miners and workmen employed in picking the ores, in smelting and amalgamating; 1896 *arastres*, or machines for reducing the ores into powder; and 14,618 mules destined to move the whims, and to tread for amalgamation the pulverized ores mixed with mercury. The *arastres* of the town of Guanaxuato bray, when there is an abundance of mercury, 568 tons of ores per day. If we recollect that the produce in silver is annually from 300,000 to 400,000 lbs. troy, we shall find by this datum, that the mean contents of the ores are extremely small.

## CHAPTER XII.

*Intendancy of Zacatecas—extent—towns—mines—geological structure.*

| Extent in north latitude. | Extent in west longitude. | Population in 1803. | Extent of surface in square miles. | No. of inhabitants to the square mile. |
|---|---|---|---|---|
| From 22° 20' to 24° 33' | From 103° 12' to 105° 9' | 153,300 | 21,195 | 7⅓ |

THIS singularly ill-peopled province is a mountainous and arid tract, exposed to a continual inclemency of climate. It is bounded on the north by the intendancy of Durango, on the east by the intendancy of San Luis Potosi, on the south by the province of Guanaxuato, and on the west by that of Guadalaxara. Its greatest length is 255 miles, and its greatest breadth, from Sombrerete to the Real de Ramos, 153 miles.

The intendancy of Zacatecas is nearly of the same extent with Switzerland, which it resembles in many geological points of view. The relative population is hardly equal to that of Sweden.

The table-land which forms the centre of the intendancy of Zacatecas, and which rises to more than 6561 feet in height, is formed of syenites, a rock on which repose, according to the excellent observations of M. Valencia, strata of primitive schistus and schistous chlorites (*chlorith-schiefer*). The schistus forms the base of the mountains of *grauwacke* and trappish porphyry. North of the town of Zacatecas are nine small lakes, abounding in muriate, and especially carbonate, of soda. This carbonate, which, from the old Mexican word *tequixquilit*, goes by the name of tequesquite, is of great use in the dissolving of the muriates and of the sulphurets of silver. M. Garces, an advocate of Zacatecas, has recently fixed the attention of his countrymen on the tequesquite, which is also to be found at Zacualco, between Valladolid and Guadalaxara, in the valley of San Francisco, near San Luis Potosi, at Acusquilco, near the mines of Bolaños, at Chorro near Durango, and in five lakes round the town of Chihuahua. The central table-land of Asia is not more rich in soda than Mexico.

The most remarkable places of this province are:

*Zacatecas*, at present, after Guanaxuato, the most celebrated mining place of New Spain. Its polation is at least 33,000.

*Fresnillo*, on the road from Zacatecas to Durango.

*Sombrerete*, the head town, and residence of a *Diputacion de Mineria*.

2 K 2

Besides the three places above named, the intendancy of Zacatecas contains also interesting metalliferous veins near the Sierra de Pinos, Chalchiguitec, San Miguel del Mezquitas, and Mazapil. It was this province, also, which in the mine of the *Veta Negra de Sombrerete* exhibited an example of the greatest wealth of any vein yet discovered in the two hemispheres.

### *Diputaciones de Mineria,* or Districts.

2. Zacatecas.
3. Sombrerete.
4. Fresnillo.
5. Sierra de Pinos.

### *Reales,* or places surrounded by mines:

Zacatecas; Guadalupe de Veta Grande; San Juan Baptista de Panuco; La Blanca; Sombrerete; Madroño; San Pantaleon de la Noria; Fresnillo; San Demetrio de los Plateros; Cerro de Santiago; Sierra de Pinos; la Sauceda Cerro de Santiago; Mazapil.

The celebrated mines of Zacatecas, called by Robertson Sacotecas, are, as we have already observed, older than the mines of Guanaxuato. They began to be worked immediately after the veins of Tasco, Zultepeque, Tlapujahua, and Pachuca. They are situated on the central table-land of the Cordilleras, which descends rapidly towards New Biscay, and towards the basin of the Rio del Norte.

The climate of Zacatecas, as well as that of Catorce, is much colder than the climate of Guanaxuato and Mexico. Barometrical measurements will one day determine whether this difference is owing to a more northern position, or to the elevation of the mountains.

The nature of the latter has been examined by two very intelligent mineralogists, MM. Sonnesschmidt and Valencia, the one a Saxon and the other a Mexican. From the whole of their observations it appears, that the district of mines of Zacatecas bears great resemblance in its geological constitution to that of Guanaxuato. The oldest rocks which appear at the surface are syenitic; they are overlaid by clay-slate, which from the beds of Lydian stone, *grauwacke* and greenstone which it contains, has a resemblance to transition clay-slate. The most part of the veins of Zacatecas are found in this clay-slate. The *veta grande,* or principal vein, has the same direction as the *veta madre* of Guanaxuato; the others are generally in a direction from east to west. A porphyry destitute of metals, and forming those naked and perpendicular rocks which the natives call *buffas,* covers in many places the clay-slate especially on the side of the *Villa de Xeres,* where a mountain rises in the midst of these porphyritic formations, in the form of a bell, the basaltic cone of the *Campana de Xeres.*

The savage aspect of the metalliferous mountains

of Zacatecas, forms a singular contrast to the great wealth of the veins which they contain. This wealth is displayed—and the fact is very remarkable—not in the ravines, and where the veins run along the gentle slope of the mountains, but most frequently on the most elevated summits, on points where the surface appears to have been violently torn in the ancient revolutions of the globe. The mines of Zacatecas produce yearly, on an average, from 2500 to 3000 bars of silver, at $82\frac{1}{2}$ ounces each*.

The mass of the veins of this district contains a great variety of minerals, viz: quartz, splintery hornstone, calcareous spar, a little sulphate of barytes and brown spar ; prismatic black silver, called in the country *azul acerado;* sulphuret of silver, *(azul plomilloso)* mixed with native silver ; black silver, (the *silber-schwärtze* of the Germans, *polvorilla* of the Mexicans) ; pearl gray, blue, violet, and leek green muriate of silver (*plata parda azul y verde*) at very inconsiderable depths ; a little red silver (*petlangue* or *rosicler*) ; and native gold, particularly to the south-west of the town of Zacatecas ; argentiferous sulphuret of lead (*soroche plomoso reluciente y tescatete*) ; carbonate of lead ; black, brown, and yellow sulphuret of zinc, (*estoraque* and *ojo de vivora*) ; copper and iron pyrites (*bronze nochistle* or *dorado,* and *bronze chino*) ; magnetic oxydulated iron ; blue and green carbonate of copper, and sulphuret of antimony. The

*From 219,866 to 263,839lbs. trov.

most abundant metals of the celebrated vein called
the *veta grande*, are prismatic black silver (*spröd-
glaserz*), sulphuret of silver, or vitreous silver,
mixed with native and black silver.

The intendancy of Zacatecas contains the mines
of *Fresnillo* and those of *Sombrerete*. The former
are very feebly wrought, and are situated in an insulated group of mountains which rise above the
plains of the central table-land. These plains are
covered with porphyritic formations; but the metalliferous group itself is composed of *grauwacke*.
According to the observation of M. Sonneschmidt,
the rock is traversed there by an innumerable quantity of veins, rich in gray and green hornsilver.

The mines of Sombrerete have become celebrated from the immense riches of the vein of the
*veta negra*, which in the space of a few months left to
the family of Fagoaga (Marques del Apartado) a net
profit of more than 834,000*l.* The greater part of
these veins are found in a compact limestone, which,
like that of Sauceda, contains flint-slate and lydian
stone. The deep red silver is particularly abundant
in this district of mines. It has been seen to form the
whole mass of veins more than three feet in width.
Near Sombrerete the mountains of secondary calcareous formation rise much above the porphyritic
mountains. The Cerro di Papareton appears to be
more than 11,000 feet above the level of the sea.

# CHAPTER XIII.

*Intendancy of San Luis Potosi—extent—climate—territorial division—towns—mines—wealth of the mine of Catorce.*

| Extent in north latitude. | Extent in west longitude. | Population in 1803. | Extent of surface in square miles. | No. of Inhabitants to the square mile. |
|---|---|---|---|---|
| From 22° 1' to 27° 11' | From 100° 35' to 103° 20' | 334,900 | 250,389 | $1\frac{1}{3}$ |

THIS intendancy comprehends the whole of the north-east part of the kingdom of New Spain. As it borders either on desert countries, or countries inhabited by wandering and independent Indians, we may say that its northern limits are hardly determined.

Of the whole intendancy of San Luis Potosi, only that part which adjoins the province of Zacatecas, in which are the rich mines of Charcas, Guadalcazar, and Catorce, is a cold and mountainous country. The bishopric of Monterey, which bears the pompous title of New Kingdom of Leon, Cohahuila, Santander, and Texas, are very low regions; and there is very little undulation of surface in them. They possess an unequal climate, extremely hot in summer, and equally cold in winter when the north winds drive before them columns of cold air from Canada towards the torrid zone.

The intendancy of San Luis Potosi comprehends parts of a very heterogeneous nature, the different denominations of which have given great room for geographical errors. It is composed of provinces, of which some belong to the *Provincias internas*, and others to the kingdom of New Spain Proper. Of the former there are two immediately depending on the commandant of the *Provincias internas;* the two others are considered as *Provincias internas del Vireynato*. These complicated and unnatural divisions are explained in the following table:

The intendant of San Luis Potosi governs,

A. In Mexico Proper:

The *Province of San Luis*, which extends from the Rio de Panuco to the Rio de Santander, and which comprehends the important mines of Charcas, Potosi, Ramos, and Catorce.

B. In the *Provincias internas del Vireynato:*

1. The New Kingdom of Leon.

2. The colony of New Santander.

C. In the *Provincias internas de la Commandancia general Oriental:*

1. The province of Cohahuila.

2. The province of Texas.

It follows, from what we have already said on the latest changes which have taken place in the organization of the *Commandancia general* of Chihuahua, that the intendancy of San Luis now includes, besides the province of Potosi, all which goes under the denomination of *Provincias internas Orientales*. A single intendant is consequently at the head of an administration which includes a greater surface than all European Spain. But this immense country, gifted by nature with the most precious productions, and situated under a serene sky in the temperate zone, towards the borders of the tropic, is, for the greatest part, a wild desert, still more thinly peopled than the governments of Asiatic Russia. Its position on the eastern limits of New Spain, the proximity of the United States, the frequency of communication with the colonists of Louisiana, and a great number of circumstances which I shall not endeavour here to develope, will probably soon favour the progress of civilization and prosperity in these vast and fertile regions.

The intendancy of San Luis comprehends more than 690 miles of coast, an extent equal to that from Genoa to Reggio in Calabria. But all this coast is without commerce and without activity, with the exception of a few small vessels, which come from the West Indies to lay in provisions either at the Bar of Tampico, near Panuco, or at the anchorage of New Santander.

The most remarkable places of the intendancy of San Luis are:

*San Luis Potosi*, the residence of the intendant, situated on the eastern declivity of the table-land of Anahuac, to the west of the sources of the Rio de Panuca. The habitual population of this town is 12,000.

*Nuevo Santander*, capital of the province of the same name, does not admit the entry of vessels drawing more than from eight to ten *palmas* \* of water. The village of *Sotto la Marina*, to the east of Santander, might become of great consequence to the trade of this coast, if the port could be improved. At present the province of Santander is so desert, that fertile districts of 90 or 100 square miles were sold there in 1802 for eight or ten shillings.

*Charcas*, or *Santa Maria de las Charcas*, a very considerable small town, the seat of a *diputacion de Minas*.

*Catorce*, or *la Purissima Concepcion de Alamos de Catorce*, one of the richest mines of New Spain. The *Real* de Catorce, however, has only been in existence since 1773, when Don Sebastian Coronado and Don Bernabe Antonio de Zepeda discovered these celebrated veins, which yield annually the value of more than from 700,000*l.* to 800,000*l.* sterling.

* From 5½ to 6.878 feet.

*Monterey*, the seat of a bishop, in the small kingdom of Leon.

*Linares*, in the same kingdom, between the Rio Tigre and the great Rio Bravo del Norte.

*Monclova*, a military post (*presidio*), capital of the province of Cohahuila, and residence of a governor.

*San Antonio de Begar*, capital of the province of Texas, between the Rio de los Nogales and the Rio de San Antonio.

*Diputaciones de Mineria*, or Districts.

6. Catorce.
7. San Luis Potosi.
8. Charcas.
9. Ojocaliente.
10. San Nicolas de Croix.

*Reales*, or places surrounded by mines :—

La Purissima Concepcion de Alamos de Catorce Matehualu; Cerro del Potosi; San Martin Bernalejo; Sierra Negra; Tule; San Martin; Santa Maria de las Charcas; Ramos; Ojocaliente; Cerro de San Pedro; Matanzillas; San Carlos de Vallecilio; San Antonio de la Yguana; Santiago de las Sabinas; Monterey; Jesus de Rio Blanco; Las Salinas; Bocca de Leones; San Nicolas de Croix; Borbon; San Joseph Tamaulipan; Nuestra Señora de Guadalupe de Sihue; La Purissima Concepcion de Re villagegido; El Venado; L. Tapona; Guadalcazar.

The mineral repository of Catorce holds at present the third rank among the mines of New Spain, classing them according to the quantity of silver which they produce. It was only discovered in the year 1778. This discovery, and that of the veins of Gualgayoc, in Peru, vulgarly called the Veins of Chota, are the most interesting in the history of the mines of Spanish America for the last two centuries. The small town of Catorce, the true name of which is *la Purissima Concepcion de Alamos de Catorce*, is situated on the calcareous table-land, which declines towards the *nuevo reyno de Leon*, and towards the province of New Santander. From the bosom of these mountains of secondary compact limestone, masses of basalt and porous amygdaloid rise up as in the Vicentin, which resemble volcanic productions, and contain olivine, zeolite, and obsidian. A great number of veins of small extent, and very variable in their breadth and direction, traverse the limestone, which itself covers a transition clay-slate; and the latter perhaps is superimposed on the syenitic rock of the *Buffa del Fraile*. The greatest number of these veins are western (*spathgänge*); and their inclination is from 25° to 30° towards the north-east. The minerals which form the lode are generally found in a state of decomposition. They are wrought with the mattock, the pickaxe, and with the gad (*pointrole*). The consumption of powder is much less than at Guanaxuato and at

Zacatecas. These mines possess also the great advantage of being almost entirely dry, so that they have no need of costly machines to draw off the water.

In 1773, Sebastian Caronado and Antonio Llanas, two very poor individuals, discovered veins in a situation now called *Cerro de Catorce Viejo*, on the western slope of the *Pichaco de la Variga de Plata*. They began to work these veins, which were poor and inconstant in their produce. In 1778, Don Barnabé Antonio de Zepeda, a miner of the *Ojo del Agua de Matchuala*, investigated during three months this group of arid and calcareous mountains. After attentively examining the ravines, he was fortunate enough to find the crest or surface of the *veta grande*, on which he immediately dug the pit of *Guadalupe*. He drew from it an immense quantity of muriate of silver, and *colorados* mixed with native gold; and gained in a short time more than 108,383*l*. From that period, the mines of Catorce were wrought with the greatest activity. That of *Padre Flores* alone produced in the first year upwards of 350,000*l*.; but the vein only displayed great riches from 160 to 330 feet of perpendicular depth. The famous mine of *Purissima*, belonging to Colonel Obregon, has scarcely ever ceased since 1788, to yield annually a net profit of 43,752*l*.; and its produce in 1796 amounted to 260,000*l*., while the expenses of working did not amount to more than 17,300*l*. The vein of *Purissima*, which is not the same with that of *Padre Flores*, sometimes reaches the extraordinary extent of 130 feet; and it was worked in 1802 to the depth of 226 fathoms. Since 1798, the value of the minerals of Catorce has singularly diminished: the native silver is now rarely to be seen; and the *metales colorados*, which are an intimate mixture of muriate of silver, earthy carbonate of lead, and red ochre, begin to give place to pyritous and coppery minerals. The actual produce of these mines is nearly 262,526 lbs. of silver annually.

# CHAPTER XIV.

*Intendancy of Mexico—extent—climate—physical aspect
—roads—principal towns—mines—Real del Monte,
Moran Biscaina, Tasco—state of mining operations—
geological structure.*

| Extent in north latitude. | Extent in west longitude. | Population in 1803. | Extent of surface in square miles. | No. of inhabitants to the square mile. |
|---|---|---|---|---|
| From 16° 34' to 21° 57' | From 100° 12' to 103° 25' | 1,511,800 | 53,343 | 28⅓ |

THE whole of this intendancy is situated under the
torrid zone. It extends from the 16° 34' to the
21° 57' of north latitude. It is bounded on the
north by the intendancy of San Luis Potosi, on the
west by the intendancies of Guanaxuato and Valladolid, and on the east by those of Vera Cruz and
La Puebla. It is washed towards the south by the
South Sea, or Great Ocean, for a length of coast
of 246 miles, from Acapulco to Zacatula.

Its greatest length from Zacatula to the mines

of the Doctor is 408 miles; and its greatest breadth from Zacatula to the mountains situated to the east of Chilpansingo is 276 miles. In its northern part, towards the celebrated mines of Zimapan and the Doctor, it is separated by a narrow stripe from the Gulf of Mexico. Near Mextitlan, this stripe is only 27 miles in breadth.

More than two thirds of the intendancy of Mexico are mountainous, and contain immense plains, elevated from 6561 to 7545 feet above the level of the ocean. From Chalco to Queretaro are almost uninterrupted plains of 450 miles in length, and 80 or 90 in breadth. In the neighbourhood of the western coast the climate is burning and very unhealthy. One summit only, the Nevado de Toluca, situated in a fertile plain, of 8857 feet in height, enters the region of perpetual snow. The elevation of the Pico del Fraile, or the highest summit of the Nevado de Toluca, is 15,156 feet. No mountain in this intendancy equals the height of Mont Blanc.

The valley of Mexico, or Tenochtitlan, is situated in the centre of the Cordillera of Anahuac, on the ridge of the porphyritical and basaltic amygdaloid mountains, which run from the S S.E. to the N.N.W. This valley is of an oval form; it contains 55 miles in length, and 37 in breadth. The territorial extent of the valley is 2,200 square miles, of which only 198 square miles are occupied by the lakes, which is less than a tenth of the whole surface.

The circumference of the valley, reckoning from the crest of the mountains which surround it like a circular wall, is 201 miles. This crest is most elevated on the south, particularly on the south-east, where the great volcanos of La Puebla, the Popocatepetl and Iztaccihuatl, bound the valley.

Six great roads cross the Cordillera which incloses the valley, of which the medium height is 9842 feet above the level of the ocean: 1. the road from Acapulco to Guchilaque and Cuervaracca, by the high summit called la Cruz del Marques; 2. the road of Toluca by Tianguillo and Lerma, a magnificent causeway, which I could not sufficiently admire, constructed with great art, partly over arches; 3. the road of Queretaro, Guanaxuato and Durango *el camino de tierra adentro,* which passes by Guautitlan, Huehuetoca, and the Puerto de Reyes, near Bata, through hills scarcely 262 feet above the pavement of the great square (*place*) of Mexico; 4. the road of Pachuco, which leads to the celebrated mines of Real del Monte, by the Cerro Ventoso, covered with oak, cyprus, and rose trees, almost continually in flower; 5. the old road of La Puebla, by S. Bonaventura and the Llanos de Apan; and, 6. the new road of La Puebla by Rio Frio and Tesmelucos, south-east from the Cerro del Telapon.

The following are the remarkable towns (*ciudades y villas*) of the intendancy of Mexico.

*Mexico*, capital of the kingdom of New Spain, height 7470 feet          Population. **137,000**

*Tezcuco*, which formerly possessed very considerable cotton manufactories. They have suffered much, however, in a competition with those of Queretaro          **5,000**

*Cuyoacan*, containing a convent of nuns, founded by Hernan Cortez, in which, according to his testament, the great captain wished to be interred, " in whatever part of the world he should end his days." This desire was never fulfilled.

*Tacubaya*, west from this capital, containing the archbishop's palace and a beautiful plantation of European olive-trees.

*Tacuba*, the ancient Tlacopan, capital of a small kingdom of the Tepanecs.

*Cuernavacca*, the ancient Quauhna huac, on the southern declivity of the Cordillera of Guchilaque, in a temperate and delicious climate, finely adapted for the cultivation of the fruit-trees of Europe.    Height 5429 feet.

*Chilpansingo* (Chilpantzinco), surrounded with fertile fields of wheat. Elevation 3542 feet.

*Tasco* (Tlachco), containing a beau-

tiful parish church, constructed and en-
dowed towards the middle of the 18th
century by Joseph de Laborde, a Frenchman, who gained immense wealth in a
short time by the Mexican mines. The
building of this church alone cost this
individual more than 83,000*l.* Towards
the end of his career, being reduced to
great poverty, he obtained from the
archbishop of Mexico permission to sell
for his benefit, to the metropolitan church
of the capital, the magnificent *custodia*
set with diamonds, which, in better
times, he had devoutly offered to the
tabernacle of the parish church of Tasco.
Elevation of the city, 2567 feet.

*Acapulco* (Acapolco), at the back of
a chain of granitical mountains, which,
from the reverberation of the radiating
caloric, increase the suffocating heat of
the climate. The famous cut in the
mountain (*abra de San Nicolas*), near
the bay *de la Langosta,* for the admis-
sion of the sea winds, was recently
finished. The population of this miserable town, inhabited almost exclusively
by people of colour, amounts to 9000,
at the time of the arrival of the Manilla
galleon (*Nao de China*).—Its habitual
population is only                    4,000

*Zacatula,* a small sea-port of the South Sea, on the frontiers of the intendancy of Valladolid, between the ports of Siguantanejo and Colima.

*Lerma,* at the entry of the valley of Toluca, in a marshy ground.

*Toluca* (Tolocan) at the foot of the porphyry mountain of San Miguel de Tutucuitlalpilco, in a valley abounding with maize and maguey (agave).—Height 8813 feet.

*Pachuca,* with Tasco, the oldest mining-place in the kingdom, as the neighbouring village Pachuquillo is supposed to have been the first Christian village founded by the Spaniards.—--Height 8141 feet.

*Cadereita,* with fine quarries of porphyry of a clay base (*thonporphyr*).

*San Juan del Rio,* surrounded with gardens, adorned with vines and anona. Height 6489 feet.

*Queretaro,* celebrated for the beauty of its edifices, its aqueduct, and cloth manufactures. Height 6374 feet. Habitual population,        35,000

This city contains 11,600 Indians, 85 secular ecclesiastics, 181 monks, and 143 nuns. The consumption of Queretaro amounted in 1793 to 13,618 loads of wheaten flour, 69,445 bushels

of maize, 656 loads of chile (capsicum), 1770
barrels of brandy, 1682 beeves, 14,949 sheep,
and 8869 hogs.

The most important mines of this intendancy,
considering them only in the relation of their
present wealth, are,

*La veta Biscaina de Real del Monte,* near
*Pachuca; Zimapan, El Doctor,* and *Tehulilote-
pec,* near *Tasco.*

*Diputaciones de Mineria,* or Districts :

           11. Pachuca.
           12. El Doctor.
           13. Zimapan.
           14. Tasco.
           15. Zacualpan.
           16. Sultepec.
           17. Temascaltepec.

*Reales,* or places surrounded by Mines :

Pachuca ; Real del Monte ; Moran ; Atolonilco
el Chico ; Atolonilco el Grande ; Zimapan ;
Lomo del Toro ; Las Cañas ; San Joseph del
Oro ; Verdozas ; Capula ; Santa Rosa ; El Potosi ;
Las Plomosas ; El Doctor ; Las Alpujarras ; El
Pinal or los Amotes ; Huascazoluya ; San Miguel
del Rio Blanco ; Las Aguas ; Maconi ; San
Christobal ; Cardonal ; Xacala ; Jutchitlan el
Grande ; San Joseph del Obraje Viejo ; Cerro
Blanco ; Cerro del Sotolar ; San Francisco Xichu ;

Jesus Maria de la Targea ; Coronilla or la Purissima Concepcion de Tetela del Rio ; Tepantitlan ; San Vicente ; Tasco ; Tehuilotepec ; Coscallan ; Haucingo, Huautla ; Sochipala ; Tetlilco ; San Esteban ; Real del Limon ; San Geronimo ; Temas Caltepec ; Real de Ariba ; La Albarrada ; Yxtapa ; Ocotepec ; Chalchitepeque ; Zacualpan ; Tecicapan ; Chontalpa ; Santa Cruz de Azulaques ; Saltepec ; Juluapa ; Papaloapa ; Los Ocotes ; Capulatengo ; Alcozauca ; Totomixtlahuaca.

The mines of Pachuca, Real del Monte and Moran, are highly celebrated for their antiquity, their wealth, and their proximity to the capital. Since the beginning of the 18th century, the vein of La Biscaina, or Real del Monte has alone been wrought with activity. The working of the mines of Moran was resumed only within these few years; and the mineral depository of Pachuca, one of the richest in all America, has been wholly abandoned since the terrible fires which took place in the famous mine del Encino, which alone furnished more than 19,689lbs. troy weight of silver annually. The wooden work which supported the roof of the galleries was consumed by fire, and the greater number of the miners were suffocated before being able to reach the shafts. A similar conflagration in 1787 put a stop to the working of the mines of Bolaños, which were only again begun to be cleared out in 1792.

The valley of Mexico is separated from the

basin of *Totonilco el Grande,* by a chain of porphyritic mountains, of which the highest summit
is the peak of the Jacal, elevated according to my
measurement with the assistance of the barometer,
10,248 feet above the level of the sea. This porphyry serves for base to the porous amygdaloid,
which surrounds the lakes of Tezcuco, Zumpango,
and San Christobal. It seems to be of the same
formation with that which, in the road from
Mexico to Acapulco, immediately covers the granite
between Sopilote and Chilpansingo, near the village
of Acaguisotla, and l'Alto de los Caxones. To
the north-east of the district of Real del Monte,
the porphyry is at first concealed under the columnar basalt of the farm of Regla, and further on
in the valley of Totonilco, under beds of secondary
formation. The Alpine limestone of a greyish
blue, in which is the famous cavern of Danto,
called also the pierced mountain, or the Bridge of
the Mother of God*, seems to repose immediately
on the porphyry of Moran. It contains near the
Puerto de la Mesa, veins of galena; and we find
it covered with three other formations of not so old
an origin, which, naming them in the order of their
superposition, are Jura limestone, near the baths
of Totonilco, the slaty limestone of Amojaque,
and a gypsum of secondary formation mixed with
clay. The position of these secondary rocks which

* *Puente de la Madre de Dios.*

I carefully observed, is so much the more remarkable, as it is the same with that which has been discovered on the Old Continent, according to the excellent observations of MM. de Buch and Freiesleben.

The mountains of the district of mines of Real del Monte, contain beds of porphyry, which, with respect to their relative antiquity, differ a good deal from one another. The rock which forms the roof and the wall of the argentiferous veins, is a decomposed porphyry, of which the base sometimes appears clayey and sometimes analogous to splintery hornstone. The presence of hornblende is frequently announced, merely by greenish stains intermingled with common and vitreous feldspar. At very great elevations, for example in the beautiful forest of oak and pine of Oyamel, we find porphyries with a base of pearl-stone, containing obsidian in layers and nodules.

What relation exists between these last beds, which several distinguished mineralogists consider as volcanic productions, and the porphyries of Pachuca, Real del Monte, and Moran, in which nature has deposited enormous masses of sulphuret of silver and argentiferous pyrites? This problem, which is one of the most difficult in geology, will only be resolved when a great number of zealous and intelligent travellers shall have gone over the Mexican Cordilleras, and carefully studied the immense variety of porphyries which are destitute of quartz, and which abound both in hornblende and vitreous feldspar.

The district of mines of Real del Monte does not display—as at Freiberg in Saxony, Derbyshire in England, or as in the mountains of Zimapan and Tasco in New Spain—a great number of rich veins of small size, on a small tract of ground. It rather resembles the mountains of the Hartz, and Schemnitz, in Europe, or those of Guanaxuato and Potosi, in America, of which the riches are contained in a few mineral depositions of very considerable dimensions. The four veins of Biscaina, Rosario, Cabrera, and Encino, run through the districts of Real del Monte, from Moran and Pachuca, at extraordinary distances, without changing their direction, and almost without coming in contact with other veins which traverse or derange them.

The *veta de la Biscaina*, of less considerable dimensions, but perhaps still richer than the vein of Guanaxuato, was successfully wrought from the sixteenth to the beginning of the eighteenth century. In 1726 and 1727, the two mines of Biscaina and Xacal still produced together 333,969 ounces of silver. The great quantity of water which filtrated through the crevices of the porphyritic rock, joined to the imperfection of the means of drawing it off, compelled the miners to abandon the works when they were yet only 65 fathoms in depth. A very enterprising individual, Don Joseph

Alexandro Bustamente, was courageous enough to undertake a level near Moran ; but he died before completing this great work, which is 7715 feet in length from its mouth to the point where it crosses the vein *de la Biscaina.* The direction of this vein is hor. 6; and its inclination is 85° to the south: its extent is from 13 to 19 feet. The direction of the porphyry of this district is generally hor. 7-8, with an inclination of 60° to the northeast, particularly in the road from Pachuca to Real del Monte. The level is at first cut through the solid rock (*querschlagsweise*) in a direction of hor. 7, towards the west; but further on it takes its way over three different veins, hor. 11-12, of which one alone, the *veta de le Soledad**, has furnished a sufficiency of silver ores to pay all the expenses of the undertaking. The level was only finished in 1762, by Don Pedro Tereros, the partner of Bustamente. The former, known by the title of Count de Regla as one of the richest men of his age, had already drawn, in 1774, a net profit of more than 1,041,750*l.* from the mine of Biscaina. Besides the two ships of war which he presented to King Charles the Third, one of them of 120 guns, he

* It is believed that this vein is the same with that which M. D'Eluyhar began to work in the pit of Cambrera, at Moran. It appeared to me, however, that the *veta de Cabrera* is rather the same with that of *Santa Brigida,* and that its principal wealth is to be found in following it towards the mine of Jesus.

lent 208,350*l.* sterling to the Court of Madrid, which have never yet been repaid him. He erected the great works of Regla at an expense of 416,700*l.* sterling; and he purchased estates of an immense extent, and left a fortune to his children, which has only been equalled in Mexico by that of the Count de la Valenciana.

The level of Moran traverses the vein of *La Biscaina*, in the San Ramon shaft, at a depth of 115 fathoms, below the level of the surface, on which the whims are placed. The profit of the proprietor has been annually diminishing since 1774. In place of driving levels for trial, to discover the vein on a great extent, they continued their sinking to a depth of nearly 53 fathoms below the level. At that depth the vein preserved its great wealth in sulphuret of silver mixed with native silver; but the abundance of water increased to such a degree that 28 whims, each of which required more than 40 horses, were not sufficient to draw it off. In 1783, the weekly expense amounted to 1875*l.* After the death of the old Count de Regla, the works were suspended till 1791, when they ventured to re-establish all the whims. The expense of these machines, which drew up the water not by means of pumps but by bags suspended by ropes, then amounted to more than 31,252*l.* per annum. At length they reached the deepest point of the mine, which according to my measurements is only 1064 feet above

the level of the lake of Zumpango ; but the ores
which they extracted did not compensate the expense of the process, and the mine was again abandoned in 1801.

It is surprising that they never thought of substituting for this wretched plan of drawing off the
water by bags, proper pump apparatus put in motion by horse whims, by hydraulic wheels, or by
machines moved by a column of water *(colonne
d'eau)*. A level begun at Pachuca, or lower down
towards Gazave in the valley of Mexico, would
have exhausted the mine of Biscaina at the pit of
San Ramon, for a depth of 202 fathoms. The
same object could be attained at less expense by
following the project of M. D'Elhuyar, in placing
the mouth of a new level near Omitlan, in the road
which leads from Moran to the place of amalgamation at Regla. This last level, before reaching
12,466 feet in length, would cut the vein of Biscaina.

The very wise plan which the Count de Regla at
present follows is, to leave off the clearing of the
old works, and to investigate the mineral repository, in points where it has never yet been worked
(*in unverfahrenem felde*). In studying at Real
del Monte the surface and undulations of the
ground, we observe that the vein of Biscaina has
furnished for three centuries its greatest riches
from a single spot, that is to say, from a natural
hollow (*enfoncement*) contained between the shafts

of Dolores, Joya, San Cayetano, Santa Teresa, and
Guadalupe. The shaft from which the greatest
quantity of silver ores has been extracted is that of
Santa Teresa. To the east and west of this central
point the vein is contracted for a distance of more
than 1300 feet. It preserves its primitive direction,
but becomes destitute of metals, and reduced to
an almost imperceptible vein. For a long time it
was believed that the vein of Biscaina was insensibly
lost in the rock ; but they discovered in 1798 very
rich metals, at a distance of more than 1640 feet,
to the east and west of the centre of the old works.
They then sunk the shafts San Ramon and San Pedro, and discovered that the vein resumed its
old power, and that an immense field was opened
to new undertakings. When I visited the mines
in the month of May 1803, the San Ramon shaft
was then only 16 fathoms in depth ; and it will be
nearly 131 fathoms to the bottom of the level of
Moran, which is itself still distant 147 feet from
the point which corresponds to the intersection of
the new shaft, and the roof of the level. In its
present state, the mine of the Count de Regla annually yields more than from 30,000 to 40,000lbs.
troy of silver.

The vein of Biscaina contains in the points of
the principal mines, milk-quartz, which frequently
passes into splintery hornstone, amethyst, carbonate
of lime, a little sulphate of barytes, sulphuret of
silver mixed with native silver, and sometimes pris-

matic black silver (*sprödglaserz*), deep-red silver, galena, and iron and copper pyrites. The same silver ores are found near the surface of the ground in a state of decomposition, and mixed with oxide of iron, like the *pacos* of Peru. Near the San Pedro shaft, the pyrites are sometimes richer in silver than the sulphuret of silver.

The mines of Moran, formerly of great celebrity, have been abandoned for 40 years, on account of the abundance of water which could not be drawn off. In this district of mines, which is in the vicinity of that of Real del Monte, near the mouth of the great level of Biscaina, there was placed in 1801 a machine *à colonne d'eau*, of which the cylinder is 10.23 inches in height, and 6.29 in diameter. This machine, the first of the kind ever constructed in America, is much superior to those of the mines of Hungary. It was executed agreeably to the calculations and plans of M. del Rio, professor of mineralogy in Mexico, who has visited the most celebrated mines of Europe, and who possesses at once the most solid and the most various acquirements. The merit of the execution is due to M. Lachausée, a Brabant artist of great talents, who has also fitted up for the school of mines of Mexico a very remarkable collection of models, for the use of students of mechanics and hydrodynamics. It is to be regretted that this fine machine, in which the regulator of the suckers is put in motion by a particular mechanism, was placed in a situation

where there is great difficulty in procuring a sufficiency of water to keep it going. When I was at
Moran, the pumps could only work three hours a
day. The construction of the machine and the
aqueducts cost 10,937l. sterling : they did not at
first calculate on more than half of the expense,
and they imagined the mass of water to be very
considerable ; but the year in which the water was
measured being exceedingly rainy, it was believed
to be much more abundant than it actually was.
It is to be hoped that the new canal which was
going on in 1803, and which will be 16,404 feet
in length, will remedy this want of water, and that
the vein of Moran (hor. $9\frac{4}{8}$ inclined 84° to the
north-east), will be found as rich at great depths,
as the shareholders of the mine suppose. M. del
Rio, on my arrival in New Spain, had no other view
but that of proving to the Mexican miners the
effect of machines of this nature, and the possibility of constructing them in the country. This
object has been in part attained ; and it will be
much more evidently attained when such a machine
shall be placed in the mine of Rayas, at Guanaxuato, in that of the Count de Regla, at Real del
Monte, or in those of Bolaños, where M. Sonneschmidt counted nearly 4000 horses and mules
employed in moving the whims.

The mines of the *district of Tasco*, situated on
the western slope of the Cordillera, have lost their
ancient splendour since the end of the last century ;

for in their present state the veins of Tehuilotepec, Sochipala, Cerro del Limon, San Estevan, and Gautla, do not altogether yield more than 36,923 lbs. troy of silver annually.   During the year 1752 and the ten following years, the mines of Tasco were wrought with the greatest activity and success. This activity was owing to the enterprising mind of Joseph Laborde, a Frenchman, who came into Mexico very poor, and who in 1743 acquired immense wealth in the mine of la Cañada of the *Real de Tlapujahua*.  We have already alluded to the reverses of fortune several times experienced by this extraordinary man.   After building a church at Tasco, which cost him 87,507*l*. sterling, he was reduced to the lowest poverty, by the rapid decline of those very mines from which he had annually drawn from 130,000 to 200,000lbs. troy of silver.   The archbishop having given him permission to sell a golden sun enriched with diamonds, with which he had adorned the tabernacle of the church of Tasco, he withdrew to Zacatecas with the produce of this sale, which amounted to 22,000*l*. sterling.  The district of mines of Zacatecas was then so entirely neglected, that it scarcely furnished 33,000 lbs. troy of silver annually to the mint at Mexico.  Laborde undertook to clear out the famous mine of Quebradilla; in which undertaking he lost all his property, without attaining his object.   With the small capital which remained to him, he began to work on the *veta*

*grande,* and sunk the pit of *La Esperanza;* when
a second time he acquired immense wealth.    The
silver produce of the mine of Zacatecas rose then
to nearly 330,000 lbs. troy per annum ; and though
the abundance of metals did not long continue the
same, he left at his death a fortune of nearly
125,000*l.* sterling.    He compelled his daughter
to enter into a convent, that he might leave his
whole fortune to an only son, who afterwards voluntarily embraced the ecclesiastical office.    In
Mexico, and every where else in the Spanish provinces, it is extremely rare to see children following the profession of their fathers ; and we do not
find there, as in Sweden, Germany, and Scotland,
families in which the business of miner is here-
ditary.

The veins of Tasco and the Real de Tehuilotepec
traverse barren mountains, furrowed by very deep
ravines.

The mining districts of Tasco and of the Real
de Tehuilotepec contain a great number of veins,
which, with the exception of the Cerro de la Compaña, are all directed from the north-west to the
south-east, hor 7—9.    These veins, like those of
Catorce, traverse both the limestone and the micaceous slate which serves for its base ; and they exhibit the same metals in both rocks.    These metals have been much more abundant in the limestone.    The mines have become extremely poor
since it became necessary to work the veins in the

micaceous slate. A very intelligent and very active miner, Don Vicente de Anza, wrought the mines of Tehuilotepec to the depth of 122 fathoms; and he cut two excellent levels for a length of 3,936 feet; but unfortunately he found that the same veins which had furnished considerable riches at the surface of the earth, were at great depths as poor in red silver ores, as they were abundant in galena, pyrites, and yellow blende.

An extraordinary event which happened on the 16th February 1802, completed the ruin of the miners of this district. The mines of Tehuilotepec, like those of Guautla, have at all times wanted the necessary water to put in motion the stamping mills and other machines which prepare the minerals for the process of amalgamation. The most abundant stream used in the works, issued from a cavern in the limestone rock called the *Cueva de San Felipe*. This rivulet was lost in the night between the 16th and 17th of February; and five days afterwards a new spring was found at five leagues distance from the cavern, near the village of Platanillo. It has been proved by researches of the greatest interest for geology, that there exists in this country, between the villages of Chamacasapa, Platanillo, and Tehuilotepec, in the bosom of calcareous mountains, a series of caverns and natural galleries, and that subterraneous rivers, like those of the county of Derby in England, traverse those galleries, which communicate with one another.

The veins of Tehuilotepec are in general western (*spathgünge*) ; they are from six to ten feet in extent, and being separated from the rock by a list of clayey loam, they form several lateral branches, which enrich the principal vein where they fall into it (*se trainent*). Their structure has this peculiarity, that the metallic mineral is rarely disseminated throughout all the lode, but is collected in a single band, which is sometimes near the roof, and sometimes near the wall of the vein. In general, the mineral depositories of Tasco and Tehuilotepec are extremely variable in their produce. As to the nature of the mass of which they are constituted, I perceived four very different formations of veins : viz.

1. Brown, red, and yellow oxides of iron, in which native and sulphuretted silver are disseminated in impalpable particles ; cellular brown ironstone, specular iron, a little galena, and magnetic iron, and blue carbonate of copper. This formation, analogous to that of the *pacos* of Fuentestiana, and Pasco in Peru, is designated at Tehuilotepec, by the name of *tepostel*. It is found at small depths from the surface (*in ausgehenden*) in the mines of San Miguel, San Estevan, and La Compaña, near Tasco, as well as at the Cerro de Garganta, near Mescala. The *tepostel* is generally not so rich as the Pasco of Peru ; but is so much the richer at Tasco, as the oxide of iron is more mixed with azure of copper : it generally, however, does not

contain more than 80 ounces of silver per ton.

2. Calcareous spar, a little galena, and transparent lamellar gypsum, containing drops of water with air, and filiform native silver.

3. Light-red silver, brittle vitreous silver (*spröd-glaserz*), much yellow blende, galena, very little of iron pyrites, calcareous spar, and milk-quartz. This formation, which is the richest of all, displays the remarkable phenomenon, that the minerals the most abundant in silver, form spheroidal balls, from 3.93 to 4.71 inches in diameter, in which red silver, mixed with brittle vitreous silver, and native silver alternate with bands of quartz. These balls, which have seldom been found but at a depth of from 50 to 200 feet, are nidulated in a course of calcareous and brown spar.

4. Much argentiferous galena, which is richer in silver in proportion as the detached pieces are of smaller grain ; much yellow blende ; little pyrites, quartz and calcareous spar, in the mines of Socabon del Re and de la Marquesa.

All these veins run through a table-land of from 5,550 to 5,910 feet elevation above the level of the sea, which enjoys a temperate climate very favourable to the cultivation of the grains of the old continent.

# CHAPTER XV.

*Intendancy of Guadalaxara—extent—climate—agricul-
tural produce—principal towns—mines.*

## V. *Intendancy of Guadalaxara.*

| Extent in north latitude. | Extent in west longitude. | Population in 1803. | Extent of surface in square miles. | No. of inhabitants to the square mile. |
|---|---|---|---|---|
| From 19° 0' to 23° 12' | From 103° 30' to 108° 0' | 630,500 | 86,408 | 7⅓ |

THIS province, part of the kingdom of Nueva Galicia, has almost twice the extent of Portugal, with
a population five times smaller. It is bounded on
the north by the intendancies of Sonora and Durango, on the east by those of Zacatecas and Guanaxuato, on the south by the province of Valladolid, and on the west, for a length of coast of 370
miles, by the Pacific Ocean. Its greatest breadth is
300 miles, from the port of San Blas to the town of
Lagos; and its greatest length is from south to

north, from the Volcan de Colima to San Andres
Teal, 354 miles.

The intendancy of Guadalaxara is crossed from
east to west by the Rio de Santiago, a considerable
river which communicates with the lake of Chapala,
and which will one day (in an advanced state of civilization) become interesting for internal navigation from Salamanca and Zelaya to the port of San
Blas.

All the eastern part of this province is the table-
land and western declivity of the Cordilleras of Anahuac.    The maritime regions, especially those
which stretch towards the great bay of Bayonne,
are covered with forests, and abound with the finest
wood for ship-building.    The inhabitants of these
districts are exposed to an unhealthy and excessively
heated air.    The interior of the country enjoys a
temperate climate, favourable to health.

The Volcan de Colima, of which the position
has never yet been determined by astronomical observations, is the most western of the volcanoes of
New Spain which are placed on the same line in
the direction of one parallel.    It frequently throws
up ashes and smoke.    This insulated mountain appears only of a moderate height when its summit
is compared with the ground of Zapotilti and Za-
potlan, two villages of 5,505 feet elevation above
the level of the coast.    It is from the small town
of Colima that the volcano appears in all its grandeur.    It is never covered with snow, but when it

falls in the chain of the neighbouring mountains
from the effects of the north wind.

According to a manuscript memoir communicated to the tribunal of the Consulado of Vera Cruz
by the intendant of Guadalaxara, the value of the
agricultural produce of this intendancy amounted,
in 1802, to 569,000*l*. sterling; in which there were
computed 1,657,000 bushels of maize, 43,000 loads
of wheat, 17,000 *tercios* of cotton, and 20,000
pounds of cochineal of Autlan. The value of the
manufacturing industry was estimated at 722,350*l*.
sterling.

The province of Guadalaxara contains 2 ciudades, 6 villas, and 322 villages. The most celebrated mines are those of Bolaños, Asientos de Ibarra,
Hostiotipaquillo, Copala, and Guichichila near
Tepic.

The most remarkable towns are:

*Guadalaxara,* on the left bank of the
Rio de Santiago, the residence of the intendant, of the bishop, and the high
court of Justice (*Audicenia*).—Population    .    .    .    .    19,500

*San Blas,* a port, the residence of the *Depar-
timiento de Marina,* at the mouth of the Rio de
Santiago. The official people (*officiales reales*)
remain at Tepic, a small town, of which the climate is not so hot and is more salubrious. Within
these ten years the question has been discussed, if
it would be useful to transfer the dock-yards, ma-

gazines, and the whole marine department from San Blas to Acapulco. This last port wants wood for ship-building. The air there is also equally unhealthy as at San Blas; but the projected change, by favouring the concentration of the naval force, would give the Government a greater facility in knowing the wants of the marine and the means of supplying them.

*Compostella*, to the south of Tepic. To the north-west of Compostella, as well as in the partidos of Autlan, Ahuxcatlan, and Acaponeta, a tobacco of a superior quality was formerly cultivated.

*Aguas Calientes*, a small well-peopled town to the south of the mines de los Asientos de Ibarra.

*Villa de la Purificacion*, to the north-west of the port of Guatlan, formerly called Santiago de Buena Esperanza, celebrated from the voyage of discovery made in 1532 by Diego Hurtado de Mendoza.

*Lagos*, to the north of the town of Leon, on a plain fertile in wheat on the frontiers of the intendancy of Guanaxuato.

*Colima*, two leagues south from the Volcan de Colima.

*Diputaciones de Mineria*, or Districts.
18. Bolaños.
19. Asientos de Ibarra.
20. Hostotipaquillo.

*Reales*, or places surrounded by Mines:—
Bolaños; Xalpa; San Joseph de Guichichila; Santa Maria de Guadalupe, or de la Yesca; Asi-

2 P

entos de Ibarra; San Nicolas de los Angeles; La
Ballena; Talpan; Hostotipaquillo; Copala; Gu-
axacatan; Amaxac; Limon; Tepanteria; Ioco-
tan; Tecomatan; Ahuatacancillo; Guilotitan;
Platanarito; Santo Domingo; Iuchipila; Mezqui-
tal; Xalpa; San Joseph Tepostitlan; Guachinan-
go; San Nicolas del Roxo; Amatlan; Natividad;
San Joaquin; Santissima Trinidad de Pozole;
Tule; Motage; Frontal; Los Aillo-Ezatlannes;
Possesion; La Serranilla; Aquitapilco; Eliso;
Chimaltitan; Santa Fe; San Rafael; San Pedro
Analco; Santa Cruz de las Flores.

# CHAPTER XVI.

*Intendancy of Valladolid—extent—climate—Volcan de Jorullo—vegetable productions—earthquakes—volcanoes —population—principal towns—mines.*

| Extent in north latitude. | Extent in west longitude. | Population in 1803. | Extent of surface in square miles. | No. of Inhabitants to the square mile. |
|---|---|---|---|---|
| From 18° 25' to 19° 50' | From 102° 15' to 104° 50' | 376,400 | 31,014 | 12 |

THIS intendancy at the period of the Spanish conquest made a part of the kingdom of Michuacan (Mechoacan), which extended from the Rio de Zacatula to the port de la Natividad, and from the mountains of Xala and Colima to the river of Lerma, and the lake of Chapala. The capital of this kingdom of Michuacan,—which, like the republics of Tlaxcallan, Huexocingo and Cholollan, was always independent of the Mexican empire,—was Tzintzontzan, a town situated on the banks of a lake singularly picturesque, called the lake of Patzquarro. Tzintzontzan, which the Aztec inhabitants of Tenochtitlan called Huitzitzila, is now only a poor Indian village, though it still preserves the pompous title of city (*ciudad*).

The intendancy of Valladolid, vulgarly called in
the country Michuacan, is bounded on the north by
the Rio de Lerma, which further east takes the
name of Rio Grande de Santiago.   On the east
and north-east it joins the intendancy of Mexico;
on the north the intendancy of Guanaxuato; and
on the west that of Guadalaxara.   The greatest
length of the province of Valladolid from the port
of Zacatula to the basaltic mountains of Palangeo,
in a direction from S. S. E. to N. N. E. is 234
miles.   It is washed by the South Sea for an extent
of coast of more than 114 miles.

Situated on the western declivity of the Cordillera of Anahuac, intersected with hills and charming
valleys, which exhibit to the eye of the traveller a
very uncommon appearance under the torrid zone,
that of extensive and well watered meadows,—the
province of Valladolid in general enjoys a mild and
temperate climate, exceedingly conducive to the
health of the inhabitants.   It is only when we descend the table-land of Ario and approach the coast,
that we find a climate in which the new colonists,
and frequently even the natives, are subject to the
scourge of intermittent and putrid fevers.

The most elevated summit of the intendancy of
Valladolid is the Pic de *Tancitaro,* to the east of
Tuspan.   To the east of the Pic de Tancitaro the
*Volcan de Jorullo* (Xorullo, or Juruyo) was formed
in the night of the 29th of September 1759.   The
great catastrophe in which this mountain rose from

the earth, and by which a considerable extent of ground totally changed its appearance, is perhaps one of the most extraordinary physical revolutions in the annals of the history of our planet.

This remarkable phenomenon has remained unknown to the mineralogists and naturalists of Europe, though it took place not more than fifty years ago, and within six days' journey of the capital of Mexico, descending from the central tableland towards the shores of the South Sea.

A vast plain extends from the hills of Aguasarco, to near the villages of Teipa and Petatlan, both equally celebrated for their fine plantations of cotton. This plain, between the *Picachos del Mortero*, the *Cerros de las Cuevas, y de Cuiche*, is only from 2,460 to 2,624 feet above the level of the sea. In the middle of a tract of ground in which porphyry with a base of *grünstein* predominates, basaltic cones appear, the summits of which are crowned with evergreen oaks of a laurel and olive foliage, intermingled with small palm-trees with flabelliform leaves. This beautiful vegetation forms a singular contrast with the aridity of the plain, which was laid waste by volcanic fire.

Till the middle of the 18th century, fields cultivated with sugar-cane and indigo occupied the extent of ground between the two brooks called Cuitamba and San Pedro. They were bounded by basaltic mountains, the structure of which seems to indicate that all this country at a very remote pe-

riod had been several times convulsed by volcanoes. These fields, watered by artificial means, belonged to the plantation (*hacienda*) of San Pedro
de Jorullo, one of the greatest and richest of the
country. In the month of June 1759, a subterraneous noise was heard : hollow noises of a most
alarming nature (*bramidos*) were accompanied by
frequent earthquakes, which succeeded one another
for from 50 to 60 days, to the great consternation
of the inhabitants of the *hacienda*. From the beginning of September every thing seemed to announce the complete re-establishment of tranquil-
lity, when in the night between the 28th and 29th
the horrible subterraneous noise recommenced.
The affrighted Indians fled to the mountains of
Aguasarco. A tract of ground from three to four
square miles in extent, which goes by the name of
*Malpays*, rose up in the shape of a bladder. The
bounds of this convulsion are still distinguishable
in the fractured strata. The *Malpays* near its
edges is only 40 feet above the old level of the
plain called the *playas de Jorullo ;* but the con-
vexity of the ground thus thrown up increases progressively towards the centre to an elevation of 524
feet.

Those who witnessed this great catastrophe from
the top of Aguasarco assert that flames were seen
to issue forth for an extent of more than half a square
league, that fragments of burning rocks were thrown
up to prodigious heights, and that through a thick

cloud of ashes, illumined by the volcanic fire, the
softened surface of the earth was seen to swell up like
an agitated sea. The rivers of Cuitamba and San
Pedro precipitated themselves into the burning
chasms. The decomposition of the water contributed to invigorate the flames, which were distinguishable at the city of Pascuaro, though situated
on a very extensive table-land 4,600 feet elevated
above the plains of *las playas* de Jorullo. Eruptions of mud, and especially of strata of clay en-
veloping balls of decomposed basaltes in concen-
trical layers, appear to indicate that subterraneous
water had no small share in producing this extraordinary revolution. Thousands of small cones, from
6 to 10 feet in height, called by the natives ovens
(*hornitos*), issued forth from the *Malpays*. Although within the last fifteen years, according to
the testimony of the Indians, the heat of these volcanic ovens has suffered a great diminution, I have
seen the thermometer rise to 202° Fahr. on being plunged into fissures which exhale an aqueous
vapour. Each small cone is a *fumorola*, from
which a thick vapour ascends to the height of
40 or 50 feet. In many of them a subterraneous
noise is heard, which appears to announce the proximity of a fluid in ebullition.

In the midst of the ovens, six large masses elevated from 1,300 to 1,600 feet each above the old
level of the plains, sprung up from a chasm, of which
the direction is from N.N.E. to S.S.E. This

is the phenomenon of the Montenovo of Naples, several times repeated in a range of volcanic hills. The most elevated of these enormous masses, which bears some resemblance to the *puys* de l'Auvergne, is the great Volcan de Jorullo. It is continually burning, and has thrown up from the north side an immense quantity of scorified and basaltic lavas containing fragments of primitive rocks. These great eruptions of the central volcano continued till the month of February 1760. In the following years they became gradually less frequent. The Indians, frightened at the horrible noises of the new volcano, abandoned at first all the villages situated within seven or eight leagues distance of the *playas* de Jorullo. They became gradually, however, accustomed to this terrific spectacle; and having returned to their cottages, they advanced towards the mountains of Aguasarco and Santa Iñes, to admire the streams of fire discharged from an infinity of great and small volcanic apertures. The roofs of the houses of Queretaro were then covered with ashes at a distance of more than 144 miles in a straight line from the scene of the explosion. Although the subterraneous fire now appears far from violent, and the Malpays and the great volcano begin to be covered with vegetables, we nevertheless found the ambient air heated to such a degree by the action of the small ovens (*hornitos*), that the thermometer at a great distance from the surface and in the shade, rose as high as

109° Fahr.  This fact appears to prove that there
is no exaggeration in the accounts of several old
Indians, who affirm that, for many years after the
first eruption, the plains of Jorullo, even at a
great distance from the scene of the explosion,
were uninhabitable from the excessive heat which
prevailed in them.

The traveller is still shown, near the Cerro de
Santa Iñes, the rivers of Cuitamba and San Pedro,
the limpid waters of which formerly watered the
sugar-cane plantation of Don André Pimentel.
These streams disappeared in the night of the 29th
September 1759; but at a distance of 6,560 feet
further west, in the tract which was the theatre of
the convulsion, two rivers having the appearance of
mineral waters, in which the thermometer rises
to 126°.8 Fahr., are now seen bursting through the
argillaceous vault of the *hornitos*.  The Indians
continue to give them the names of San Pedro and
Cuitamba, because in several parts of the Malpays
great masses of water are heard to run in a direction from east · to west, from the mountains of
Santa Iñes towards *l'Hacienda de la Presentacion*.
Near this habitation there is a brook, which dis-
engages itself from the sulphureous hydrogen.  It
is more than $21\frac{1}{2}$ feet in breadth, and is the most
abundant hydro-sulphureous spring which I have
ever seen.

In the opinion of the Indians, these extraordinary transformations which we have been de-

2 Q

scribing,—the surface of the earth raised up and
burst by the volcanic fire, and the mountains of
scoria and ashes heaped together,—are the work of
the monks; the greatest, no doubt, which they have
ever produced in the two hemispheres! In the
cottage which we occupied in the *playas* de Jorullo,
our Indian host related to us, that in 1759, Capu-
chin missionaries came to preach at the plantation
of San Pedro, and not having met with a favourable reception (perhaps not having got so good a
dinner as they expected), they poured out the most
horrible and unheard-of imprecations against the
then beautiful and fertile plain, and prophesied,
that in the first place the plantation would be
swallowed up by flames rising out of the earth, and
that afterwards the ambient air would cool to such
a degree that the neighbouring mountains would
for ever remain covered with snow and ice. The
former of these maledictions having already produced such fatal effects, the lower Indians contemplate in the increasing coolness of the volcano
the sinister presage of a perpetual winter. I have
thought proper to relate this vulgar tradition, because it forms a striking feature in the picture of
the manners and prejudices of these remote countries. It proves the active industry of a class of
men who too frequently abuse the credulity of the
people, and pretend to suspend by their influence
the immutable laws of Nature for the sake of found-
ing their empire on the fear of physical evils.

The extent of the intendancy of Valladolid is one-fifth less than that of Ireland ; but its relative population is twice as large as that of Finland. In this province there are 3 *ciudades* (Valladolid, Tzintzontzan, and Pascuaro) ; 3 *villas* (Citaquaro, Zamora, and Charo) ; 263 villages ; 205 parishes ; and 326 farms. The imperfect enumeration of 1793 gave a total population of 289,314 souls, of whom 40,399 were male Whites, and 39,081 female Whites ; 61,352 male Indians, and 58,016 female Indians ; and 154 monks, 138 nuns, and 293 individuals of the secular clergy.

The Indians who inhabit the province of Valladolid form three races of different origin ;—the Tarascs, celebrated in the sixteenth century for the gentleness of their manners, for their industry in the mechanical arts, and for the harmony of their language, abounding in vowels ; the Otomites, a tribe yet very far behind in civilization, who speak a language full of nasal and guttural aspirations ; and the Chichimecs, who, like the Tlascaltecs, the Nahuatlacs, and the Aztecs, have preserved the Mexican language. All the southern part of the intendancy of Valladolid is inhabited by Indians. In the villages the only White figure to be met with is the *curé*, and he also is frequently an Indian or Mulatto. The benefices are so poor there, that the bishop of Mechoacan has the greatest difficulty in procuring ecclesiastics to settle in a country where Spanish is scarcely ever spoken, and where, along

the coast of the Great Ocean, the priests, infected
by the contagious miasmata of malignant fevers, frequently die before the expiration of seven or eight
months.

The population of the intendancy of Valladolid
decreased in the years of scarcity of 1786 and
1790; and it would have suffered still more, if the
respectable bishop of the diocese had not made
extraordinary sacrifices for the relief of the Indians.
He voluntarily lost in a few months the sum of
9,600*l.* sterling, by purchasing 50,000 bushels of
maize, which he sold at a reduced price, to keep
within bounds the sordid avarice of several rich proprietors, who, during that epoch of public cala-
mities, endeavoured to take advantage of the misery of the people.

The most remarkable places of the province of
Valladolid are the following :

*Valladolid de Mechoacan,* the capital
of the intendancy and seat of a bishop,
which enjoys a delicious climate. Its
elevation above the level of the sea is
6,396 feet; and yet at this moderate
height, and under the 19° 42′ of latitude, snow has been seen to fall in the
streets of Valladolid. This sudden
change of atmosphere, caused, no doubt,
by a north wind, is much more remarkable than the snow which fell in the

streets of Mexico the night before the Jesuit fathers were carried off! The new aqueduct by which the town receives potable water, was constructed at the expense of the last bishop, Fray Antonio de San Miguel, and cost him nearly 21,000*l.* sterling.

18,000

*Pascuaro*, on the banks of the picturesque lake of the same name, opposite to the Indian village of Janicho, situated at a distance of two or three miles, on a charming little island in the midst of the lake. Pascuaro contains the ashes of a very remarkable man, whose memory, after a lapse of two centuries and a half, is still venerated by the Indians,—the famous Vasco de Quiroga, first bishop of Mechoacan, who died in 1556 at the village of Uruapa. This zealous prelate, whom the natives still call their father (*Tata don Vasco*), was more successful in his endeavours to protect the unfortunate inhabitants of Mexico than the virtuous bishop of Chiapa, Bartholomé de las Casas. Quiroga became in an especial manner the benefactor of the Tarasc Indians, whose industry he encouraged. He prescribed one particular branch of commerce to each Indian village.

These useful institutions are in a great
measure preserved to this day.   The
height of Pascuaro is 7,217 feet.

Population.

6,000

*Tzintzontzan,* or Huitzitzilla, (the old
capital of the kingdom of Mechoacan,)
of which we have already spoken.

2,500

The intendancy of Valladolid contains the mines
of Zitaquaro, Angangueo, Tlapuxahua, the Real
del Oro, and Ynguaran.

*Diputaciones de Mineria,* or Districts.
33. Angangueo.
34. Inguaran.
35. Zitaquaro.
36. Tlalpujahua.

*Reales,* or places surrounded by Mines:
Angangueo; El Oro; Tlapaxahua; San Au-
gustin de Ozumatlan; Zitaquaro; Istapa; Los
Santos Reyes; Santa Rito de Chirangangeo; El
Zapote; Chachiltepec; Sanchiqueo; La Joya;
Paquaro; Xerecuaro; Curucupaseo; Sinda; In-
guaran; San Juan Guetamo; Ario; Santa Clara;
Alvadeliste; San Nicolas Apupato; Rio del Oro;
Axuchitlan; Santa Maria del Carmen del Som-
brero; Favor; Chichindaro.

# CHAPTER XVII.

## Summary recapitulation.

HAVING presented our readers with all the details which appeared relevant to the purpose of this work, we will now briefly recapitulate what has been said concerning the present state of Mexico.

*Physical aspect.*—In the centre of the country a long chain of mountains runs first from the south-east to the north-west, and afterwards beyond the parallel of 30° from south to north ; vast table-lands stretch out on the ridge of these mountains, gradually declining towards the temperate zone ; under the torrid zone their absolute height is from 7,550 to 7,870 feet. The ascent of the Cordilleras is covered with thick forests, while the central table-land is almost always arid and destitute of vegetation. The most elevated summits, many of which rise beyond the limits of perpetual snow, are crowned with oak and pine. In the equinoctial region the different climates rise as it were by strata one above another : between the 15° and 22° of latitude, the mean temperature of the shore, which is humid and unhealthy for individuals born in cold countries, is from 77° to 80° Fahr.; and that of the central table-land, which is celebrated on account of the great salubrity of the air, is from 60° to 62°. There is a want of rain in the interior, and the most populous part of the country is destitute of navigable rivers.

*Territorial extent.* — One million sixty-two thousand square miles, of which two thirds are under the temperate zone; the other third, lying under the torrid zone, from the great elevation of its table-lands, enjoys generally a temperature similar to that which is experienced in spring in Spain and the south of Italy.

*Population.*—Five millions eight hundred and forty thousand inhabitants; whereof two millions and a half are copper-coloured Indians, one million Mexican Spaniards, seventy thousand European Spaniards; scarcely any Negro slaves. The population is concentrated on the central table-land. The clergy alone consists of fourteen thousand individuals. The population of the capital 135,000 souls.

*Agriculture.*—The banana, the manioc, maize, cerealia, and potatoes, are the foundation of the nutriment of the people. The cerealia cul-

tivated under the torrid zone, wherever the surface
rises from 3,900 to 4,300 feet of elevation, produce
twenty-four for one. The maguey (*agave*) may be
considered as the Indian vine. The cultivation of
sugar-cane has lately made a rapid progress;
and Vera Cruz annually exports Mexican sugar to
the value of 282,000*l*. The finest cotton is produced on the western coast. The cultivation
of cocoa and indigo is equally neglected. The
vanilla of the forests of Quilate produces annually
900 *millares*. Tobacco is carefully cultivated
in the districts of Orizaba and Cordova; wax
abounds in Yucatan; the cochineal harvest of
Oaxaca amounts to 880,000 lbs. per annum.
Horned cattle have greatly multiplied in the *Provincias internas* and on the eastern coast between
Panuco and Huasacualco. The tithes of the
clergy, the value of which points out the increase
of territorial produce, have increased two-fifths
within the last ten years.

*Mines.*—Annual produce in gold, 4,289lbs.
troy; in silver, 1,439,832lbs.; in all, to the value
of 5,000,000*l*. sterling, or nearly the half of the
precious metals annually extracted from the mines
of North and South America. The mint of Mexico
has furnished, from 1690 to 1803, more than
293,150,000*l*.; and from the discovery of New
Spain to the commencement of the nineteenth century, probably 878,800,000*l*., or nearly two fifths of

2 R

the entire quantity of gold and silver which in that interval of time has flowed from the New Continent into the Old. Three districts of mines, Guanaxuato, Zacatecas,and Catorce, which form a central group between the 21° and 24° of latitude, yield nearly the half of all the gold and silver extracted from the mines of New Spain. The vein of Guanaxuato alone, richer than the mineral depository of Potosi, furnishes at an average 286,000 lbs. troy of silver annually, or a sixth of all the silver which America annually throws into circulation. The single mine of Valenciana, in which the expense of working exceeds 180,000*l.* per annum, has for the last forty years never ceased to yield annually to the proprietors a net profit of more than 120,000*l.* : this profit has sometimes amounted to 240,000*l.* ; and it amounted to 800,000*l.* in the space of a few months for the family of Fagoaga at Sombrerete. The produce of the mines of Mexico has tripled in fifty-two years, and sextupled in a hundred years ; and it will admit of greater increase as the country shall become more populous and industry and information be more diffused. The working of the mines, far from being hostile to agriculture, has favoured cultivation in the most uninhabited regions. The wealth of the Mexican mines consists more in the abundance than in the intrinsic riches of the silver minerals, which amount at an average only to ·0002 (or from 60 to 80 ounces per ton). The quantity of minerals extracted bymeans of mercury is to that produced by smelting in the proportion of $3\frac{1}{2}$ to 1. The process of amalgamation used is long, and occasions a great waste of mercury : the consumption for all New Spain amounts to 1,540,000 lbs. per annum. It is to be presumed that the Mexican Cordilleras will one day supply the mercury, iron, copper, and lead, necessary for internal consumption.

*Manufactures.*—Value of the annual produce of manufacturing industry from 1,500,000*l*., to 1,700,000*l*. The manufacture of hides, cloth, and calicoes, has been on the increase since the conclusion of the last century.

*Commerce.*—Importation of foreign produce and goods, 4,400,000*l*; exportation in agricultural produce and manufactures of New Spain, 1,300,000*l*. The mines produce in gold and silver 5,000,000*l*., of which about 1,750,000*l*. are exported on account of the king : consequently if we deduct from the remaining 3,250,000*l*., 3,034,000*l*. to pay the excess of imports over the exports, we find the specie of Mexico hardly increases 216,000*l*.

*Revenue.*—The gross amount of the revenue is 4,400,000*l*. ; whereof 1,192,000*l*. from the produce of the gold and silver mines, 816,000*l*. from the tobacco farm, 650,000*l*. from the alcavalas,

282,000*l.* from the Indian capitation tax, and 173,000*l.* from the duty on *pulque* or fermented juice of the agave.

*Military defence.*—It consumes the fourth of the total revenue. The Mexican army is 30,000 strong, whereof scarcely a third are regular troops, and more than two thirds militia. The petty warfare continually carried on with the wandering Indians in the *provincias internas,* and the maintenance of the *presidios* or military posts, require a very considerable expense. The state of the eastern coast and the configuration of the surface of the country facilitate its defence against any invasion attempted by a maritime power.

## ADDENDA.

Since my return to Europe I have received the following particulars, which carry on our information on the subjects in question to the year 1806.

The road from Vera Cruz to Xalapa, and from thence to Perote, begun in the month of February 1803, has been continued with great activity. It was executed in 1806, between las Vigas and la Rinconada, for a length of 79,228 varas, or 198,601 feet. As the work was executed by a great number of condemned criminals, an hospital was established at la Rinconada, capable of receiving 1700 patients. The arches of the bridge of the Rio de la Antigua, begun near the Ventilla, were destroyed by the extraordinrry swell which took place in 1806. The *Consulado* of Vera Cruz immediately constructed new pillars, more solid than the former and closer to each other. The beautiful giratory light-house (*fanal de la Vera Cruz*), of which I have spoken, was completed in the month of May 1804. It will require nearly 650*l.* annually keep it up.

Notwithstanding the rise in the price of iron, the working of the mines has been continued with the same activity as before the commencement of the last war. There has been coined at the mint of Mexico in gold and silver;

In 1804,—5,201,687*l.*; in 1805,—5,885,942*l.*; in 1806,—5,359,471*l.*

Of the 5,201,687*l.* coined in 1804; 5,094,483*l.*, or 1,696,404lbs. troy were silver, and 107,187*l.* or 2,235lbs. troy were gold.

The coinage of the year 1805 has even exceeded that of 1796. The extraordinary increase of the public revenue since the commencement of the eighteenth century, as well as the augmentation of tithes of which we have already spoken, proves the progress of population, great commercial activity, and the increase of national wealth.

**THE END.**

Printed by Richard Taylor,
Shoe-Lane, London.

Printed in the United States
By Bookmasters